Social Intelligence

The New Science of Success

Karl Albrecht

JOSSEY-BASS
A Wiley Imprint
www.josseybass.com

Published by Jossey-Bass
A Wiley Imprint
989 Market Street, San Francisco, CA 94103-1741
www.josseybass.com

For additional copies/bulk purchases of this book in the U.S. please contact 800-274-4434.

Jossey-Bass books and products are available through most bookstores. To contact Jossey-Bass directly call our Customer Care Department within the U.S. at 800-956-7739, outside the U.S. at 317-572-3986, fax 317-572-4002, or visit www.josseybass.com.

Jossey-Bass also publishes its books in a variety of electronic formats. Some content that appears in print may not be available in electronic books.

Library of Congress Cataloging-in-Publication Data
Albrecht, Karl.
  Social intelligence : the new science of success / Karl Albrecht.
    p. cm.
  Includes bibliographical references and index.
  ISBN-13: 978-0-7879-7938-6 (alk. paper)
  1. Social intelligence. 2. Interpersonal relations. 3. Success. I. Title.
  HM1106.A53 2006
  302.1'2--dc22
                          2005025923
ISBN-10: 0-7879-7938-4
ISBN-13: 978-0-7879-7938-6

Acquiring Editor: Lisa Shannon	Production Editor: Dawn Kilgore
Director of Development: Kathleen Dolan Davies	Editor: Rebecca Taff
Manufacturing Supervisor: Becky Carreño	
Printed in the United States of America	

Printing   10   9   8   7   6   5   4

CONTENTS

FOREWORD

Professor Warren Bennis

Karl Albrecht has his ways. He has such good, fresh ideas and knows how to write about them. Like the title of this book, he incarnates the "social intelligence" he tells us about. He invites us into his world of ideas in a beguiling way, and subtly re-arranges our thinking about what we thought we'd already arranged. His latest effort, this thoroughly charming and well-researched book, *Social Intelligence,* breaks new ground on the terrain we thought we understood.

Building on the work of Howard Gardner, Daniel Goleman, and others, Karl freshly imagines the intimate ins and outs of everyday life, those micro-interactions, little hurts and joys, and clarifies these crawl spaces of our hearts with a language and with laughter that stay with you. It's a page-turner, this book; the next page and the next page and the next: all gave me the pleasure of finding things out, about how to live life in a terrific social (and intelligent) space. As I said, Karl Albrecht has his ways, and, as you'll see, he'll have his way with you.

As Victor Hugo reportedly declared: "There is one thing more powerful than all the armies of the world, and that is an idea whose time has come." Social intelligence, particularly as articulated so clearly in this groundbreaking book, may be such an idea. And the time could not be more ripe for a new understanding of ourselves, both as individuals and as members of the human community.

Technological change is rapidly accelerating. We are now beginning an era in which people's knowledge and approach can become obsolete before they have even begun the careers for which they were trained. We are living in an era of runaway inflation of knowledge and skill, where the value of what one learns is always slipping away. The age of "virtual" relationships is upon us, with people changing careers, uprooting themselves, moving their families to follow new opportunities, and constantly forming new but ever more transitory relationships. The traditional concept of community as a localized experience is giving way to a social model that looks more like an airport than a village. Perhaps this partly explains the feelings of futility, alienation, and lack of individual worth that are said to characterize our time.

As the Information Age and its awesome technology inexorably transform us into a virtualized society, I believe that even the most wired—and wireless—among us still experiences the craving for a sense of personal connectedness. As artificial and virtual communities become ever more common, our need for a real sense of community will deepen, not lessen. Ironically, the digital age will demand greater social competence of us, not less.

The Nobel laureate John Franck once said that he always knew when he had heard a good idea because of the feeling of terror that seized him. Good ideas tend to do that—they invite us to a journey of discovery that can be both fearful and joyful; we may fear the overturning of our emotional and intellectual apple carts, but at the same time our deeper wisdom invites us to joyfully explore their possibilities.

Karl Albrecht provides us with a simple but elegant framework for understanding social intelligence as a set of five primal competencies for life and leadership: Situational Awareness, Presence, Authenticity, Clarity, and Empathy. I could expound at length on the role each of these concepts has played in my understanding of leadership, social influence, and the workings of human society, but I'll let him do that, as he does so well in the following pages.

ACKNOWLEDGMENT

I would like to acknowledge the contributions to this book by Dr. Steve Albrecht, my colleague, partner, mentor, and best friend. As an experienced consultant, speaker and seminar presenter, author, and subject-matter expert, he has provided invaluable advice and assistance in the development of this book.

Thanks, mate.

PREFACE

"You're wrong. You're dead wrong, and I'll tell you why."

That statement, and a few others that came after it, may have caused the loss of several million dollars worth of business for a company I was employed with many years ago.

The person on the receiving end was a high-ranking civilian technical expert working for the U.S. Department of Defense. The person on the delivering end was an associate of mine, Jack (not his real name), a young man with considerable technical knowledge but few discernible social skills.

He and I were meeting with the government expert for the first time. Our mission was to begin building a relationship that would enable us to acquaint him and his colleagues with our technical capabilities as a firm, and by that means create a competitive advantage for our firm as a contractor for Defense business.

The government expert had just voiced a rather strong—and largely unsupportable—opinion about the future prospects of a particular type of technology. My colleague Jack, apparently blind to the larger context for the conversation, could not let this act of technical blasphemy go unanswered. He had to set this man straight. In short order, they were engaged in a heated debate.

Far from achieving our objective of starting a successful relationship, we were rapidly achieving exactly the opposite. Before I was able to shift the discussion back to neutral ground, the damage had been done. We never succeeded in getting another meeting with him or any of his colleagues.

I eventually came to understand that my colleague Jack was well supplied with *abstract intelligence*—the "IQ" kind—but short on *social intelligence*.

In the more than two decades since this enlightening episode, I've been fascinated to observe the differences in the ways people manage the interpersonal experience. I gradually came to believe that this ability to "get along with people" represents a kind of "intelligence" in itself, quite apart from the usual "IQ" kind of intelligence that academics, psychologists, and educators have studied so diligently. I began studying this particular set of competencies, trying to discern or create a coherent framework for describing it, observing it and—most importantly—developing it if possible.

My first priority, selfishly, was to understand my own capacity for connecting with and influencing people, and to learn ways to do it better. Aside from that, however, it was always very clear that some sort of descriptive model of social competence could be a useful resource in various aspects of human development.

The concept of social intelligence, or "SI," as one of a set of key life competencies is surely an idea whose time has arrived. It crystallizes much of what we know about an important dimension of human effectiveness.

SI is perhaps best understood as one of a larger set of interwoven competencies. For some years now, Harvard professor Howard Gardner and others have been preaching the idea that human intelligence is not a single trait, as the devotees of the IQ cult have always claimed. According to Gardner, we humans have a whole range of distinct intelligences, or primary dimensions of competence. Even the public education establishment has come to accept Gardner's view, at least in principle. How well they apply the concept to educational design remains an open question.

It's time for us to bring professor Gardner's multiple-intelligence, or "MI" concept, into our everyday consciousness. Taking a few minor liberties with his evolving theory and translating his various categories of intelligence into a street language vocabulary, I identify six primary intelligences: *Abstract Intelligence* (symbolic reasoning, of the "IQ" type); *Social Intelligence* (the topic of this book); *Practical Intelligence* (getting things done); *Emotional Intelligence* (self-awareness and the management of inner experience); *Aesthetic Intelligence* (a sense of form, design, literature, the arts, music, and other holistic experiences); and *Kinesthetic Intelligence* (whole-body competence such as sport, dance, music, or flying a jet fighter).

These six basic intelligences, like the faces of a cube, all come together to form a whole. Surely the "Renaissance human," the success model most of us admire, would have a strong and well-integrated combination of all intelligences.

In recent years, Dr. Daniel Goleman has launched popular interest in the developmental possibilities for the multiple-intelligence model with his book *Emotional Intelligence:Why It May Be More Important than IQ.* The growing acceptance of "EI"—or "EQ" as some fans prefer to call it—has legitimized the notion of an intelligence as a dimension of competence which people can study, think about, learn, and improve.

Considered together, Gardner, Goleman, and other contributors to the multiple-intelligence theory have done a great service—notably by legitimizing the multiple-intelligence concept, and also by inviting our attention to the other dimensions. By advancing a model for describing, assessing, and developing social intelligence, we can now add another important piece to the MI picture.

We can characterize SI as a combination of a basic understanding of people—a kind of strategic social awareness—and a set of component skills for interacting successfully with them. A simple description of SI is:

> . . . *the ability to get along well with others and*
> *to get them to cooperate with you.*

We can think of the extremes of SI—very low and very high—in metaphorical terms as either "toxic" or "nourishing," respectively. *Toxic behaviors,* by this definition, are those that cause others to feel devalued, inadequate, intimidated, angry, frustrated, or guilty. *Nourishing behaviors* cause others to feel valued, capable, loved, respected, and appreciated.

People with high social intelligence—those who are socially aware and basically nourishing in their behavior—are magnetic to others. People with low social intelligence—those who are primarily toxic to others—are anti-magnetic. In this regard, the old expressions about having "a magnetic personality" may be fairly accurate.

We seem well overdue to make SI a developmental priority in our early education, public schooling, adult learning processes, and in business. Children and teen-agers need to learn to win the fellowship and respect they crave. College students need to learn to collaborate and influence others effectively. Managers need to understand and connect with the people they're appointed to lead. High-tech professionals like Jack need to understand the social context and achieve their objectives by working from empathy. All adults, in their careers and personal lives, need to be able to present themselves effectively and earn the respect of those they deal with. Social intelligence can reduce conflict, create collaboration, replace bigotry and polarization with understanding, and mobilize people toward common goals.

This book is certainly not the last word, and in fact it's not the first word. My modest aspiration is that it can contribute in some way to building acceptance, interest, and application of these important principles in our culture, in business, and in education. This is not a "cookbook" or a motivational self-help book for "getting along with people." It contains lots of stories, examples, suggestions, and self-assessment and development methods. But fundamentally its purpose is to stimulate deep reflection.

The legendary fiction writer and social commentator H.G. Wells said, "Civilization is more and more a race between education and catastrophe." Not to put too grand an interpretation on it, but social intelligence may be, in the long run, one of the most important ingredients in our survival as a species.

1

A DIFFERENT KIND OF "SMART"

"There is one thing more powerful than all the
armies of the world, and that is an idea whose time
has come."

—Victor Hugo

SURELY, EACH OF US KNOWS at least one person, and probably several, whose company we do not enjoy. Not rarely do we hear people say things like:

> "I dread having to visit my parents this weekend; I just know my mother will pick a big fight with my father, and she'll criticize me the whole time I'm there. I don't even know why I still go to visit them. Guilt, I suppose."

Others may say things like:

"I hate my job; my boss finds fault with everything I do. I guess I'll have to start looking around for something better."

Or:

"Maybe we should kind of 'forget' to invite him to go out with us. If he goes along, we'll argue all night."

Or:

"I feel like we should invite her to join us for lunch, but I can't bear to hear about her divorce one more time. She can't seem to talk about anything else."

Most of us can more adroitly spot deficits in social intelligence on the part of others than virtues—I know it when I don't see it. We may unconsciously gravitate toward people who have it, but we consciously steer away from those who don't. And those in between, at the middle of the scale of interpersonal competence? We can "take them or leave them."

How many people consider their parents or close family members a negative influence in their lives, rather than counting them among their best friends? How many people have parted company with their families, at least emotionally if not physically? How many parents complain that their children neglect them or seem to have no desire to visit them?

People who enjoy close and supportive family relationships often seem baffled by the difficulties others describe in dealing with their close kin. But even within so-called happy families, certain individuals may treat others in ways that alienate them.

Conversely, most of us have at least a few acquaintances we consider special—people with whom we feel comfortable, respected, affirmed, and cared about. Put two examples of the extremes side by side for a moment—compare a person you tend to avoid with a person whose company you eagerly seek out, and contrast their behaviors. It quickly becomes obvious, not only that one person simply behaves in a more positive, supportive way than the other, but you also get the sense that the positive person somehow knows more about people than the negative one. The positive ones seem to "get it"—they understand people and their interactions reflect that understanding, more than simply consisting of some set of "nice" behaviors.

What we will call social intelligence in this book consists of both insight and behavior. We seek to understand human social effectiveness at a level beyond simple formulas—beyond saying "please" and "thank you," beyond the normal social courtesies, beyond the so-called "people skills" supposedly valued in the workplace. We seek to understand how highly effective people navigate social situations so skillfully, and how they know—at least most of the time—how to engage others in ways appropriate to the context.

To begin with a working definition, we can think of social intelligence, or "SI," as:

> *The ability to get along well with others and to get them to cooperate with you.*

OLD WINE IN NEW BOTTLES?

I've often heard people I deal with every day—from teachers, trainers, personnel people, and conference organizers to business managers, consultants, publishers, editors, and journalists—express a kind of automatic, stereotyped reaction to the phrase "social intelligence." Frequently such a person will say, "Oh yeah—'people skills'—very important in today's world."

By slotting the concept of social intelligence into an old familiar category and recoding it with an old familiar name, they risk misperceiving its potential significance. This sense of the simple and familiar may have held back the perception and understanding of SI as a more deeply layered, more comprehensive view of human affairs. An expression from the ancient tradition of Zen philosophy advises:

"The biggest obstacle to learning something new is the belief that you already know it."

Academic researchers and theoreticians have chewed on the notion of social intelligence for decades, with mostly ambiguous results. As far back as 1920, eminent researchers such as E.L. Thorndike tried to identify a unique set of skills, separate from those associated with the traditional idea of intellectual intelligence, that could measure a person's social competence, and possibly predict his or her success in dealing with others. In the other camp, "IQ" pioneers like David Wechsler, as early as 1939, argued that "social intelligence is just general intelligence applied to social situations." Attempts to correlate measures of sociability with the early intelligence tests yielded inconclusive results. Academics have kept themselves profitably occupied ever since, trying to deconstruct the concept of social effectiveness into an acceptable set of dimensions, or categories, in hopes of designing scientifically rigorous ways to measure them.

Meanwhile, life goes on, and we ordinary civilians have struggled on our own to define the essence of social effectiveness. In the business world particularly, personnel experts, trainers, consultants, executives, and managers have sought to define practical social skills, presumably for the purpose of helping their employees develop or improve, or at least to select the ones who "have it" and place them in the right jobs. This search has also met with relatively limited success.

For many years, and particularly over the past few decades, business educators have talked often about "communication skills," "interpersonal skills" and "people skills," usually with very little in the way of working definitions to support their conversations. For example, many employee performance evaluation forms include a section on communication skills, but mostly leave it to the worker's boss to assess a dimension of performance based on subjective impressions and opinions. Lacking a comprehensive operating definition of these skills, managers and others have little to rely on other than a sense that "I know it when I see it."

Frequently, if I ask a manager who assesses an employee as having poor communication skills, "What particular skills do you see as lacking, or in need of development?" the manager may think for a moment and then begin to enumerate certain specific malfunctions he or she has observed. They can often identify certain behaviors and idiosyncrasies they consider ineffective or dysfunctional.

However, if I ask the same manager to enumerate a fairly complete set of skills that make up the package of "people skills," he or she will typically struggle with the challenge. After quickly listing the obvious and familiar skills such as listening and explaining things clearly, the inventory typically degenerates to a vague set of personality traits— aspects such as "considerate," "cooperative," and "articulate."

These traditional platitudinal definitions of interacting skills have limited our understanding of social intelligence as a broader concept and have led many people to settle for clichés instead of seeking a more robust operational model. We have typically settled for a few skills and techniques—"active listening," for example, or "I-messages," in which a person expresses his or her own feelings and reactions—and have not seriously sought a more comprehensive view.

The argument in favor of developing a more comprehensive model of human effectiveness, which goes beyond the older construct of "people skills," posits that such a model can serve a person as a mental platform for understanding social situations, or contexts in which interactions take place, and it can also enable a person to design a response to a unique situation without feeling dependent on some fixed inventory of things to say, ways to say them, or pre-programmed conversational tactics.

It seems reasonable to posit that the ability to behave skillfully in a wide range of social situations—talking to one's boss, taking part in a meeting, making a presentation to a group, sharing experiences with a spouse or significant other, interviewing for a job—rests on something more than simply knowing a set of specific skills or procedures. It implies a depth and breadth of life knowledge, a deep knowledge of one's culture—and possibly other cultures—the accumulated wisdom that comes from constantly observing and learning what works and what doesn't in human situations.

For example, simply "reading" the context of a situation—the multitude of cues that encode and signal the relationships, rules for behavior, and the attitudes and intentions of the participants—requires a deeply embedded understanding and know-how. To reduce the idea of human effectiveness to some simple package of "people skills" seems to discount the richness of understanding and resourcefulness that can make people more effective in their dealings with one another.

GOING BEYOND IQ

For many experts and students of human performance, the publication of Harvard professor Howard Gardner's 1983 book *Frames of Mind* marked a turning point in understanding and defining the sources of mental competence. For some, it represents a turning point of immense importance.[1]

Gardner overturned one of the most fundamental assumptions of the psychological and educational establishments, namely that human mental competence arises from a single trait called "intelligence." Beginning with the work of Alfred Binet in France, who tried to measure the "mental age" of children, to the early attempts of the U.S. Army to identify measurable mental characteristics of soldiers that could predict their success in various tasks, and Cattell and others in California, who searched for measures that could predict the academic success of schoolchildren, the "IQ" concept has held sway in Western cultures for seventy-five years.

Many leading thinkers in the field of developmental psychology have advocated eliminating intelligence testing from American schools, but with little success. The eminent intelligence psychologist Arthur Jensen wrote, "Achievement itself is the school's main concern. I see no need to measure anything other than achievement itself."

The notion that a single three-digit number assigns a person to a certain level of potential for success in life became an article of faith, particularly for educators and administrators who believed in designing educational systems and experiences around presumed levels of competence. Argument and speculation continue as to whether the use of numerical IQ scores has done more harm than good in Western society. Aside from its presumed usefulness in classifying and assigning students, real benefits of the IQ system and ideology seem hard to find. Many anti-IQ advocates argue that its only real impact has consisted of making some people feel less worthy than others and leading some to consider themselves somehow superior to others.

The method of measuring IQ has come in for even more criticism than the concept of IQ itself. Critics charge—quite rightly, I think—that standardized pencil-and-paper IQ tests cannot possibly assess the full range of mental competencies available to a person. In particular, the designer of a standardized written test has to define each problem in terms of a closed set of possible answers. Any other means of assessment, such as written essays, commentary, or physical demonstration of a skill, would require a scoring system run by trained evaluators, which would make the testing process very costly and difficult to administer.

The lack of a method for inviting *original responses* to questions or problems completely rules out the measurement of *divergent production,* the basis for what we call creativity. Asking a question like "How many things can you do with a small coin?" invites an unbounded range of replies; no computer software could possibly evaluate them all. At a minimum, this restriction to *convergent responses,* that is, the "one right answer," eliminates a whole range of mental skills that play an important part in human success. Some critics of IQ testing contend that relying on written IQ measurements has caused educators to favor—consciously or unconsciously—students who perform well on preprogrammed tasks, at the expense of those who lean toward unstructured, creative forms of thought. They argue further that the design of the educational experience in public institutions reflects the "one right answer" approach and shows little respect for the "more than one right answer" concept that forms so much of the basis for creative thinking, the arts, literature, music, and other subjective aspects of human experience.

Enter Professor Howard Gardner. Beginning in about 1980, Gardner became interested in some fundamental questions arising from psychological testing: Why do some people with very high IQ scores fail miserably in their personal lives? Do tests of mental competence miss certain obvious aspects of human ability, such as artistic, musical, athletic, literary, and social competence? Gardner came to the inevitable conclusion: the concept of "intelligence" as a singular measure of competence has to go. He posited that human beings have a *range* of key competencies—intelligences—and they exist in various proportions in various persons.

With Gardner's model of multiple intelligences, theory finally caught up with common sense. Theoretical questions remain about how best to subdivide or categorize these various intelligences, and that discussion will probably continue for some time. Gardner himself has apparently not arrived at a fully satisfying taxonomic structure; as of this writing he continues to explore various categorical dimensions. But his "MI" concept has reached the tipping point of acceptance in certain sectors, particularly education and business, at least in the United States. Some of the more rigorous academic advocates of the single-number "g-factor" theory of IQ still vigorously oppose Gardner's concept, and the controversy will almost certain rage for decades to come. In particular, Gardner's research methods do not involve exactly the same experimental tools as those favored by the single-IQ fans, so the two lines of investigation do not necessarily yield comparable results.

We'll have our hands full in this book exploring just one of these multiple intelligences, the domain of social intelligence, so we have no cause to enter the theoretical fray surrounding the MI concept itself. We must content ourselves with placing SI clearly within the MI framework and then understanding its implications within that framework.

Placing SI within Gardner's MI framework requires a bit of conceptual acrobatics, inasmuch as Gardner himself—at least at the time of this writing—continues to evolve his categories and definitions. The bulk of his early work involved a set of some seven independent intelligences. He has also posited the existence of an eighth dimension, less clearly defined. Some other researchers have diced up the macro-intelligences into other categories.

Consequently, for our exploration, we will need to settle on some working definition of these multiple intelligences, in order to place SI clearly into that perspective. While Gardner uses rather scientific sounding labels for his categories—verbal-logical, mathematical-symbolic, spatial, kinesthetic, interpersonal, intrapersonal, and musical—we probably do little harm by recoding them into street language and simplifying them conceptually. With appropriate respect for Professor Gardner and his theory, I've found it helpful to rearrange these "multiple smarts" into six primary categories:

1. *Abstract Intelligence:* symbolic reasoning.
2. *Social Intelligence:* dealing with people (the topic of this book).
3. *Practical Intelligence:* getting things done.
4. *Emotional Intelligence:* self-awareness and self-management.
5. *Aesthetic Intelligence:* the sense of form, design, music, art, and literature.
6. *Kinesthetic Intelligence:* whole-body skills like sports, dance, music, or flying a jet fighter.

Others might argue for a somewhat different set of subdivisions, but these six categories work fairly well, and they have the modest extra advantage of spelling out a memorable acronym: ASPEAK.

This notion of multiple intelligences seems to fit with our common experience. Consider the disparity between abstract intelligence—the

IQ kind—and social intelligence. I've met many members of Mensa, the international society of people with high IQs—the only requirement for membership. I've often marveled at the number of them who, despite their impressive cognitive credentials, seemed incapable of connecting with other people and, in some cases, incapable of maintaining a reasonable degree of emotional resilience. Presumably the "Renaissance human," the success model most of us admire, would have a strong and well-integrated combination of all six intelligences.

EI, SI, OR BOTH?

Since the 1995 publication of Daniel Goleman's landmark book *Emotional Intelligence: Why It Can Matter More Than IQ,* the concept of "EI" or "EQ"—an emotional quotient—has taken hold significantly in the business sector.[2] Trainers, personnel people, consultants, coaches, and managers have embraced EI as an important element of personal effectiveness. A series of other books, training programs, seminars, and conferences have, predictably, followed in its wake. As typically happens with a breakthrough concept, some people have even accorded the EI movement a kind of cult-like status. For a few, EI explains just about everything; for most, it explains many things and fits well with other concepts of human development.

Goleman's first attempts to frame a practical model of EI identified five dimensions of competence:

1. Self-awareness.
2. Self-regulation.
3. Motivation.
4. Empathy.
5. Relationships.

One of Goleman's five original dimensions, however—the relationship dimension—seems to stretch the model and the concept beyond its practical boundaries. The first four primary competencies do clearly identify elements of the internal emotional landscape, which influence one's behavior in fundamental ways. And certainly they influence in a very fundamental way a person's capacity to interact well with others. But in trying to force-fit social competence into an already broad model of emotional competence, we risk doing too little with too much.

By folding motivation into self-awareness, later work streamlined the EI model into four domains—as of this writing termed self-awareness, self-management, social awareness, and relationship management—each of which links to clusters of specific EI competencies, eighteen in all.[3] Relationship management, for example, is associated with seven leadership-oriented competencies, including inspirational leadership (guiding and motivating with a compelling vision), developing others (bolstering others' abilities through feedback and guidance), and change catalyst (initiating, managing, and leading in a new direction).[4]

If we widen our conceptual zoom lens to reconsider Howard Gardner's multiple intelligences, we can more readily place Goleman's overall EI concept in terms of its relationships to the other intelligences. We can also begin to identify the ways in which we can combine the various intelligences in a synergistic way, to build a portrait of the competent human—the true "Renaissance person."

With appropriate respect for the contributions of both Gardner and Goleman, it seems worthwhile to link together both of these useful concepts as complementary views. We can look at EI as a dimension of *internal competence*—self-awareness and skillful deployment of one's emotional responses. Then we can clearly delineate our model of social intelligence in terms of *externally oriented competencies*. In other words, we need both of these intelligences for interpersonal success.

Indeed, as previously explained, Professor Gardner does exactly this in his formulation: he posits an *intrapersonal* intelligence—emotional intelligence, for all practical purposes—and an *interpersonal* intelligence—competency in human situations. The value of this clearer delineation of concepts may lie in the opportunity to coordinate and interrelate them, rather than trying to squash them into a single conceptual container.

For example, consider the syndrome of shyness, a pattern of behavior that relates strongly to low self-esteem, lack of self-confidence, and feelings of low self-worth. Learning to interact more skillfully and confidently with others requires not only acquiring new social skills—eye contact, using a stronger voice, taking up more space—but it also involves revising one's inner self-estimate—re-owning one's rights as a person, acknowledging one's worth as a human being, and learning different emotional responses to social interactions. Taken together, EI and SI can go a long way toward explaining social pathologies such as shyness and offering developmental strategies for overcoming them.

As another example, consider a person who exhibits what many people call the "abrasive personality." This person's abusive behaviors—criticizing others, disputing and arguing with them, putting people down, using aggressive language, voicing dogmatic opinions—may arise from a low sense of self-worth, that is, low EI. At the same time, such a person may simply lack sufficient insight into his or her impact on others, and may not grasp the value of helping other people feel good about themselves as an avenue to achieving his or her own ends.

FROM TOXIC TO NOURISHING

A personal experience, more than a decade ago, finally brought the concept of SI, as a behavioral proposition, into focus for me. I had been teaching a series of management seminars for a university extension program in northern California. The program ran for five consecutive week-ends, each with a Friday evening session and an all-day Saturday session. The same managers attended all sessions.

During the first session I introduced a self-assessment questionnaire I had drafted as an attempt to profile behaviors that contributed to alienation, conflict, and animosity, in contrast to behaviors that led to empathy, understanding, and cooperation. I also introduced the terms "toxic" and "nourishing," respectively, to denote the contrast between the two.

Toxic behaviors, by this definition, cause others to feel devalued, inadequate, angry, frustrated, or guilty. *Nourishing behaviors* cause others to feel valued, capable, loved, respected, and appreciated. People with high social intelligence—those who are primarily nourishing in their behavior—become magnetic to others. People with low social intelligence—those who exhibit primarily toxic behavior toward others—act as anti-magnetic. In this regard, the old expression about having "a magnetic personality" may have some value.

During the session, the managers filled out the draft questionnaire and scored it. Most of them reported that they found the profile personally useful, particularly in that it gave them a specific set of behaviors to think about. At the next session one of the managers offered to share an experience he'd had during the intervening week:

"I have one particular employee who's very toxic in almost all of his interactions with others. I've been urged to fire him many times. I haven't been able to figure out what to do with him, until now.

"Last Monday, after our week-end seminar, I invited him to sit down with me and I showed him this questionnaire. I just said, 'I've been taking a management course, and the instructor gave us a questionnaire that I thought was kind of interesting. I'd like to ask you to read it.'

"I sat there without saying a word while he read the list of toxic and nourishing behaviors. When he got to the bottom, he looked up at me. He said 'This is me, isn't it? All of the things on the toxic side are the things I've been doing. I never really thought about it this way.'

"I only said one thing to him: 'Maybe it's something you want to consider.'"

"Well, I've never seen someone's behavior change so fast in my whole life. From one day to the next, he went from the complete grouch to being helpful, considerate, and even friendly. His coworkers keep asking me 'What did you do to him? Did you inject him with something? Did you send him off to therapy? Suddenly he's become Mr. Personality!'"

Many times since that episode I've seen convincing evidence that the biggest single cause of low social intelligence comes from simple lack of insight. Toxic people often become so preoccupied with their own personal struggles that they simply do not understand the impact they have on others. They need help in seeing themselves as others see them. And to make sense of that insight, we turn to our model of social intelligence—and some examples of social incompetence from everyday life.

BLIND SPOTS, LENSES, AND FILTERS

Try the following experiment: light a very small candle or switch on a small pocket-sized flashlight and hold it out in front of you at arm's length. Fix your vision straight in front of you, focusing on some convenient object or a point on a wall, and don't let your eyes move as you carry out this procedure. Close your left eye if you have the light source in your right hand, or close your right eye if you have the light source in your left hand. Now, starting with the light source directly in line with the center of your open eye, and continuing to gaze directly forward, slowly swing the light source in an arc, outward from the center line of your nose. Keeping your eyes focused straight ahead, but remaining aware of the light source, you'll discover a point—located at about a 15-degree angle outward from the center line—at which the light source will disappear. On either side of this "blind spot," you'll become aware of the light again; within the blind spot, you simply can't see it.

This physiological blind spot resides at the point where the optic nerve leaves the eye; you have no nerve cells at that small point, and so you cannot see anything in that particular place in your visual field. Most of us rarely notice this blind spot, and many people don't know they have one. How can we have an area of no perception right in the middle of our visual field and not notice it? The answer lies in the way the brain processes the information coming to it. Our eyes move about more than they stay still; our survival instincts cause us to scan our environment rapidly, except when we choose to concentrate on one thing for some reason. As the eyes move about, they feed a complete picture to the brain, which works around the blind spot and constructs an apparently complete picture by filling in the missing data.

Just as our brains work around our visual blind spots, so too do they work around our social or psychological blind spots. We don't see what we don't want to see. And we do see what we want to see.

The commonplace expressions we use in our culture indicate that we understand, at some level, that we human beings do not actually perceive reality—*we create it at the instant of perception.* Each of us ingests his or her own unique reality, which becomes the net result of our perceptions, reactions, interpretations, and distortions. We often refer to our blind spots—aspects of our experience that we block out of our consciousness, either through simple inattentiveness, subconscious repression, or outright denial. However, the fact that we frequently refer to these blind spots in ordinary conversation does not guarantee that we actually understand them or that we consciously act to see through them or see past them.

All of us have blind spots, lenses, and filters permanently installed between our sensory channels and our brains. Our unique blind spots block out those parts of reality that we have chosen not to deal with. Our personal lenses magnify those aspects of reality we preoccupy ourselves with. And our filters selectively exclude or rearrange various aspects of reality to suit our existing brain patterns.

These blind spots, lenses, and filters operate dynamically—they shift from moment to moment, from situation to situation, programmed by our values, beliefs, desires, expectations, fears, and evaluations.

A personal experience brought the concept of social blind spots home to me in a very direct way. I discovered that several of my acquaintances, with whom I've enjoyed many evenings in interesting conversations, felt that I made a practice of monopolizing the discussions. In particular, several of them who usually had little to say seemed to feel that I interpreted their silence as a license to take the conversational ball, and they felt that I should have made a more proactive effort to invite them to participate. Unfortunately, none of them saw fit to break this news to me; I began to suspect it based on other sources of evidence. When I sought their feedback, they agreed with my diagnosis. "You always have interesting points of view and interesting things to say," they assured me. "But others may not feel encouraged to share their views unless you take a back seat for a while."

If we knew about our blind spots, they wouldn't exist, or at least we could adjust to them and work around them. Unfortunately, even our best friends may hesitate to tell us about our blind spots—as they perceive them—and we sometimes have no other way of discovering them except by accident.

My way of dealing with that particular blind spot, now brought into consciousness, included silently reciting a personal mantra before entering into any conversation: "A conversation is not a lecture by Karl Albrecht." This has helped considerably, at least according to the feedback I've received from my friends. I only wish that all of us had felt more free and less anxious about helping me discover and reduce my particular blind spot.

Do I have other such blind spots? How would I know?

SOCIAL HALITOSIS, FLATULENCE, AND DANDRUFF

Recently I was sitting in my favorite local coffee shop, reviewing some information for a project I was engrossed in, when two men came in and sat at the table next to mine—a few feet away. One of them chatted to the other animatedly for several minutes. At a lull in the conversation, he leaned over in my direction and said "Pardon me, sir. That's a great-looking ring you're wearing. Is it 'lapiz'?"

"Thanks," I said. "It is."

He immediately took this as an invitation; he got up and came over to my table, depositing himself in the chair across from me. "May I see it?" he asked. I took off the ring and he made a show of admiring it. "I see you're writing quite a bit. What do you do for a living?"

As he continued to chatter I quickly discovered that he had an objective in mind. He set off in a tirade about a "fantastic new business opportunity," using "the Internet—which is a whole new way of doing business."

"This is not a franchise," he assured me. "It's not a multi-level marketing scheme. It's a fabulous way to achieve financial independence, and I'm proud to be able to help so many people realize their dreams."

As I listened to a few more of his breathless platitudes, I mused about how little he cared about me and how he seemed perfectly entitled to exploit a complete stranger. In a surreal moment of imagination, I seemed to lose awareness of his smiling, handsome face. I pictured a bright yellow "smiley face" superimposed on his head—a kind of mindless happy guy who was completely oblivious to the social impropriety he was committing.

Social Halitosis

I've come to refer to this kind of inauthentic, inconsiderate behavior as a form of "social halitosis," the conversational equivalent of bad breath. I suppose Mr. Smiley Face was consumed with enthusiasm for his new-found moneymaking enterprise. I also suppose that he often told himself and his associates something like "Everybody's a customer for this. I can make a sale in any situation." And to prove it, he accosted an innocent bystander in a coffee shop.

The conversation had become a rather comical experience for me. As soon as he'd bridged over from the artifice of admiring my ring to the set-up for his sales pitch, I said, "This sounds like a sales pitch. Is that why you wanted to talk to me?"

Probably unaccustomed to hearing normally polite people refer directly to his rudeness, he stalled for a few seconds, and then found his feet again. "Oh no, I just thought that you seemed like a really intelligent person who's probably interested in making a lot of money. We all want to be successful, don't we?"

Then he launched again into his story about this fantastic new opportunity. When he stopped for a breath, I said, "You really seem to be consumed by this." Startled again, he began to lose altitude. "Well, yes, I am excited about it. I can't understand why anybody wouldn't be interested in an opportunity to make money."

I said, "Well, thanks for considering me, but I'm really not interested." Finally out of steam, he mumbled some polite form of departure and slunk back to the other table to join the other man.

This little vignette holds several lessons, I believe. One is that some people are completely capable—either through ignorance and lack of insight, or through willful disregard for the social rights of others—of treating another person like a thing, a piece of furniture, a non-being who exists only for the fulfillment of their own selfish purposes.

I don't know whether Mr. Smiley Face ever recovered from his social pathology, but I wouldn't be surprised to discover that he has very few real friends. Maybe he came to his senses, or maybe he jumped on another "fabulous opportunity"—possibly sold to him by another member of the Smiley Face clan.

A second lesson—or conclusion—I've arrived at after being accosted by members of the Smiley Face clan is that I have no obligation to listen politely while they're treating me like a thing. I've developed the habit of telling them to their faces that I don't want to listen to their stories. Usually I do it politely, and sometimes I do it bluntly.

The Smiley Face clan seems rather numerous, actually. Some of them are religious proselytizers. They accost people in public places, purport to strike up banal conversations, and then segue into a sales pitch for their church. Years ago many of the followers of a personal growth movement known as EST (which originally stood for "Erhard Seminars Training") became known as zombie-like recruiters for the cause. I found it a surreal experience to meet one of them at a social function and suddenly find myself on the receiving end of a strangely patterned recitation that seemed devoid of all originality or spontaneity.

I don't think all persons who try to sell things to strangers deserve to be classified as afflicted with social halitosis—just those who can't or won't treat human beings like human beings. Military recruiters, car salespeople, telemarketers, and quite a few others get paid to pitch us their products. The difference, it seems, lies in the *meta-verbal* cues— the choice of words, inflection, phrasing, and pacing, the cadence of their conversation tell us whether we're getting the canned spiel or we're being addressed as real human beings and individuals. Perhaps if it doesn't sound like a spiel, then it doesn't matter if it is.

This malfunction takes on comic proportions for me when I hear a telemarketer launch into a robotic, mindless recitation of a scripted message—before I interrupt and politely hang up. I think of it as hearing someone who knows the words but doesn't know the tune; after the thousandth recitation, the sales rep's brain goes "off line" and leaves behind the equivalent of a recorded message. This partly explains the low success rate of telemarketing calls.

Another variation of the social halitosis affliction is the person who has only one "story" and who insists on telling it over and over to everyone who will hold still. Sometimes their subject is so important or so personally compelling to them that they interpret the slightest expression of interest—even feigned interest—as an invitation to tell the whole story. Unable or unwilling to deliver the "elevator" version of the story and let the conversation move on to other topics, the monostory person gets caught up in his or her own preoccupation and overloads the listener. A surprising number of them never seem to detect or consider that they're sharing much more about penguins than others want to know.

For some, their religious views dominate their discussion. Sometimes people going through difficult life situations, such as divorce or major health problems, feel compelled to dump their suffering on others, and to elaborate and dramatize it well beyond the limits of ordinary sympathy. Some people suffer from occasional and circumstantial bouts of social halitosis. For others it becomes a long-term affliction, with a set of unconscious benefits that make it difficult to give up.

I recall one person in particular, who seemed to have only one subject of conversation: a particular medical disorder she struggled with. She had built a support group of people who coped with this disorder, and every conversation I had with her—before I began navigating toward other people at the social functions where I encountered her—revolved around this most interesting medical condition. She recited the statistics of its occurrence, shared the latest research findings, and regaled anyone who would listen with the experiences of her support group. I began to notice the subtle signals of withdrawal on the part of her listeners, but apparently she did not.

Some psychologists interpret the mono-story syndrome as evidence of a form of covert hostility—the impulse to victimize others who feel bound by the rules of polite conversation. They may derive a measure of enjoyment—usually unconsciously—from keeping their "victim" pinned down like a prize butterfly, knowing that most people will not violate the unspoken rules of etiquette.

Social Flatulence

Quite a few years ago I was visiting Dallas on a business trip. I was out for the evening with the marketing representative of the firm I was dealing with, a likable but somewhat uncouth fellow with a loud voice and a pronounced New Jersey accent. He had just recently relocated to Texas and didn't know the city very well yet.

We were having a drink in a lounge in the central business district, prior to heading out somewhere for dinner. This happened only a few years after the assassination of President John Kennedy had occurred.

Benny (not his real name) expressed interest in driving past the site of the assassination event, and asked whether I knew how to get there. I did not.

In his best "Jersey" accent, he yelled out across the room to the bartender who was standing at the other end of the bar, "Hey! Where's the place downtown where JFK got it?"

Suddenly, the room got very quiet. All eyes turned to us. I began shifting my body in the direction of the door. The bartender walked over to us and explained, in a quiet voice, how to get to the Dealey Plaza site. I felt mortified, and very grateful that the bartender had chosen to overlook the insensitive statement. I had already known that many Texans, and especially those in Dallas, felt especially distressed about the event, even years later, and that many of them worried that other Americans might unfairly characterize Dallas as a violence-prone place.

Benny's peculiar form of insensitivity and lack of situational awareness demonstrates what organizational consultant Edward Hampton calls "social flatulence." Hampton is somewhat less delicate in his choice of language. According to Hampton:

> "Some people have a knack for saying something so inappropriate, inconsiderate, or crude, showing so little appreciation for the immediate context, that it's the social equivalent of passing gas in church, or at a wedding or a funeral. I call it a 'social fart.'"

I must agree with Hampton's characterization. Social flatulence originates in ignorance, lack of situational awareness, or—possibly worse—a lack of respect for the accepted norms for behavior.

Social Dandruff

While riding on a sightseeing bus in some now-forgotten tourist city, I had the misfortune of sitting behind a teen-aged girl who decided to vigorously brush her long hair. After a few seconds of watching her hair flying in all directions, and considering the hygienic implications of her beauty maintenance, I tapped her on the shoulder and politely requested that she stop brushing her hair in my face. She did, but only after a sullen comment and an expression that clearly conveyed that I had violated her civil rights in some way. She apparently saw nothing wrong with sharing her dandruff with a total stranger.

Inasmuch as we've used metaphors of personal hygiene—social halitosis and social flatulence—we might as well complete the triad: consider social dandruff, a pattern of behavior that selfishly imposes one's interests on others.

Many examples spring to mind: the teenagers in the car beside you at the traffic light, who feel entitled to share their musical preferences with you by playing their car stereo at maximum volume. Or the young men loudly displaying their ethnic pride by carrying a "boom box" playing their favorite counter-cultural music. Or the group of ten people who come into the restaurant and "take over" the place, laughing loudly and yelling across the table as other patrons try to enjoy their meals in peace. Or the coworker who walks into your office uninvited, sits down, and props his feet up on your desk, assuming you have nothing better to do but talk to him.

Social dandruff also includes the person who imposes on the politeness of others to ask for favors inappropriate to the relationship. It includes the "get my way" person, who insists on deciding where the group shall go for lunch. It includes the person who feels free to spray everybody in sight or hearing with his or her political views or religious convictions. It includes the narcissistic person who sweeps into the room with a grand air, expecting others to stop what they're doing or talking about and acknowledge his or her entrance.

All three of these forms of toxic behavior—social halitosis, flatulence, and dandruff—arise from the same social pathology: lack of insight or lack of concern for one's impact on others. They all represent various versions of self-centered, selfish, and self-serving behavior, lacking in altruism or consideration for others.

THE "DILBERT" FACTOR

The world of Scott Adams' popular cartoon character Dilbert offers a valuable window into the social dynamics of an important subculture of the Western business world—the "techies." Dilbert and his workmates represent a highly stereotyped but very real subpopulation, which we in the business world haven't really taken seriously or tried to understand. Jokes and anecdotes about high-tech people abound, and yet their influence on the rest of us remains largely unexamined, and the ways in which their techno-theology shapes the choices in our lives deserves much more careful thought.

These people design the web pages and computer screens we see, decide how our software works, write the manuals and help screens we read as we struggle to understand their software, answer the help calls we make, create the formats for bank statements—and authors' royalty reports—and they make far-reaching decisions about how technology fits—or fails to fit—the hands of human beings. Ridiculing them or looking down on them does little good; we need to understand them, and figure out how to integrate them more successfully into the social structures of our world.

We can temporarily borrow Adams' trademarked character and transform him from an individual into a generic profile, for the purposes of understanding the handicaps that limit his—or her—social and professional success, and understanding how the education of a dilbert—in the generic sense—may also benefit society at large.

Stereotypes get to be stereotypes partly because they contain a certain core element of truth. Although the cruel or unthinking use of stereotypes can do great injustice, on the other hand, denying their core truths can also have destructive effects. While many engineers, computer experts, scientists, and technicians do not fit the stereotypical pattern of techies, geeks, and nerds, many of them do.

For this discussion, we characterize dilberts as not all technically or intellectually oriented people, but rather those who more or less fit a distinctive psychosocial profile—a stereotype, to be sure. At the extreme, dilberts tend to show the following characteristics:

- Arrested or retarded social development, accompanied by marked introversion and limited self-insight
- Limited awareness and insight into social contexts and the motivations of others
- A compensated sense of low self-esteem; gaining feelings of self-worth through intellectual or technical achievements
- Eccentric social and political ideologies; ostentatious rejection of social conventions and views; attempts to present themselves as different, unclassifiable, and unique
- An adolescent-like sense of humor and a truncated sense of imagination, often manifested in ways others perceive as eccentric rather than creative
- A well-rationalized disdain for authority, rules, and social structures; characterizing bosses and non-technical authority figures as stupid, ignorant, and ego-motivated

The recurring stories in Adams' "Dilbert" cartoons consist mainly of the bumbling incompetence of the boss, his Machiavellian disregard for the humanity of the dilberts as underlings, the stupidity and incompetence of the seldom-seen top executives, nonsensical policies that waste time and resources, and occasionally the nerdy personalities of the protagonist and his coworkers.

Where do these dilberts come from? What makes dilberts behave like dilberts? I believe they constitute the flawed outputs of our educational system, at both high school and university levels. From personal experience, having received my early education as a physicist, I can testify that high schools and colleges have done little in the past to acquaint prospective dilberts with the need to function socially. While this state of affairs has changed somewhat, at some institutions, for the most part the dilberts tend to pass through the educational system unchanged. Having worked with and managed dilberts, I have also found that business organizations do very little to help them acculturate to the diversified working societies in which they have to function.

Many technically or intellectually inclined students choose careers in engineering, the sciences, and in technologically oriented fields precisely because they anticipate working with things rather than with other people, or at worst working with other people like themselves. Seldom does their educational experience alert them to the fact that they will one day have to explain their ideas to others, persuade others of the value of their opinions, and sell their ideas and themselves. Like innocent sheep, they enter the political environments of large organizations assuming that their great ideas will sell themselves, that only a stupid person would fail to grasp the value of their contributions.

After a big dose of reality, they often conclude that fortune has cruelly implanted them in the midst of an astonishing number of stupid people. Too often, they rationalize their failures and frustration by retreating into the dilbert syndrome: "These people are too stupid, incompetent, or misguided to understand or appreciate me." Dilberts tend to disdain "company politics," which they consider despicable and unproductive. Consequently, they typically do not develop the kinds of political smarts necessary to advance in a career. In their naïve, oversimplified world view, one should advance strictly on technical merit, not on one's ability to "play politics." Many of them discover the truth slowly, if at all.

CAN WE BECOME A SOCIALLY SMARTER SPECIES?

At the risk of veering too far off into the philosophical realm, it may be worth reflecting on the broader implications of a science of social intelligence, and on where the study of such a discipline might be leading us.

An observer from a distant planet, presumably from a culture wiser and more successful than ours, might look with dismay at the incapacity of human beings to cooperate and to forbear from inhuman behavior. To be fair, such a being should credit human beings with great acts of collaboration and common effort, as well as condemn them for their colossal atrocities. One cannot sneeze at the Great Pyramid, the Panama Canal, the moon landing, the Internet, and the Ice Capades.

On the other hand, such an extraterrestrial observer might point out, we humans have proven that we can inflict destruction and suffering on a grand scale, just as we can build and collaborate on a grand scale. And parenthetically, many of our proud grand schemes have also involved considerable "collateral damage." After the most gifted artisans in India completed the Taj Mahal, emperor Shah Jahan had them killed; he had the principal architects blinded so they could never repeat their masterwork. Historical accounts note that over 5,000 workers lost their lives building the Panama Canal.

Looking at the broader sweep of history, our extraterrestrial observer could justifiably declare us a murderous species—"the only one," in the words of Mark Twain, "that, for sordid wages, goes forth in cold blood to exterminate his own kind." Over the past century or so, we've averaged something over 1,000,000 people per year killed in wars and similar violent episodes. That only counts people professionally killed; the collateral damage—the deaths due to starvation, disease, and social collapse—would run the score up to much more impressive levels.

The renowned British writer and futurist H.G. Wells observed, "Civilization becomes ever more a race, between education and catastrophe." Anthropologists like the late Steven Jay Gould have labeled us a relatively young, unproven species, and see no good evidence to conclude that we will outlast the cockroaches.

To venture into the realm of the grandiose for a moment, I would say that we as a species need three things to improve our chances of surviving and living in a reasonably peaceable state. None of them individually will solve the problem of man's inhumanity to man, and taken together they can probably only reduce its severity. But as we progressively lose them, we seem to drift further in the wrong direction.

First, we need leaders who model high social intelligence. In particular we need leaders who can articulate a positive vision of development and progress—even if it doesn't make all of us happy. We need leaders who appeal to our higher selves and invite us to grow as individuals and as a society, rather than leaders who pander to our primal fears and selfish greed.

Second, we need an educational system that honors the principles and behaviors associated with high social intelligence, and that teaches our young people to understand the cultures and subcultures through which they must navigate in this modern world, and that emphasizes the value of collaboration over conflict. We need an educational system that equips young people to express their ideas clearly, to make themselves understood, and to seek to understand others before reacting to their behavior. They need at least a workable alternative to the standard seventeen-word teenager vocabulary—"awesome," "weird," "I'm like. . .," "Ohmygod!," "whatever," and the rest.

And third, we need a media environment that serves the higher values of the culture and not simply the commercial interests of corporations whose executives feel entitled to sell anything they choose, to anybody they can influence, by any means possible. By shifting our discussion from the vague, undefined entity called "the media" and focusing instead on the leaders of the commercial enterprises that operate, populate, and manage the media environment that surrounds us all, we may succeed to some extent—possibly to a greater extent than we do now—in holding them accountable and inducing them to feel responsible for the powerful consequences of the image environment on our children, our leaders, our attitudes, our institutions, and our politics.

Order in the Court

The phrase "civility in the courtroom" doesn't come to mind too often these days. In the wake of televised celebrity trials, where we get to know defendants on a first-name basis—like football star "O.J." (Simpson), entertainer "Michael" (Jackson), TV cooking-show host

"Martha" (Stewart), actor "Robert" (Blake), accused wife-murderer "Scott" (Peterson), and sports star "Kobe" (Bryant), there seem to be fewer and fewer lay or law people still clinging to the musty old courthouse traditions of decorum, order, and politesse.

Since exceptions are often useful, consider the example set by Baltimore, Maryland, Judge Anselm Sodaro (1910–2002). Judge Sodaro became known, not just statewide, but nationally, for his courtesy, civility, and positive demeanor toward everyone who entered his courtroom.

In an age of increasing discourtesy, disrespect for institutions, and incivility, Judge Sodaro set such a standard of excellence for courtroom courtesy that, in 1998, the Maryland State Bar Association created the "Judge Anselm Sodaro Judicial Civility Award." This prize is given annually to a sitting judge who best demonstrates the practices of its namesake.

Known in his early law career as an example of the "fair but relentless prosecutor," Judge Sodaro became a Maryland Circuit Court Judge in 1956, Chief Judge in 1975, and continued in that capacity until his retirement in 1980.

His span as a judge was consistently noted for his use of courtesy and graciousness toward civil litigants, criminal defendants, witnesses, victims, bailiffs, and each of the attorneys who addressed his court. With each session, he tried to create an atmosphere of fairness for all parties.

Judge Sodaro may have best exemplified what it really means to have "order in the court."

S.P.A.C.E.: THE SKILLS OF INTERACTION

Returning to Planet Reality for the remainder of this discourse, I would like to complete this chapter by offering a fairly simple but relatively comprehensive model for describing, assessing, and developing SI at a personal level.

Inasmuch as I possess no formal credentials as a psychologist or academic researcher, I choose to invoke a kind of "diplomatic immunity" as I attempt to construct a workable and useful framework that may apply in the business and professional environment. Not having any obligations to the traditions of psychometric research, I feel relatively free to start with Professor Gardner's concept of social intelligence as a legitimate dimension of human competence, and to attempt to build a model based largely on experience and common sense.

Having chewed on the idea of SI myself off and on for over twenty years—mostly off—I've gradually evolved to a set of dimensions that seem promising as a framework for defining, measuring, and developing it. I make no claims for the statistical validity or psychometric rigor of this model or these dimensions, other than that they seem to pass the test of common sense. It will, of course, have to stand or fall on its merits over time.

Five distinct dimensions, or categories of competence, have emerged over the many years of chewing. We will explore each of them later in considerable detail, so we simply enumerate them here as follows:

1. *Situational Awareness.* We can think of this dimension as a kind of "social radar," or the ability to read situations and to interpret the behaviors of people in those situations, in terms of their possible intentions, emotional states, and proclivity to interact.
2. *Presence.* Often referred to as "bearing," presence incorporates a range of verbal and nonverbal patterns, one's appearance, posture, voice quality, subtle movements—a whole collection of signals others process into an evaluative impression of a person.
3. *Authenticity.* The social radars of other people pick up various signals from our behavior that lead them to judge us as honest, open, ethical, trustworthy, and well-intentioned—or inauthentic.
4. *Clarity.* Our ability to explain ourselves, illuminate ideas, pass data clearly and accurately, and articulate our views and

proposed courses of action, enables us to get others to cooperate with us.

5. *Empathy.* Going somewhat beyond the conventional connotation of empathy as having a feeling *for* someone else, or "sympathizing" with them, we define empathy as a shared feeling *between* two people. In this connotation we will consider empathy a state of *connectedness* with another person, which creates the basis for positive interaction and cooperation.

Putting these five common-language dimensions together, we have a working definition and a diagnostic tool for SI, which we will refer to by its acronym S.P.A.C.E. The following chapters will define, explore, and interrelate each of these key dimensions and will propose ways in which we can use the S.P.A.C.E. framework as a diagnostic and developmental model.

Exploring S.P.A.C.E.

If you would like to develop and practice the five dimensions of social competence—Situational Awareness, Presence, Authenticity, Clarity, and Empathy—a good way to start is to make yourself more fully aware of all of them on a daily basis. Once you've read the following individual chapters, consider concentrating on each of the five dimensions on each of the five week-days.

- On Monday, pay special attention to Situational Awareness. Observe others in various situations, and study the situations you personally experience.
- Spend each Tuesday paying careful attention to the dimension of Presence—yours and others'.
- Spend Wednesdays observing and learning about Authenticity.
- Devote Thursdays to Clarity of both thought and expression.

- On Fridays, concentrate especially on Empathy, observing it, learning about it, and developing it.
- On the week-end, deliberately tune in to all five dimensions.

Other things you can do to develop your S.P.A.C.E. skills:

- Keep some note cards handy and jot down your observations, discoveries, and realizations.
- Discuss these ideas with others. Explain them to others as a way to strengthen your own understanding. Teach them to the children in your life.
- Form a discussion group to share the learning process with others.
- Have the courage to seek helpful feedback from others, so you can gain greater self-insight. Provide others with helpful feedback if they ask for it.
- Make social intelligence an everyday experience of observation, learning, and development.

Notes

1. Gardner, Howard. *Frames of Mind.* New York: Basic Books Inc., 1983. See also Gardner, Howard. *Intelligence Reframed.* New York: Basic Books Inc., 1999.
2. Goleman, Daniel. *Emotional Intelligence: Why It Can Matter More Than IQ.* New York: Bantam, 1995. See also Daniel Goleman, *Working with Emotional Intelligence.* New York: Bantam, 1998, and Daniel Goleman, Richard Boyatzis, and Annie McKee, *Primal Leadership: Learning to Lead with Emotional Intelligence.* Boston: Harvard Business School Press, 2002.
3. Goleman, Boyatzis, and McKee, *Primal Leadership.*
4. Ibid.

2

"S" STANDS FOR SITUATIONAL AWARENESS

[About a particularly argumentative river boat pilot he worked under] "He did his arguing with heat . . . and I did mine with the reserve and moderation of a subordinate who does not like to be flung out of a pilothouse that is perched forty feet above the water."

—Mark Twain

THE "S" FACTOR in the S.P.A.C.E. model represents your Situational Awareness, a.k.a. your situational "radar." Are you able to understand and empathize with people in different situations? Can you sense their feelings and possible intentions? How well do you "read" situations based on a practical knowledge of human nature? Situational Awareness includes a knowledge of the cultural "holograms"—the unspoken background patterns, paradigms, and social rules that govern various situations. It means having an appreciation for the various points of view others might hold, and a practical sense of the ways people react to stress, conflict, and uncertainty.

Having a good situational radar means having a respectful interest in other people. If you are self-centered, preoccupied with your own feelings, needs, and interests, and not open to the feelings, needs, and interests of others, it will probably be more difficult for you to get them to accept you, share themselves with you, like you, and cooperate with you.

SITUATIONAL DUMBNESS AND NUMBNESS

It's hot. You're tired. You're trying to fly home after a long business or vacation trip. The airport waiting area for your flight is crowded, so, of course, your plane will be packed to the seams as well. The gate crew announces the boarding process and you and your traveling companions begin the slow trudge into the jetway and down to the entry door.

You're about the tenth passenger in line and as you approach the door of the plane, you see a guy wheeling what looks like the largest suitcase ever created by human hands. His assigned seat is in the front of the plane and so he stops to begin the process of trying to stuff this refrigerator-sized bag into an overhead bin. People who are assigned to seats past his can't get through and he seems oblivious to their heavy sighing, frequent watch checking, and shifting from foot to foot. Our intrepid traveler is oblivious to his aisle-blocking performance and as he breaks into his third hard sweat, the flight attendant makes the mistake of telling him he'll have to door-check his bag. The ensuing five-minute argument blocks the road even more, and finally one brave passenger says, "Sir, please step inside the aisle so the rest of us can get past!"

After a snarl and a sneer, Mr. Suitcase Grande finally steps out of the way to allow the remaining 134 people in line to pass. His bag finally lands in the bowels of the plane and your flight finally leaves the ground.

A classic case of situational numbness or dumbness. Situational dumbness can also take some remarkable forms.

Case in point: the director of a county department, long known as a pompous, ego-driven leader, was home on a long injury leave. Under the guise of getting some work done and building "team unity," he decided to hold a staff meeting at his home. Because he had injured his foot in an off-the-job auto accident, he was on crutches and unable to move around the room without considerable pain and effort.

During the staff meeting, the group, which included his department heads and their (completely female) support staff, covered a number of issues. As one of his people was talking, the director (and from this point on, you may use this term loosely to describe his leadership abilities) suddenly realized he needed to relieve himself. Either unwilling or unable to muster the strength necessary to rise from his chair, mount his crutches, and hobble to the bathroom, he reached down by his side, picked up a plastic bottle and proceeded to urinate into it.

Not surprisingly, his staff was more than a bit taken aback. Perhaps in other circumstances, on a good day, with overt permission from the group, a blanket to cover his lap, and a loud stereo playing in the background to provide some "white noise," just maybe he could have done this somewhat surreptitiously. But no, he decided to expose his full bladder issue to the group. Is there a better example of a lack of situational awareness? Did this director fail to turn on his "situational radar" when he got out of bed that morning? Or did he have one?

What is it in our culture that allows, causes, or permits people to victimize others with their rude behavior, selfish actions, or complete lack of insight about what they do and say, and how it affects others?

Why do we sit by as people shout into their cell phones at the movies, church, restaurants, libraries, bookstores, restrooms, sporting events, airplanes, shared vehicles (the rental car bus from the airport is another favorite locale for this), and even in the next stall in a public restroom? Why do we put up with figurative party crashers, who inflict their brand of social ineptness on us and our shared gatherings, meetings, or events?

And perhaps a larger question is: How do we help them see the self-destructive impact of their lack of social intelligence? At a minimum, what can we as the affected parties do to deal successfully with the afflicted parties? And, how can we as a society raise a new generation of people who can get along effectively with one another?

BALLISTIC PODIATRY: MAKING THE WORST OF A SITUATION

The expression "shooting yourself in the foot" conjures up a range of self-defeating behaviors, some arising from situational unawareness, some from lack of experience, and some from sheer thoughtlessness. Expert practitioners of this art can even shoot other people in the feet.

Case in point: George Millay was a visionary who, starting in 1964, helped found the Sea World theme parks around the country. His ideas included Shamu, the world's first trained and performing killer whale, pearl drivers, hydrofoil rides, whale-shaped baby strollers, and a trained sea otter exhibit.

Some of his brilliant ideas never made it to the public's eye. While in Japan, Millay saw a bird show featuring a bevy of peacocks flying majestically together down a mountainside. Intrigued by the beauty of these birds, when he returned to San Diego, he told Sea World's curator of birds to prepare three peacocks for a show of their own.

They took the birds to the top of a 320-foot observation tower (then known as the PSA Sky Tower and now known as the Southwest Airlines Tower) for a practice run.

"Release the peacocks!" shouted Millay.

The birds were set free and proceeded to drop like three stones to their deaths.

Millay was as shocked as everyone else in attendance and spent several years wondering why Asian peacocks flew better than American peacocks. He later found out that the bird curator, not wild about the idea of using the peacocks in this public fashion, had clipped their wings prior to the rehearsal and thereby sent them to their doom. So score four for the bird man, who shot himself and Millay in all four feet.[1]

In his book, *The Comic Toolbox,*[2] situation comedy writing expert John Vorhaus talks of a favorite stock character found in many "ensemble" comedies: The King of the Wildly Inappropriate Remark. Many good comedies (and some bad ones) have this character, whose off-center commentary gives a twist to the humor. The Kings say the exact wrong things at the exact right times and that's what makes them so funny. They *specialize* in ballistic podiatry and even revel in situational "unawareness." Consider this list of Kings from some of the most popular TV shows:

- Cosmo Kramer on "Seinfeld"
- Cabbie Jim Ignatowski on "Taxi"
- Bartender Woody Boyd on "Cheers"
- Corporal Max Klinger on "M.A.S.H."
- The "Major" on BBC's "Fawlty Towers"
- Joey Tribiani on "Friends"
- Cartoon character Homer Simpson on "The Simpsons"

These characters apply the wrong skills in the wrong situations, and as archetypes of ballistic podiatry, they win the gunshot sneaker award every time.

The antidote for bullet holes in your penny loafers is to respect and develop the art of Situational Awareness. Know when to speak and when to hold your tongue. Be able to size up the situation you find yourself in, rather quickly, and make the best response based on both your intuitive radar and real-time intelligence. So if it's you with the cell phone in the public place, keep it turned off until you're more alone. (Unless you're a transplant surgeon with a liver or a heart in your bag, your call can probably wait until the plane has stopped moving.)

Much of social dumbness comes from missing all the clues, both what is said and what is "non-verbalized" by others in the situation. If you enter a room where two people are standing with their backs to each other and one is red-faced and the other is drying some tears, maybe it's not a good time to ask them both to join you for coffee.

READING THE SOCIAL CONTEXT

All human interaction takes place in a context. Regardless of who's interacting with whom, where, or how, there is always a setting of some kind in which they engage one another. When we understand that there can be no human interaction without a context in which it takes place, we begin to understand how context *creates meaning,* and how the meaning supplied by the context shapes the behavior of those who are engaged in it.

Case in point: a man parks his car, locks it, opens the trunk, and takes out a revolver. He looks around, checks the revolver to confirm that it's loaded, and puts it inside his coat. He closes the trunk, looks around again, and walks into an office building.

As he steps inside, someone says, "The boss is looking for you."

He replies "Yeah—I'm looking for him, too."

He walks down the hall and enters the corner office.

Is this a disgruntled employee, about to shoot his boss? No—it's a police detective starting his shift.

Without understanding the context, we can't understand the behavior.

Why does a teenager become silent and sullen when Mom and Dad come to the school on parents' night to have a conference with the teacher? Because their presence changes the context. With the authority figures in the room, the teen no longer feels free to talk and act the way teenagers do around their friends. The presence of the parents demotes the youngster from a self-assertive member of a miniature society to a humble subordinate. This explains why many teenagers— although certainly not all—consider it the height of humiliation to be spotted in the company of their parents at the shopping mall. In their minds, it contradicts their grown-up status and reinforces their status as children.

Why do consultants and trainers advise managers not to scold subordinates in front of their workmates? It's because a private conversation, with the boss's office door closed, creates a very different context from the one created during a meeting or a gathering in a common work area. The statements and the behavior may be the same, but the context gives an entirely different meaning to the interaction.

A key aspect of the skill of Situational Awareness is being aware of, attentive to, and wise about contexts and the meanings they create. All normal human beings have some general sense of the importance of context, but for many of them this situational savvy doesn't go very far. Most of us know we're not supposed to make jokes at a funeral; we don't go out in public without our clothes on; and we know how to behave in a restaurant. But quite a few people are so self-preoccupied that they don't accurately perceive various important contexts, and consequently may not know how to behave appropriately.

Case in point: while sitting with friends over dinner at a soup-and-salad buffet restaurant, I heard a great clatter behind me—dishes and cutlery being thrown about with great energy. We all looked around and saw a young bus-boy—an energetic fellow of perhaps eighteen years—covered with sweat and working feverishly to clear the tables left by the recent surge of diners who had now cleared out of the restaurant. He dashed from one cluttered table to another, grabbing up the implements and throwing them into a large collecting tub, which he lugged between tables.

One member of our party caught his attention and said, "Excuse me. I know you're working hard, and I don't want to offend you, but the noise is making it difficult for us to carry on a conversation. Could you please work a little more quietly?"

He stopped and stared at her. Then his expression clouded, as if he didn't know whether to be angry or embarrassed. He muttered something like "I'm just doing my job," and proceeded to go about his work, albeit somewhat less noisily.

We surmised that he created such noise and commotion for two reasons: (1) he took pride in working hard and getting a lot done in a short time (youthful enthusiasm and testosterone, I suppose); and (2) he simply had little insight about the impact of his behavior on others. His only priority was the one at the center of his particular world: getting the tables cleared off. Presumably, after the discussion he began to open up his mental "bandwidth" to include a perception of the needs and interests of others.

WHAT TO LOOK FOR

If we're going to train ourselves to observe the dynamics of social contexts and to make effective use of what we observe, it may help considerably to know what to look for. A simple way to analyze a typical social context could come in handy.

Although social contexts can be remarkably complex and richly diversified, we can start with a fairly simple subdivision, or set of dimensions. For the sake of simplicity, we can think of three dimensions, or subcontexts, as a way to observe what's going on:

1. *The Proxemic Context:* the dynamics of the physical space within which people are interacting, the ways they structure that space, and the effects of space on their behavior.
2. *The Behavioral Context:* the patterns of action, emotion, motivation, and intention that show up in the interactions among the people who are engaged within the situation.
3. *The Semantic Context:* the patterns of language used in the discourse, which signal—overtly and covertly—the nature of the relationships, differences in status and social class, the governing social codes, and the degree of understanding created—or prevented—by language habits.

We can explore each of these three subcontextual dimensions further, and then recombine them to see how they operate *in toto*.

THE PROXEMIC CONTEXT

proxemics, noun.
1. *The relative degree of physical proximity tolerated by an animal species or cultural group.*
2. *The use of space as an aspect of culture.*
3. *The study of differences in distance, contact, posture, and the like in communication between people.*

If you've ever had the experience of walking into St. Peter's Basilica in The Vatican, you probably responded immediately to the sheer immensity of the space within it. You look up, and up, and up—the towering columns, the massive stone structures, the opulent use of gold and vivid decorations—all conspire to induce an immediate sense of smallness and humility. One feels utterly dwarfed by the gigantic structures. This is the power of space.

If you observe the other visitors walking around, standing around, or participating in any religious rituals that might be going on at the moment, you can easily see how their behavior responds to the proxemic context. They typically talk in quiet voices, they keep children close at hand and admonish them to be quiet, and they usually show considerable respect for the religious significance of the place. One seldom hears a person call out in a loud voice to a friend who may be standing some distance away.

Every human-designed space has its apparent meaning—what it "says" to those who enter it. A Japanese garden may say "serenity." A shopping mall may say "spend." A hotel lobby may say "luxury." A royal palace may say "power." Some professionally decorated homes look like museums—they seem to say, "Be careful where you sit. This place is to be seen and not touched." Others seem to say, "Make yourself comfortable. You're welcome here."

Proxemic Politics

After the Spanish Civil War (1936–1939) General Franco, who ruled Spain with an iron hand, commissioned the construction of an enormous cathedral, ostensibly to commemorate those who died in the conflict and to establish some sort of reconciliation with the Catholic church. North of Madrid, the Valley of the Fallen features a 500-foot cross on top of a mountain, under which lies a huge basilica carved straight back into the granite face.

In a gesture of reconciliation—and self-glorification—Franco arranged for himself to be buried under the basilica, along with the leader of the defeated opposition party. In addition, some 40,000 of the one million soldiers who died during the civil war are also buried in the site.

After the basilica was completed—a twenty-year project that nearly ruined the government's treasury—the Vatican's representatives let it be known that it would not be eligible for consecration.

The reason for withholding consecration: the length of the basilica—the distance from the entrance to the back wall—was 252 meters (860 feet). This made it longer than St. Peter's Basilica in Rome.

To satisfy the Vatican representatives, the architects installed a false wall with a second set of doors, sealing off part of the length of the structure and making it shorter than St. Pete's.

Human beings both structure space and interpret the meaning of space. They behave according to the signals transmitted by the space around them. In arranging those elements of a spatial context that they can control, people express—both consciously and unconsciously—their intentions toward one another.

Case in point: I attended a meeting with a group of managers in an aerospace company, in the office of a senior project manager who coordinated the contributions of their various work groups. The senior manager—who conducted many meetings in his office—had placed a work table perpendicular to the front of his desk, making a "T" formation, and placed chairs along both sides of the table. This arrangement allowed him to sit at his desk and run the meeting. This proxemic context reinforced his role as the authority figure in the room. While the rest of us sat upright in our chairs, with our notepads on the table, he was free to lean back in his chair, put his feet up on the desk, and be the boss. I got the feeling that the rest of us were like the people pulling oars on one of those huge Viking boats, and he was the guy banging the drum to keep us all working.

Interaction Zones

I've often noticed that executives communicate their attitudes and intentions about power, status, and social distance by the arrangement of their offices.

Television news stories sometimes portray big important negotiation meetings between powerful parties, such as representatives from countries in a state of conflict, showing them facing each other across a huge conference table, lined up like two symbolic armies. Perhaps something as simple as changing the seating arrangement can signal a less polarized, antagonistic relationship.

Human beings even structure imaginary space, that is, the empty space between structural elements, by locating themselves in particular ways and inviting others to take up certain locations. Anthropologists who study the science of proxemics identify four basic spatial zones that human beings demarcate, and which they use to express and control their relationships to one another:

- *Public space*—the extended area, within which people can co-exist without "officially" interacting in any meaningful way. Examples: a shopping mall, department store, or public park.
- *Social space*—a more immediate zone, within which people interact somewhat directly, or are expected to interact.

Examples: the area associated with a table in a restaurant, an area surrounding a group of people who are having a conversation, or a living room. Interestingly, a relatively confined space, such as the inside of an airplane, can operate as both public space and social space; the passengers are conscious of an enforced relationship, however distant, during the flight. Elevators also enforce a kind of social interaction, or at least acknowledgment, between strangers who find it necessary to share the same small space for a few minutes. It's public space, but it becomes social space when the door slides shut.

- *Personal space*—the proxemic "bubble" surrounding one person, which marks off his or her personal boundaries, and within which others are expected to acknowledge that person's individuality. Examples: the area around a person standing on a crowded train or bus, the area within which someone like a dentist or hair stylist performs a personal service, and the space between two people who are conferring over a document of some kind. It's axiomatic that the typical size of this personal bubble varies from one culture to another. The privilege of closely approaching a person, or even touching another person, varies considerably according to cultural codes, including codes that dictate how differences in rank or status are nonverbally expressed.

- *Intimate space*—the small region surrounding and directly touching a person's body, within which direct contact with another person implies a close personal, emotional, or sexual interaction. While standing among a group of strangers in a fully packed train car, you may be sharing your intimate bubble with two or three strangers at the same instant; however, the prevailing social codes contradict the implication of intimacy.

In addition to marking off these four invisible concentric zones of interaction, human beings also tend to arrange themselves within a spatial environment in ways that serve and solve a variety of psycholog-ical and social needs.

Case in point: several years ago, I met with a group of Japanese executives who were touring the United States to study management practices in outstanding service organizations, a topic for which I was one of the recognized experts at the time. They had requested a half-day meeting, a kind of informal seminar, to examine my concepts and theories. The evening before the session, I met with the bicultural interpreter they had hired, a young woman who had lived and studied in the United States as well as Japan. She was explaining to me how the session would probably proceed.

"I haven't met them yet, but they're Japanese, so I can probably guess how they'll handle the meeting," she said. "They haven't met one another before this trip, but by some process they will all have figured out the relative ranks in their own organizations, and those ranks will become the order of social status within the group while they're together.

"They'll have you sit at the end of the conference table, and the highest-ranking guy will be sitting on your right. The next-highest-ranking guy will be on his right, and so on around the table. The most junior person will be at the end of the chain, and I'll be on your left."

I was intrigued by the confidence with which she predicted the proxemic context of the meeting. The next day, I found she was com-pletely accurate. They arranged themselves exactly as she had predicted.

Further, she had coached me about the question-and-answer pro-cedure. "When you invite them to ask questions, be sure to allow a very long time for them to respond. What will happen is that they'll all look at the number one guy; he gets to ask the first question. If he doesn't have a question, he'll look down the line toward the others. If the number two guy has a question, he'll ask it; if not, he passes the invisible baton down the line. If you assume nobody has a question, you might move on too soon, and the lowest-ranking guy might not get to ask his question."

Again, she was exactly accurate. A group of—heretofore—strangers had all agreed on the same proxemic context, and the same rules for behavior, without ever discussing it.

Subconscious Spaces

Proxemic contexts are everywhere—once we start looking for them. The fact that they're omnipresent might help to explain why we tend to be unaware of them most of the time. Consider the evolving proxemic context set up by the interaction of people driving their cars on streets and highways. Have you noticed that a fairly large percentage of drivers—especially males—will accelerate slightly when you overtake them and begin to pass? How about the way many drivers enter a freeway from an on-ramp: they accelerate sufficiently to enter the first lane—where you happen to be driving—and then they slow down? It's as if they are signaling to you: "See, I've claimed this piece of moving territory, and there's nothing you can do to get it back." If you anticipate this maneuver and move over to the next lane, the person may accelerate as he enters the first lane, so as to stay ahead of you.

"Staying ahead"—proxemically speaking—is an important subconscious impulse for many people. Proxemic behavior in automobiles seems to be a matter of claiming ownership of a moving patch of territory—usually extending ahead of one's vehicle for a distance that depends on the speeds involved and the instinctive reactions of the drivers involved. Human beings in most cultures also seem to relate to people who are standing—or driving—behind them as socially inferior, and perhaps they strive to position themselves "ahead" of others in order to gain feelings of potency and proxemic superiority.

The proxemic context can include other elements in addition to the arrangement of physical space. Attached to this space, or—more accurately stated—woven through it, we have sounds, the effects of light, and even odors of all kinds. Consider the proxemic context of a frenetic dance club or disco, with the strobe lights, smoke, and pounding music.

All of these elements influence the feelings and behavior of people who interact within the space. The dim light of a church or temple, the smell of incense, the sounds of chanting or singing, all lend meaning to the proxemic context we experience.

THE BEHAVIORAL CONTEXT

An experience I had as a seventh-grader long ago left a life-long impression on me about the ways human beings respond to context. This episode involved both proxemic and behavioral contexts. It helped me begin to understand that we human beings delude ourselves most of the time when we tell ourselves that we continuously invent our behavior according to deliberate choices we make. In fact, we usually don't. Usually, we react unconsciously to the many cues of the context—proxemic, behavioral, and semantic—and on rare occasions do we consciously think about how to react.

In my seventh-grade experience, I was one of the "country kids" who rode the school bus to and from our school every day, in the small town of Westminster, Maryland. The same group of kids would be collected every day, standing outside their houses or at the end of the lanes leading to their farmhouses. We all knew one another, if not necessarily on a first-name basis.

On one particular day, a strange pattern began to emerge. Quite by chance—I presume—I and about a dozen of the other kids who got picked up first along the route happened to sit on the left side of the bus. As it happened, the next half-dozen kids also sat on the left. At some point, it became obvious that nobody was sitting on the right side. Every new kid or small group of kids would board the bus, look around, and take seats on the left side.

As the bus began to fill up, we looked around in bemused fascination; we watched carefully as every new kid who entered the bus chose a seat on the left side. I could also see, by looking in the bus driver's mirror, that he was reacting to this strange pattern as well. Normally taciturn and borderline crabby, he kept glancing into the mirror and scowling more intensely as this situation developed. Finally, he reached his breaking point.

With the bus virtually full, and with all seats taken but one, the next kid who boarded tried to take the last empty seat on the left side. The kid sitting in that seat didn't want to move over and let him sit down; he snarled, "Sit over there!" Not knowing what was going on, and possibly suspecting some sort of practical joke, the last kid insisted on taking the last seat. A shoving match ensued, with the occupant insisting that the new kid sit on the completely empty right side of the bus, and the new kid demanding that he move over.

The whole situation became quite bizarre. Finally, the driver blew up. He stopped the bus and began yelling at us. "You kids are trying to drive me crazy! Move over to the other side of the bus!" He forcibly rearranged us so that both sides of the bus were occupied. "Get over there!" After that, the other kids who boarded, having no knowledge of the strange developments before they arrived, seated themselves randomly on both sides of the bus.

To this day, I'm not sure I understand what happened in that little episode, what caused it, or why we all engaged in such strange collective behavior.

One can see vividly the strength of proxemic and behavioral contexts—situations in which certain behavioral patterns dominate—by observing situations in which people bring very different expectations with them.

Case in point: an acquaintance of mine spent several years in the 1970s as an "ESL" teacher—English as a Second Language. Having a background in social work, she specialized in working with Asian refugees, particularly the ethnic group known as the Hmong, a group from the highlands and mountains of Laos. The Hmong had been a highly isolated ethnic group, with very well-defined customs and very little knowledge of the outside world. Most of them were doubly illiterate, that is, they couldn't read or write in their own language, to say nothing of English. Because of the double-illiteracy factor, she could not use the normal print materials typically available for ESL training. She also discovered that most of the refugees, who had recently arrived, were so overwhelmed by an unfamiliar environment that they didn't understand how to behave in situations Westerners take for granted. Many of them had never seen buses, television sets, or even pencil and paper—familiar artifacts of Western culture. "The women would bring their infants to class," she said. "They thought it was kind of a social gathering. A lot of them didn't know what went on in a classroom situation; they didn't even know they were supposed to sit facing the front of the room. They talked freely; I had to ask them to be quiet so I could teach them the recitation exercises."

As on our bus, much of the behavioral context in any situation is encoded nonverbally: body postures, movements, gestures, facial expressions, tone of voice. For example, people signal authority and deference by where and how they sit or stand, who sits and who stands, who has the right to touch whom, who enters and leaves a room first, and countless other details that skilled observers can pick up. People signal affiliation—or lack of it—by various gestures, expressions, and interactions. Can you look at a couple sitting at a table in a restaurant and guess whether they've recently met or they have a long-term relationship?

Sociologists identify many other signaling systems, such as those involving clothing, jewelry, hats, tattoos, and other adornments as *class marks*—indications of affiliation with a well-defined subculture. Certain combinations of clothing can identify a person as belonging to a street gang, an ethnic group, or a distinct socioeconomic level. The business suit has long served as a class mark for the commercial subculture.

Cartoonist Scott Adams, creator of the everyman technical worker Dilbert, cautions managers to dress for success, especially if they have neither brains nor talent going for them. According to Dilbert's companion Dogbert, in *Dogbert's Top Secret Management Handbook:*[3]

> "Clothes make the leader. Employees probably won't ever respect you as a person, but they might respect your clothes. Great leaders throughout history have understood this fact.
>
> "Take the pope, for instance. If you took away his impressive pope hat, his authority would be seriously diminished. Ask yourself if you would take advice on birth control from a guy wearing, let's say, a John Deere hat. I don't think so."

Part of any behavioral context, in any situation, is the set of shared rules, customs, expectations, and norms for behaving that the participants bring with them. To the extent that they share the same behavioral codes, they typically get along successfully. If one or more of the people in a particular situation does not share—or chooses to violate—certain of those codes, conflict can arise.

Case in point: one does not touch the Queen of England. It just isn't done, by anybody, under any circumstances, except by those few people who have a special familial relationship or an intimate relationship of personal service. In 1992, the Australian Prime Minister Paul Keating earned the caustic label "Lizard of Oz" from the British press for touching the Queen on the back. While showing her around some public building, he gestured to show the way, and then put his arm across her back, with his palm on her side. While many people would take this as an amicable gesture, the Queen stiffened, paused, and gave him a look that clearly communicated that he had violated the official behavioral code. Many in England were angered and offended on behalf of the Queen. In contrast, many in Australia were angered at what they considered British snobbery—a replay of the continual antagonism between Aussies and Brits.

Brian Tobin, the Premier of Newfoundland and Labrador also scandalized the Commonwealth, as he was photographed touching the

Queen's back as he accompanied her up a flight of stairs; he protested that he was simply trying to help an elderly lady avoid falling. In 2000 another Australian PM, John Howard, felt it necessary to vigorously deny having touched the Queen.

Experts in cross-cultural communication cite unique behavioral codes that people in certain cultures follow almost unconsciously, but which make little sense to people from other cultures. In many Arab cultures, for example, people do not pick up food with their left hands, nor do they pass food to others with the left hand. They typically use the left hand to attend to various bodily functions, and even with modern standards of sanitation and hygiene, tradition dictates that the left hand is unclean.

Similarly, in many Mediterranean cultures, presenting the bottom of one's foot or shoe to another person constitutes a serious nonverbal insult. Sitting in such a way as to display the sole of the shoe, or putting one's feet up on a desk, signals disrespect for others.

To the Balinese, the soul resides in one's head, and for this reason it is a serious offense for a stranger to pat a small child on the head. Balinese consider it very unwise, spiritually, to stand on one's head, or even to place one's feet higher than one's head. One of the gravest of insults in that culture is to say "I'll beat your head!"

In strict Islamic cultures, behavioral codes dictate when males and females can be alone together, and even when they can be in the same room. Westerners doing business in Saudi Arabia, for example, may find it frustrating that male and female workers are not allowed to work together in the same room. Female representatives of foreign companies, female diplomats, and female journalists often find these restrictions very difficult to cope with.

THE SEMANTIC CONTEXT

Physician Frederic Loomis, in his classic book *Consultation Room,* cited an incident in which an innocent remark invoked an undesired *semantic reaction:*

"I learned something of the intricacies of plain English at an early stage in my career. A woman of thirty-five came in one day to tell me she wanted a baby but that she had been told that she had a certain type of heart disease which might not interfere with a normal life but would be dangerous if she ever had a baby. From her description I thought at once of mitral stenosis. This condition is characterized by a rather distinctive rumbling murmur near the apex of the heart, and especially by a peculiar vibration felt by the examining finger on the patient's chest. The vibration is known as the 'thrill' of mitral stenosis.

"When this woman had been undressed and was lying on my table in her white kimono, my stethoscope quickly found the heart-sounds I had expected. Dictating to my nurse, I described them carefully. I put my stethoscope aside and felt intently for the typical vibration which may be found in a small but variable area of the left chest.

"I closed my eyes for better concentration, and felt long and carefully for the tremor. I did not find it and with my hand still on the woman's bare breast, lifting it upward and out of the way, I finally turned to the nurse and said, 'No thrill.'

"The patient's black eyes snapped open, and with venom in her voice she said, 'Well isn't that just too bad? Perhaps it's just as well you don't get one. That isn't what I came here for.'

"My nurse almost choked, and my explanation still seems a nightmare of futile words."[4]

Words are much more than mere lifeless symbols and signals. *They are the very structure of thought.* Many famous leaders have understood and capitalized on the psychology of language, and have used this knowledge to arouse and mobilize people, for both good and evil. Poetry, literature, popular slogans, metaphors, and patriotic songs all have the power to move people in profound ways.

The study of *rhetoric* deals with the primal patterns of language, and how a skillful turn of phrase conveys meaning beyond the mere symbolic level of words. For example, at the time of the American declaration of independence from Britain, Benjamin Franklin reportedly made one of the most memorable statements of the time. When one of his fellow statesmen said, after the group had passed the Declaration of Independence, "Now gentlemen, we must all hang together," Franklin said, "Indeed, we must, or assuredly we shall hang separately."

Alfred Korzybski, a respected scholar and researcher who studied the psychology of language, proposed a kind of "theory of relativity" of knowledge, in his book *Science and Sanity,*[5] published in 1933. He coined the term *general semantics* to describe his theory of how the structure of language shapes human thought, and particularly how certain language habits contribute to conflict, misunderstandings, and even psychological maladjustment.

According to Korzybski, we live in a *semantic environment*. This environment consists of the shared language habits, traditions, symbols, meanings, implications, and connotations within which we interact and try to make ourselves understood to one another. Actually, most of us navigate through a variety of semantic environments, depending on the people we associate with and interact with.

Korzybski asserted that there is no such thing as "universal truth" or "universal knowledge," and in contradiction to the teachings of a long line of Western philosophers starting with Socrates, Plato, and Aristotle, he believed that the structure and psychology of language made it impossible for any two people to ever share exactly the same "reality." Speakers of English, he maintained, do not construct the same reality with their words as speakers of Japanese, Swahili, or Spanish. Since different languages represent concepts in different ways, the structural differences of those languages impose inescapable limitations on our mental models of reality.

Korzybski often referred to *verbal maps*. By verbal maps, he meant that the things we say—either vocally or in writing—are our best attempts to "map" the inner structure of knowledge and meaning we carry around in our nervous systems into a shared medium of exchange. Try to describe a small child, for example, to a person who has never met the child, and you'll become conscious that "the map is not the territory," as Korzybski often said. No matter how many words you use, and no matter how many ways you try to capture your experience of the child in words, you can never do it completely. The verbal map the other person takes away from the conversation can never be more than a vague and incomplete approximation of your personal experience of the child.

Even worse, Korzybski argued, any two speakers of the same language do not share exactly the same reality, because each person grows up learning his or her own unique meanings for the many words in his or her native language.

Korzybski believed that Aristotle, although greatly respected as an historical figure, was trapped inside a "mental box" that he could not detect: the structure of his own native language. His attempts to define abstract concepts such as truth, virtue, responsibility, and man's relationship to nature and God were, Korzybski argued, doomed to failure. They would always be confined to the implications of the ancient Greek world-view as encoded in the Greek language. He referred to this syndrome, disparagingly, as "Aristotelian thinking."

Many Meanings

To state the theory of general semantics in its simplest terms:

> No two brains contain exactly the same "meaning" for any word expression, or concept; the meanings are embedded in the people, not in the words.

The influence of language on human thinking is easy to see, once you start paying attention to it. Consider, for example, the use of various terms in any particular language—and "language culture"—to describe kinship roles. In English-speaking cultures, the word *uncle* generally refers to the brother of one's father or mother. There is no widely used English word—and consequently no clearly identified concept—to signal whether the uncle one is referring to is the father's brother or the mother's brother. Some other cultures, however, have a unique word for each type of brother, but no generic word for this relationship. There may be additional words—and conceptual "handles"—for other males who have brother-like relationships with one's parents. In those cultures, it would seem very peculiar to refer to such a male relative generically, without using words that signaled the important elements of family lineage.

More serious issues arise from the effects of language on thought and behavior. For example, arguments over the meanings of abstract terms like "democracy," "capitalism," and "justice" are ultimately futile, because they have differing personal meanings for different people. Wars and ethnic conflicts often start as a result of, or in connection with, reckless use of highly charged language.

In my occupation as a management consultant, I've frequently heard people argue about the difference between "management" and "leadership," as if each term has some fundamental, god-given definition and that all we have to do is find it. They don't seem to understand that any symbol—a word, or a collection of words—has no innate meaning. Its meaning is embedded in the nervous system of the person saying it or hearing it. This is why arguments about the "true" meanings of words are ultimately futile. The Red Queen in the children's story "Alice in Wonderland" is technically correct when she says, "A word means what I want it to mean, nothing more and nothing less," but she misses the larger issue of whether it means the same thing to other people.

Most political debates degenerate to a pushing match in which each party seeks to impose its favorite verbal map on the other. Each builds a self-consistent verbal structure that works for him or her. And in order to avoid being conquered by the other in verbal combat, each must reject the other party's verbal map. Finding agreement ultimately comes down to sorting out the verbal maps being used by the various parties and arriving at a few key verbal maps they can agree to.

Our practical experience tells us that human beings tend to use multiple *linguistic frames,* or "semantic territories" demarcated by certain vocabularies and styles of usage. These linguistic frames also serve as class marks, identifying people with certain socioeconomic or cultural classes. One linguistic frame might involve considerable use of profanity, treating "fancy" language as the province of outsiders. Another might favor an erudite or academic style of language, with profanity considered a mark of lower social or intellectual status. Each linguistic frame has its rules—which forms of expression are accepted and which are considered foreign.

Case in point: a colleague hired a contractor to paint his home. He had known the contractor socially for many years and this was his first opportunity to use his services. The contractor, a smart and talented man, ran his painting business while working full time as a city employee. He had about six to eight workers on his crew, including a man we'll call "Dave."

Because the contractor knew that my colleague wrote business books, he must have mentioned it to Dave. During a break in the paint work, Dave came over to my colleague to make small talk:

Dave, cleaning his brushes: "So, I hear you're an arthur [sic]."

Colleague: "I'm sorry, a what?"

Dave: "I said I heard you were an arthur."

Colleague: "I'm sorry, I'm confused. What's an 'arthur'?"

Dave (getting frustrated): "You know, an arthur, a guy what writes books."

Colleague (the light finally coming on): "Oh! An author. Yes, I write books."

If you're a skillful navigator of these linguistic frames, you know how to speak one language to a small child, another language to a teenager, another language to the construction foreman who repairs your roof, another language to the clerk in the supermarket, and another language to your doctor.

Beyond Logic

Besides using different linguistic frames, each person's verbal map—the symbolic translation of his or her inner reality into a message—encodes his emotional state as well as the structure of what we like to think of as logic. For example, psychologists recognize an aspect of nonverbal signaling associated with the use of language—an element unrelated to the actual words being spoken. *Meta-verbal signals* are the "between the lines" cues that can indicate an unconscious mental state, an emotion, or an apprehension the speaker would like to conceal. One can observe the interplay between subconscious mental process and social behavior, in the shift of language. Many people, when discussing their own behavior and prospectively having to admit that they may have behaved in socially unacceptable ways, will shift from the "first-person" form—"I did such-and-such"—to the less direct "third-person" form—"people do such-and-such." Or they may shift to the generic familiar form, "you," as a way to implicate the listener as a fellow protagonist.

An excerpt from a news report illustrates this phenomenon of *displacement*—taking one's self out of the conversation by changing the "person" form of the language. An article on the CNN.com news site, during the highly contentious 2004 U.S. Presidential elections, quoted the supervisor of elections for Florida's Palm Beach County as saying:

> "'Our staff knows we're being held to a much higher standard, and we're doing everything we can to make sure nothing happens,' said LePore, designer of the 'butterfly ballot.' 'But we're human, sometimes *mistakes are made.*'"[6]

Note the shift in "person"—probably unconscious—from "*we're* human" to "mistakes *are* made." Somebody makes mistakes, but the speaker doesn't say "*we* make mistakes."

This verbal behavior of displacement actually occurs quite frequently in human language behavior. It serves a subconscious need for ego-defense—shielding the speaker from the anticipated stress of disapproval. Once you recognize it and begin listening for it, you may be surprised how often it appears, and how deftly people use it.

Skilled interrogators know that subtle shifts in the use of language can telegraph internal and subconscious feelings of guilt, apprehension, suppressed anger, and various other emotional states that the person under interrogation would prefer not to reveal. This is why they often engage their subjects in wide-ranging conversations, designed to elicit these inadvertent signals of internal conflict.

Returning to the theme of Situational Awareness, we can see that reading the semantic context, and picking up the linguistic cues that signal deeper levels of meaning, can be a very useful skill. We can learn to quickly identify the different linguistic frames that come into play in various situations: a conversation among teenagers, a business meeting, a dinner party, a classroom, a gathering of friends in a pub. We can exercise Situational Awareness and establish empathy with those involved by matching the language they use—within reason. In a sense, we may need to be multi-lingual within a single language.

NAVIGATING CULTURES AND SUBCULTURES

The more you know about an in-group, the easier it is to understand why its members react the way they do in certain situations. Review the following characteristics of a certain subculture in our society and see if you can guess which one it describes:

- Distrustful of non-group members
- Overprotective of family members
- More comfortable socializing with other group members than with outsiders
- Perceive themselves as hard-hearted and tough

- Male dominated
- Militaristic
- Special language and tools

If you guessed "professional sports athletes" or "Navy fighter pilots," you'd be close. If we added in "Need for personal space is wider," "controlled and action-oriented," "tend to see things in black and white, yes or no, for or against, and legal or illegal," you might say we were describing "police officers" and you'd be correct.

Every subculture is really just a part of our larger full culture. But even though they belong to our meta-world, they see their miniature worlds as more important. Every member of a subculture tends to see himself or herself as unique, different, special or specialized, and more socially or operationally significant than those who are outside their membership.

So who lives in these distinctive subcultures? Besides members of law enforcement, we can add firefighters; military members (with each branch having its own subculture within the military subculture, that is, Marines don't hang out with Army soldiers, Airmen don't socialize with Coasties, etc.); rock stars; movie and TV celebrities; professional athletes; medical doctors; academics (Ph.D. holders); and even gang members.

And in a way, aren't all of these subcultures rather like street gangs? There are many commonalities that make very different groups more similar than one might first imagine. It's hard to get into the group, hard to leave it or get out of it completely, there are "uniforms," coded jargon and special language, and there are rules of behavior that can get you kicked out if you violate them.

Street gangs, typically a rather violent subculture, follow a precise set of "entrance requirements." You have to live in their neighborhood, have their skin color, and/or identify with their belief systems. They operate under a rule of "blood in and blood out," meaning that they will shed some of your blood when you join (a ritualized beating for new initiates) and shed perhaps even more of your blood should you choose to leave the group "early."

Subcultures tend to flourish and thrive when the barriers to entry are stringent. When not everyone can get in, the existing members generate a tremendous sense of cohesion, pride, and self-worth among themselves. Medical doctors, police officers, firefighters, military pilots, actors, singers, and professional sports figures know intuitively that their ranks are special, small, and even elite. Not everyone can do what they do, and only a finite number, like themselves, are or were willing to subject themselves to the rigorous entry process to get in, stay, and succeed.

To say these belief systems help to create an "us versus them" mentality understates it. The reason these members eat together, socialize together, meet outside of work, dress similarly, date and even marry each other suggests their innate social distance from outsiders. The phrase, "You can't understand what it's like to be me unless you do what I do," makes it difficult for even family or friends to pierce this veil of togetherness, and alienates those who don't really "know what it's all about."

Some subcultures are so well-bounded that even the levels inside a group will divide it. In other words, cops don't usually hang out with parking controllers; doctors don't usually eat lunch with nurses (unless there is dating going on); airline pilots don't usually eat dinner with flight attendants (see doctor-nurse exception); and professors don't socialize with their graduate assistants. Birds of a feather don't always flock together, especially when one bird sees the other as less bird-like.

This subculture specialization leads to norming behavior, where you stay inside by not allowing the outside in. Membership in these subcultures is usually difficult, requiring a special skill (good eyesight, exceptional body control, raw courage, fearlessness), good genes (beauty, brains, nice hair), and a rare degree of perseverance (long years in medical school and residency; academies, boot camps, and flight schools; years of failed auditions and readings; acting or singing lessons since early childhood; lots of time spent in the minor leagues).

All this being true, it's easy to see why members fight so hard to keep others out and why staying in requires conformity. The best way to get along, in any subculture, from certified public accountants to skateboarders, is to go along.

CODES OF CONDUCT: VIOLATE THE RULES AT YOUR PERIL

Every culture, and indeed every situation and every context, has some kind of code of conduct that people impose on themselves. Formal or informal, conscious or unconscious, these codes have the effect of making humans highly predictable to one another. Indeed, no organized society could function without the myriad subconscious "deals" people make with one another about how to behave. People who have adapted to a particular culture have internalized these codes and typically follow them quite automatically and unconsciously. And the person who violates an important social code—the rebel, the renegade, the radical—will almost certainly arouse the disapproval and even the animosity of others who follow that code.

Case in point: a few years ago I conducted an informal seminar in California for some visiting Japanese executives. The meeting convened at about 5:15 p.m. in a small conference room, shortly after the end of the day's sessions at an international conference. They had traveled to the conference as a group, but most of them had not known one another before the trip. They began to assemble in the conference room to get ready for our seminar. All of them wore suits with ties— typical for Japanese executives in business situations. However, one of their number, an outgoing young man with considerable experience working in Western cultures, had decided to go to his room before the meeting and change clothes.

When he walked into the room dressed in shorts, running shoes, and a T-shirt, all heads turned in his direction. More than one of his colleagues gave him a "once-over" and a disapproving stare, implying strongly with their gaze that he had violated the dress code.

The disapproving glances, which seemed to say "Hey! No fair! If we have to wear suits, what gives you the right to dress any way you want?" had no apparent impact on him. After a few minutes, some of them began to remove their jackets, the ties began to come off, and a new dress code emerged.

Some social codes, however, have more power over their subjects than others, and some involve sanctions much more severe than disapproving looks.

Case in point: some years ago, while working in Australia, I read a newspaper account of aboriginal tribal justice, which had both social and political overtones for the Australian government and for the broader society. It seems that a group of Aborigines in the Northern Territories region—the true "outback," as Aussies know it—had put several of their members on trial for their lives. Their crimes involved failing to prevent the desecration of a sacred site—a place long revered by their clan for its spiritual importance.

Apparently, the stock ranch that incorporated the sacred site—not recognized as sacred by its white owners, of course—changed possession. The new owner, noting that part of "his" property showed signs of squatter activity (Aborigines, like many "primitive" peoples, do not conceive of individual ownership of land), decided to clean it up. He brought in earth-moving equipment, razed the site, and re-fenced the area.

According to the news reports, several of the clan's members bore the responsibility for protecting and preserving the site and, in the eyes of the clan's elders, they had failed to carry out a sacred and very serious duty. The sentence handed down by the council: death by stoning.

The case drew considerable press attention, forcing the state government and the Australian Commonwealth government to take a position. Inasmuch as Australia as a nation does not allow capital punishment, the peculiar political relationship between the Commonwealth and the various aboriginal groups came into question once again.

While various government agencies moved to block the execution of the tribal members, the men facing punishment seemed to accept their fate with relative equanimity. One of them, interviewed by the press, simply said, "It was our job to protect the site, full stop. We didn't do it and the site got destroyed. Now we gotta cop it."

Ultimately the government blocked the execution and provided a face-saving means for the men to escape death. The process illustrated vividly the power of social codes.

Women in many cultures have suffered for centuries under oppressive, male-dominant behavior codes.

Case in point: during the first attempt to install a democratic government into the failed state of Afghanistan, in October 2004, women—theoretically, at least—acquired the right to vote. But in many areas of the country, particularly those far away from the main urban centers, older cultural codes conflicted with this new and novel code that presumably permitted women to behave in very untraditional ways.

In many areas, tribal elders and local military chieftains, whose word carried the force of law, simply forbid women to go to the polling places. Under the strictest of the Islamic and tribal codes, women could not move about freely in public. They required specific permission from the senior surviving male in their family—a father, a husband, or even an elder brother. In many cases, the codes dictated that women could not leave their homes unless in the company of a male member of the family.

In other cases, the senior males might permit their wives, daughters, or sisters to go to the polls, but they ordered them to vote for certain candidates. Many women, in interviews with journalists and investigators, felt they could never violate the instructions of the senior male members of their families. Others felt, as a result of their social isolation, limited education, and lack of access to political news, that they could not make reasonable judgments in any case.

Women did manage to get one female candidate on the ballot, although she had even less chance of winning than the male candidates who opposed the U.S.-backed president. Some female thought leaders and organizers concluded that the availability of voting rights for females, while largely inconsequential in its impact, nevertheless represented a change of great symbolic significance. Many felt that, realistically, they would have to settle for a small step, as they could see clearly what happens when new and unaccepted codes of behavior collide with old, deeply entrenched codes.

Part of growing up in a world run by adults (bosses, parents, teachers, etc.) means learning how to behave. And learning how to behave means following the rules created by those in charge. Most often, we learn the "right" ways to operate successfully through the most common and old-fashioned methods: trial and error, crimes and punishments. As a child, when you do well (you manage to keep your hands out of the wedding cake), you get rewarded (with cake). When you misbehave (purposely kick the football into the scary neighbors' backyard), you get punished (no more football).

Same goes for adults. Aren't there codes of behavior for these situations?

- In a meeting alone with your new boss? In a group meeting with your new boss?
- In front of your in-laws versus your oldest friends?
- Face-to-face with someone you're physically attracted to at a party?
- In a social situation where your kids are terrified you'll embarrass them, that is, at a parent-teacher meeting, a conference with their teacher, at a sporting event where they're playing on the field?
- In front of a business client or co-worker whom you're trying to impress?

It gets more complicated when subcultural norms come into play. One of the problems with subcultures is that the members can become so conditioned to the rules, roles, and responsibilities that, whenever someone deviates from the norm, chaos erupts. Breaking the rules of the subculture is the fastest way to fall from favor; breaking the "code" gets you put out of the tribe. Consider these examples of subcultures in crisis:

- Lawyers suing other lawyers for malpractice
- Doctors criticizing other doctors for surgical or administrative errors (except in Morbidity and Mortality meetings or "Disruptive Physician Committees," where the gloves come off)
- Cops telling Internal Affairs about other cops who have broken the law or injured someone under the color of their authority
- Expert witnesses criticizing each other's findings and conclusions in court cases
- Mafia members singing to federal prosecutors about their criminal colleagues to avoid prosecution for their own crimes
- Union members siding with the "suits" in a labor dispute, by crossing a picket line or failing to visibly support union brothers and sisters

This last example brings to mind an example of codes of conduct in the workplace. In his insightful book, *Rivethead,*[7] about the inner experience of the assembly-line worker, General Motors worker Ben Hamper tells many tales of the tensions between the "suits" and the assembly-line workers. Each subculture was always seeking to punish the other, often in unique and painful ways.

During one particularly tense period of labor unrest, company management thought it useful to take various other "suits" on tours of the GM truck assembly plant. These walking tours usually included GM executives from other facilities, vendors, car dealers, politicians, and other VIPs.

Some of the workers, who were both bored and bugged, decided to have a little fun by throwing bolts, nuts, and other hot or sharp pieces of metal at the tourists. It only took a few flying projectiles to hit their targets' heads, necks, and backs before the plant tours were quickly suspended.

Of course, with turnabout being fair play, thereafter, whenever the union shop stewards asked their managers for a favor or for a break in the tedious and repetitive duties for their people, they were quickly met with a firm "no way." You throw bolts at us, we'll make your working lives miserable.

The penalties for breaking other workplace subcultures' rules may be more subtle but no less severe. Keeping your situational radar well focused can help to reduce the conflict and stress, whether you're working on the shop floor or in the executive suite.

BUILDING THE SKILLS OF SITUATIONAL AWARENESS

Things you can do to increase your skills in the dimension of Situational Awareness include:

- Sit in an airport, at a mall, or some other public place and watch people go by. Try to figure out the kinds of relationships you see between couples, families, and groups. How do they signal their relationships and their affiliation? Do they convey affection and affirmation, or do they seem cold or even antagonistic?
- Study the proxemic contexts you find yourself in. How does the physical arrangement of space and structure influence the way people behave? Who sits where in the business meeting? How does the arrangement of someone's office communicate status or authority?
- Practice identifying the various linguistic frames you encounter in a day. How do people at various levels of social status signal their

membership through their language, slang, figures of speech, use or avoidance of profanity, and specialized vocabularies?

- Study the nonverbal signals people use to define and reinforce their relationships. How does the boss convey authority or approachability? How do people signal deference toward others in authority or of higher status?

- Watch a TV show or a movie with the sound turned off. Pay attention to the way the actors move, how they arrange themselves in relation to one another, and how they communicate their roles without sound. Do the nonverbal behaviors contribute to and reinforce the integrity of the scene, or do they seem artificial or contrived?

Notes

1. Rowe, Peter. "Whale Rider: A Sea World founder recounts both his park and his life's journey." *San Diego Union-Tribune,* October 3, 2004.

2. Vorhaus, John. *The Comic Toolbox: How to Be Funny Even When You're Not.* New York: Silman-James, 1994.

3. Adams, Scott. *Dogbert's Top Secret Management Handbook.* New York: HarperCollins, 1997, section 1.4 (pages unnumbered).

4. Taken from Irving J. Lee, *Language Habits in Human Affairs.* New York: Harper & Row, 1941, p. 46. Lee attributes it to Frederic Loomis, M.D., *Consultation Room.* New York: Knopf, 1939, p. 47.

5. See Korzybski, Alfred. *Science and Sanity: An Introduction to Non-Aristotelian Systems and General Semantics.* Cambridge, MA: Colonial Press, 1933. This is a rather dense, academic-sounding book, but one which is considered the classic foundation work of General Semantics. For other, perhaps more readable publications, contact the Institute for General Semantics, at general-semantics.org.

6. News item on CNN website, CNN.com, November 4, 2004.

7. Hamper, Ben. *Rivethead: Tales from the Assembly Line.* New York: Warner Books, 1986.

3

"P" STANDS FOR PRESENCE

"O wad some Pow'r the giftie gie us,
to see oursels' as ithers see us:
It would fra monie a blunder free us,
and foolish notion."
—Robert Burns (Scottish poet)

THE "P" FACTOR in the S.P.A.C.E. model represents Presence. It's the
way you affect individuals or groups of people through your physical
appearance, your mood and demeanor, your body language, and how
you occupy space in a room. Are you approachable? Do you convey a
sense of confidence, professionalism, kindness, and friendliness or do
you communicate shyness, insecurity, animosity, or indifference? We all
need to pay special attention to the sense of presence we communicate,
especially if we want to be accepted and taken seriously.

BEING THERE

In Hollywood, if budding TV and movie stars are to succeed, they must have something called "screen presence." It's an abstract concept, but we know it when we see it. "Look at her," said Robert Redford about Michelle Pfeiffer, who starred in the 1996 movie *Up Close and Personal*. "The camera falls in love with her."

People who have screen presence can communicate their emotions, using the smallest of gestures or facial expressions, in such a natural way that they break the boundaries of the screen and become almost three-dimensional.

But screen presence may not always translate into personal presence. It's a unique and special skill to connect with a movie camera; it's quite another thing to connect with people on an individual basis. And it's another thing entirely to connect with a large number of people—a one-to-many state of empathy. Some famous figures have had one or more of these capabilities; a few have had all three.

For us mortals, who don't live in front of movie cameras, personal presence is a more practical matter—a bearing, a physicality that gives and gets respect and attention. It lives in the moment, involves listening with skill, and creates and provides a quality of self-assurance and effectiveness that allows you to connect with a person or a group. It can be as simple as the expression one habitually carries around on one's face. The stone-faced, sourpuss expression can put people off before there's a chance to make a connection. An extremely repressed, shrinking demeanor can also keep people at a distance. A boisterous, "take-over" presence can also drive them away. Looks count, but the first key element of a positive Presence—or at least one we can control—is an inviting demeanor.

Case in point: while meeting with a group of Japanese executives a few years ago, I noticed some of the signals of Asian gender politics, and particularly how some Japanese women have chosen to cope with the situational rules in business.

I attended the meeting with my Japanese agent, a middle-aged divorced woman with whom I'd worked for some years, as well as a professional translator—also a woman.

The only other female in the meeting was the administrative assistant to the managing director of the organization, a young woman in her mid-twenties. She sat beside the director throughout the meeting, prepared to assist in any way if needed.

Throughout the meeting I noticed how she communicated and confirmed, nonverbally, her subordinate status. She sat motionless, face forward and eyes downward, with knees and feet together and her hands resting on her lap. She had a small note pad and a ballpoint pen on the conference table in front of her. She spoke only when spoken to and occasionally made notes if asked to by the director.

This intelligent and capable young woman had turned herself into a piece of furniture. I contrasted her patterns to those of my agent and the translator, both of whom had built successful careers dealing with male Japanese executives. Both of them had learned to "take their place" at the table, albeit with the usual Japanese demeanor of politeness and deference. Both volunteered ideas, asked questions, and participated fully in the discussion.

Our young colleague, for any of a number of reasons—some cultural, some emotional and related to self-esteem, and possibly some related to the unspoken rules of that particular organization—chose to reduce her Presence to an absolute minimum. To convey a stronger Presence, as a minimal starting strategy, she needs to simply take up more space, that is, change to a more open, less retracted body posture, put a few personal items on the table, move around somewhat more, and look around the room instead of sitting like a potted plant. From there she can progress to speaking without being spoken to, asking questions, adding to the conversation, and maybe even going to the whiteboard to record the findings of the meeting. The behaviors her culture once deemed outrageous for a woman are increasingly considered normal in business, and she might as well begin to behave in more assertive ways.

IS CHARISMA OVER-RATED?

Noted MIT economist Professor Rudiger Dornbusch defines an economist as "somebody who's good with figures, but doesn't have the charisma to be an accountant." Self-effacing as it is, the comment signals our general recognition of that special "something" that sets people apart.

In everyday life, charisma is one of those vaguely defined and little understood concepts that we think of as familiar but which seem to resist being captured in a simple definition. We know that the bottom end of the charisma spectrum is occupied by people who seem to project very little social energy, those whom psychologists describe as presenting a "flat affect," a monochrome and monotone sort of expression, use of language, and physical energy. This flat-affect presentation of self typically arises from an inner inhibition, a holding back of one's emotional energy. This is usually also associated with a low sense of self-worth.

The range of variation along the charisma spectrum, and particularly the high end, is somewhat more difficult to pin down. It may help to understand charisma better by viewing it in three of its distinct forms, based on its impact on others. There is "official" charisma, "artificial" charisma, and "earned" charisma. Each has its own trappings, ceremonies, and attached notables.

Official charisma is that which is attached to a world leader, a well-known politician, a highly visible businessperson, or anyone who gets a built-in, large-scale, often public ceremony, anytime he or she arrives. Whether it's the current head of the United Nations or Queen Elizabeth of the United Kingdom, the charisma comes with the territory more than the persons themselves.

Case in point: when the President of the United States steps into a crowded room, comes down the stairs of Air Force One, or steps off Marine One (the presidential helicopter) it's hard not to feel, deep in one's bones, the absolute awe of that moment. And here's the part where his charisma takes over: even if you personally cannot abide the President's politics or personality (or both), the animus tends to fade away during that moment when you hear the sounds of "Hail to the Chief" and you see the awesome power of the United States government on display. The collection of Secret Service agents, squads of police, the impressive machinery, the podium and the Seal, and the roar of the crowd might momentarily sway even the staunchest political opposite into conceding that "maybe he's not such a bad guy after all." This is the power of official charisma at work, and it has its moments and its uses.

Artificial charisma is that which is "created" for the media darlings of the moment. It's based largely on timing over talent, big breaks over exemplary behavior, and the ability to be more beautiful, more outrageous, and more provocative than others who have not wanted to sacrifice their humanity or dignity for fame. Some ordinary mortals try—usually in vain—to award themselves a kind of charisma by dressing expensively, acting dramatically, and making grand entrances. The gold standard of this variant of artificial charisma are the pretentious TV preachers with their fancy hairdos, floozy wives, and their trappings of wealth, whom the legendary country guitarist Chet Atkins parodied in a song he titled "Would Jesus Wear a Rolex on His Television Show?"

Earned charisma is the special province of a rare few, who know they have it, yet who don't often exploit it. At this level, the owners of this type of charisma have *earned* it through the importance of their life work. It's deeply rooted, not in money or elected political power, but in achievement, greatness, and a sense of self that says, "I will do this, not for what it gets me, but for what it allows me to give." Mohandas Gandhi, Mother Teresa, and the Dalai Lama accomplished great things without ever asking, "Will this get me on TV?" Paradoxically, their brand of charisma arose from humility.

Earned charisma is not about amassing fame and collecting followers; it's about the sum total of their lives. Mohandas Gandhi met the

King and Queen of England, wearing not a business suit, but the clothing made from his native land, a homespun cotton loincloth and cover called *khadi*. He espoused that khadi had a "transformative power" and that "through wearing it people could actually become more worthy."

When Mother Teresa died in 1997 in her convent in India, her funeral was attended by leaders from all over the world, not just East Asia. Why did such a small and frail woman have such an impact on the globe, outside her own Calcutta? How could the Nobel Committee have seen fit to award her the Nobel Peace Prize in 1979? Her strength was not found in her level of fame, but in the smallest of actions, as she comforted the poor, the abandoned, and the dying over the entire span of her life.

As the exalted spiritual leader of the "Government of Tibet in Exile" His Holiness the 14th Dalai Lama has earned the right to travel with a large entourage, and yet he does not. His needs are simple and his message, given to world leaders and large crowds alike, is this: "*For as long as space endures, and for as long as living beings remain, until then may I, too, abide to dispel the misery of the world.*"

Real charisma could be characterized as having "it," with "it" being that rare combination of grace under pressure, energy, passion for your purpose, and a kind of a life essence that seems to attract energy and attention wherever you go. Unassuming people can have it (think again of Mohandas Gandhi, small and slight, wrapped in his homespun robes and leading his followers through civil disobedience) and larger-than-life blowhards will never get it, no matter how much they puff.

Maybe the essence of real charisma—the earned kind—is what goes on inside. Those who perceive someone as affirmative, admirable, and compellingly attractive may be reacting to the outward and visible signs of that person's inner commitment to life. One gets the sense that great spiritual leaders—Gandhi, Mother Teresa, the Dalai Lama—would go where they go and do what they do regardless of whether others chose to follow them. Paradoxically, maybe others follow them not because they lead, but because they know who they are and where they're going.

DO LOOKS MATTER?

"Live fast, die young, and leave a
good-looking corpse."

—James Dean, actor

If you want to "make it" in the media-based societies of today's world, it doesn't hurt to look good. The blunt truth is that if you're not a bit of a "looker" (moderately handsome male, better-than-average attractive female), you'll have to work harder and smarter.

Hollywood movies that spoof the never-ending American fascination with looks only create more of a divide between the truly beautiful and the truly average. And related clichés, true or otherwise, abound: the "distinguished looking older gentleman" can stay on a local or network newscast for decades; when an anchorwoman starts to look her age, out she goes for younger fare. The richer, older man with the "trophy wife" is far more common than the reverse. And sociological study after study has used variations on the same experiment to prove this reality: fat people are less favored during job interviews, on video dating services, in auditions for movie roles and TV parts, and even in housing, at fitness centers, or on airplanes. Similar studies suggest that taller people tend to get higher-paying jobs, get promoted faster, and have greater influence in their work environments than shorter people. The message is: Tall, good-looking and charming will take you a long way.

This, of course, doesn't have to mean that those of us who arrived on the planet without movie-star looks can't succeed in business on character and the skills of social intelligence. It just means that we don't get extra points in the competition.

READING (AND SHAPING) THE "RULES OF ENGAGEMENT"

Any interaction between human beings generally involves a set of mutual expectations about how the participants will behave—the "rules of engagement," so to speak. When all parties know and abide by the generally accepted rules, the interaction may unfold amicably and successfully. When one or more parties violates the social compact by behaving in unapproved ways, serious conflicts can arise.

These rules of engagement may come ready-made—the "accepted" way of doing things—or they may take shape under the influence of one or more dominant parties. Further, the capacity to influence, shape, or define the rules of engagement puts a person in a leadership position. At a minimum, we need to be able to anticipate situational rules, or to detect them as they arise or take shape. To shape the rules, we need to develop an effective Presence.

Case in point: during my service as a U.S. Army officer, stationed in the Washington, D.C., area, I frequently had occasion to attend meetings at the Pentagon. Often these meetings would involve a mixture of officers and civilian specialists. Having traveled from the base where my office was located, I would typically be dressed in full uniform— during fall and winter months, this would usually be the standard Army green suit—pants and jacket (or "blouse" as the Army called it).

Typically, when a meeting got underway, I could usually tell immediately what kind of discussion would ensue, based on whether the senior ranking officer kept his jacket on or took it off. If he had his jacket on, with the metal insignia of his rank clearly showing, I could generally surmise it would not be a free-wheeling, creative discussion. The implied message was: The person with the highest rank is the one who is most "right." Those of us of lesser rank—junior officers like me— were expected to speak when spoken to.

If the top guy removed his jacket, the rest of us did, too. Without the jacket, the uniform at that time did not advertise one's rank. Only the black stripe running down the outside of each pants leg signaled one's status as an officer. In the no-jacket behavioral context, it would generally be understood that the discussion could be somewhat less formal, and possibly open to alternative points of view. I also noticed that certain senior officers frequently removed their jackets, while others almost always kept theirs on.

Consider two contrasting examples of how the way you assert your Presence influences the rules of engagement by meeting the requirements of the context or failing to:

Case #1: A police officer on patrol in a large city sees a man in an expensive luxury sedan run a red light. The officer hits his overhead lights and the driver, nervously looking for a safe place to pull over, travels through two intersections before he finally stops his car. By the time the officer gets out and stomps up to the driver's window, we can see by his face that he's furious.

"Hey pal! What are you, blind or something? Didn't you see my lights? Why didn't you stop when I told you to? Give me your license and registration, right now!"

The confused and embarrassed driver hands over his license and sits steaming in his car while the officer writes him a citation. When the officer returns to have him sign the ticket, he scratches his name quickly, snatches the copy from the officer's hand, and drives away, feeling that his day has been ruined. Upon arriving at his office, he calls the police station and makes a formal complaint against the officer, citing his actions, behavior, words, and body language in great detail to a police supervisor.

Case #2: Another police officer is working in a crime-ridden neighborhood, late at night and alone. He sees a large, muscular man covered with prison tattoos, walking through the parking lot of a convenience store. He recognizes the man from a previous arrest and knows he is on parole and has an outstanding warrant for his arrest.

He pulls his patrol car near the man and calls for him to stop. As he gets out of his car to talk the man, the parolee turns and starts cursing at the officer.

The officer responds back, "Sir, you can't speak to me that way. I'm an officer of the law. Cursing is not appropriate in this situation. Please come over here. You're under arrest."

The angry ex-prisoner starts to run toward the officer, pulling a knife from his back pocket. The officer realizes the fight for his life has begun.

Both of these scenarios are based on a hard truth: some police officers choose the wrong words and then the wrong approach for the situations they face.

In the first scenario, the officer overreacted, lost his temper, and let his emotions interfere with his need to stay professional. In the second scenario, the officer didn't use enough "force presence," through his words, the symbols of his profession (badge, uniform, firearm), and his tactical actions, to take control of a dangerous person in a dangerous situation.

Police officers in particular face a very difficult psychological challenge. Many times in a single day, they must adjust their "presence pattern" to rapidly changing situations. An officer who goes into a restaurant for a meal break needs to "present" in a non-threatening manner to the other patrons. He or she is expected to play the role of the friendly local constable.

In a different situation, or in an instance where a threat suddenly arises, he or she must instantly switch to the "command presence" mode. Few citizens—and not all city officials or police commanders—fully appreciate the psychological challenge and the stress associated with this sudden change of context.

THE UGLY AMERICAN SYNDROME

Rick Steves, who hosts well-known television and radio programs about travel, spends most of the year abroad, producing his TV show, "Rick Steves' Europe." Because of his work overseas, he finds himself in a unique position to study a controversial variation of Presence: the proverbial "Ugly American."[1]

The epitome of the Ugly American is a U.S. traveler, abroad and in unfamiliar surroundings (amid "foreign" cultures filled with "foreign" people), who acts like he or she is strolling down Main Street, U.S.A. "Don't expect me to adapt to your country and culture; I've brought mine with me," says the behavior of the U.A. Mr. or Ms. U.A. is contemptuous of understanding the country and culture he or she is visiting or even learning a few simple foreign phrases to help forge friendships or at least build empathy. "Just point the way to the nearest McDonald's, so I can get some 'real food.'"

Not surprisingly, this lack of social intelligence sends a message to the local people that says, "I don't *really* want to be here, experiencing new sights, sounds, and tastes outside my comfort zone. I just want to buy a T-shirt, take some postcard-style snapshots with my new digital camera, and then get on back to the Land of the Big Wal-Mart."

Says Rick Steves,

"If Americans traveled more, we'd better understand our place on this complex planet and fit in more comfortably. And eventually, perhaps, we wouldn't need to spend as much as the rest of the world combined on our military to feel safe. Though many Americans travel, millions more don't venture out to see or experience the world. About 80 percent of Americans *do not hold a passport.* Many of those have stubbornly held world-views based on little more than TV news. Travel gives us a firsthand look at the complexity and struggles of the rest of the world, enabling us to digest news coverage more smartly. Travel helps us celebrate—rather than fear—diversity."[2]

Having Presence includes being respectful of the people around you and showing real rather than manufactured interest in them. One of the cross-complaints of many Westerners in general and Americans in particular comes to bear when they have to deal with foreign-born people as part of their work or social interaction. If we could read their minds, we might hear, "Why can't they be more like me?"

And if we could hear the internal monologue of the foreign-born person, we might hear, "I'm trying hard to understand this confusing culture; why doesn't this person make any effort to understand mine?"

Presence in SI is more about "giving to people" versus "getting from people." Part of the solution to the cultural diversity issue facing Americans may simply start with patience.

MORE OF YOU, LESS OF ME

Clint Eastwood has screen presence; otherwise he wouldn't have had a distinguished acting career. His work as an actor and director spans sixty films, a career as a cowboy actor in the fledgling days of American TV (the serial "Rawhide"), and many acting and directing awards.

And partly because of his long career he has learned not only how to direct movies, but how to direct actors. His own acting style—spare, direct, and what critics hail as "minimalist"—serves him well on the set of his own productions.

Eastwood's approach as a director is classically simple and brilliantly successful: bring in good people, make sure they understand what the film needs, and let them do it. His production team and shooting/set crews have been with him for decades; he knows what he wants. He so respects actors and the craft of acting that he doesn't find it necessary to scream at people on his set. He gives the actors and actresses their scripts and asks them to be ready to work from day one.

Ignoring the usual movie directing clichés, he doesn't even like to yell "Action!" to begin the scene. He'll simply say, "Okay" or "Let's go" or "Whenever you're ready" to cue his players. He sees no need to *raise* the tension level on his movie sets, because he knows acting is tough enough without being shouted at.

With little interest in long rehearsals or shooting take after take after take, he works in a sparing, precise fashion. Eastwood sees no need for retakes, when he so frequently gets what he wants early in the process. He uses what he has, shoots the scenes he wants, moves on to the next ones, and finishes on time. If the light is going, he wraps it for the day. If his actors have suggestions for improvement, he considers them. Eastwood feels this approach makes him a better director (shooting thirty takes wastes film and gives him too much to look at) and makes for a happier cast. His Academy Awards in 1992 for *Unforgiven,* 2005 for *Million Dollar Baby,* and 2004 nominations for *Mystic River* suggest that his ways work. It's a respectful process, a set of work rules that appreciates the contributions of others, and appreciates the craft of acting.

Compare the approach of Clint Eastwood (or Steven Spielberg or Woody Allen, who both work in a similar productive, collaborative fashion as well) with other legendary directors, whose narcissistic self-importance has made many a movie shoot a trying and stressful experience. The late Stanley Kubrick, whose films *2001, Dr. Strangelove,* and *The Shining* have certainly earned great respect, seemed to like keeping his cast and crew in a constant state of anxiety.

While filming the 1999 Tom Cruise-Nicole Kidman film *Eyes Wide Shut,* Kubrick was in his usual histrionic form: eccentric behavior on and off the set, a sixteen-month shooting schedule (one of the longest ever recorded for a popular feature film), and forcing his actors through as many as *fifty to sixty takes* before being satisfied. (Cruise and Kidman spent so much time on the project that they lost income, because it limited their ability to take on roles in other films.)

Like the chef who creates a high-stress kitchen because he thinks it will reinforce his prima donna image, perhaps the screaming director feels it's better to be feared than loved. Many times, great Presence may be more subtle than demonstrative.

Attitude Counts

William F. Buckley, a noted intellectual, author, and founder and editor-in-chief of the conservative magazine *National Review,* had a way of intimidating others with his intellectual demeanor. Born into a family of wealth and privilege, educated abroad and constantly challenged by his intellectual family and tutors, and a skilled debater at Yale, he became an icon of conservative intellectualism.

Exuding that special combination of intellectual aristocracy, condescension, and dry wit, he held court with other big thinkers such as
Norman Mailer, Germaine Greer, the Dalai Lama, and Groucho Marx on
his television show "Firing Line."

In one particular exchange, a guest presumed to paraphrase something Buckley had said. "Mr. Buckley," he said, "a while ago you
referred to such-and-such, by which I presume you meant so-and-so. Is
that correct?"

Buckley fixed him with his patrician countenance and stopped
the conversation momentarily with, "If I had meant that, I would have
said that."

A CASE OF ATTITUDE

While we tend to think of Presence from the external point of view—
as others perceive us—it also has an important inward dimension.
One's own state of mind, or "emotional demeanor," also influences the
presentation of self. Here we have another important connection to
the sister concept of emotional intelligence.

Presence is partly about living in the moment, being available, not
just physically, but emotionally as well, for your spouse or significant
other, for your kids, for your co-workers and colleagues, or for people
who need you at that moment, to be aware of their issues or needs. It's
also a question of balance, being able to parse your emotional commitment for those situations in which a human connection is called for,
and not overreacting or losing perspective. This requires being emotionally self-aware and centered.

Perhaps we can take some lessons from Zen thinking. One of the
key principles of Zen study is to live fully and completely in the
moment. Zen, which many people interpret more as a philosophy, or
"a way," than a religion, teaches one to fully engage whatever moment
one experiences.

A Zen-like approach to life invites you to be present; it helps you take pleasure in life's little moments: a good cup of coffee in the morning; a great song that you haven't heard in years on the radio as you drive in to work; a clean, comfortable, and peaceful place to do your work; a satisfying meal; a good book; a great joke; the warm sun when you're out and about or a pounding rainstorm when you're inside and dry.

Consider the way in which a Zen-like equanimity—a mode of thinking about the present experience—can give you better choices, either in dealing with others or with important situations.

A common example: you drive to the grocery store and in the last few seconds as you climb out of your car, you realize, as the door shuts tight, that you've locked your keys inside.

The usual response (pounding on the car roof, kicking a tire): "I can't believe it! I didn't just do that! I'm so stupid! Now I'm really screwed! How could I have been so dumb? I can't believe I did that! Now what am I gonna do?"

The Zen-like response (looking at the keys inside): "I wish I hadn't done that. I did." (You spend some time feeling your anger rise and fall, ebb and leave. Deep breaths. A shrug of the shoulders, then back to the moment.) "Now, who can I call to get some help here? My spouse? The Auto Club? The police? Do I call a tow truck or a locksmith? Can I get a wire coat hanger from inside the store? Well, I still have my cell phone. I'm not running late for anything today. And I haven't bought any milk or ice cream yet, so nothing is going to spoil in my car. There's time to deal with this. . . ."

This internal dialogue might seem impossible, impractical, or naïve in the face of the obvious facts (the keys are inside!), so it may help to break it down:

1. Can you change the situation by raging about it? No.
2. Does it help get the keys back when you criticize yourself? No.
3. Does pounding/kicking the car get your keys out? No.

4. Does repeating the phrase, "I can't believe it!" get the keys back? No.

5. Does it help to complain about what just happened, which, we know for a fact, you can't undo? No.

6. Can you really allow your anger to rise and fall and then dissipate? Yes.

7. Are there, in fact, many solutions available to you, if you can think calmly about them? Yes.

8. Could you even do something out-of-the-ordinary, like go have lunch and deal with the keys later or walk home to get your spares? Yes.

9. Is there a positive side to any of this? Yes. (No one is hurt; the world hasn't come to an end; it's just keys.)

10. Does a Zen-like approach invite you to think about solutions and alternatives rather than staying stuck in the past, with the problem? Yes.

This concept of living in the present, being in the moment, and staying focused on the world of possibilities will take some people a lot of time to adapt to. For some people, getting and staying angry is their form of psychic exercise; they secretly like it when their blood boils. For others, with a negative world view, locked car keys prove (once again) that the world is an unfair and unfriendly place.

The Zen philosophy posits that "human beings suffer" and "the cause of suffering is desire." The way to put an end to suffering is to stop *wanting* everything, all the time. There is great freedom in living in the moment. It's clarifying to enjoy what's right in front of you, even if it's the smallest of things, like the breeze across your face.

Your mother's expression "Count your blessings" may seem trite, but it's no less true than it ever was. People who live in the wealthy societies cope with "personal problems" every day that would be the envy of most of the rest of the world.

It's easy to take flush toilets, electric power, clean water, TV, the Internet, and good coffee for granted, especially if you've never lived without any of these luxuries. What's more difficult is to enjoy each of these things, with the kind of gratitude that comes from living in a country that *provides*. All of us could take seriously the humble reminder "I had no shoes, and I complained—until I met a man who had no feet."

Living in one of the wealthy countries of the world, even at the U.S. poverty level of $9,300 per year, is still better than the best day in the Sudan, Iraq, or Haiti. Americans, for example, represent 5 percent of the world's total population, but control 50 percent of the global wealth. Nearly half the people on the planet live on less than $2 per day.

One of the most valuable tools for attitude adjustment I've ever found was given to me by a friend many years ago. When I start to feel my problems are mounting and my stress level is going up, I recall her advice: "Think about the level you're complaining from."

Would that we all could live in the moment and enjoy what we can out of what we have; then we would really know what it is to be Present. And being Present, both emotionally and behaviorally, enables us to reach out to others and build the connections that can contribute not only to our success, but also to theirs.

BUILDING THE SKILLS OF PRESENCE

Things you can do to increase your skills in the dimension of Presence include:

- Don't try to "present" like a movie star (or anyone else); find your most natural way of telling who you are by the way you stand, walk, talk, dress, and interact. Find and express your own "voice." Try to imagine what the experience of meeting you for the first time would be like for another person. How do you want it to be?

- Write a brief description of yourself, as another person might describe you after having met you. What would you like people to say about you? Start working on specific aspects of that ideal description to make sure they're real.
- Leave a long message on your voice-mail system and play it back a few days later. Get an idea of how you sound to a stranger. Make a note of any aspects of the way you speak that you would like to change.
- Record a conversation with friends, either in audio or video format. Make it long enough that everybody forgets they're being recorded. Study yourself and the other participants and note any habits or behaviors that contribute to or inhibit empathy, clarity of communicating ideas, and authenticity.
- Ask one or more close friends, preferably individually, to share with you the impressions they got when meeting you for the first time. This might also be a way to gently invite them to share with you any aspects of your interaction they feel could be improved.

Notes

1. Coined by William J. Lederer and Eugene Burdick, in their 1958 text on Asia and the American struggles against the growing Communism movement there, the phrase "Ugly American" has infiltrated the popular lexicon of cultures all over the world.
2. Steves, Rick. "Travel can help mend a fractured world." *USA Today.* October 18, 2004.

4

"A" STANDS FOR AUTHENTICITY

"I yam what I yam, and dat's all what I yam."
—Popeye (cartoon character)

THE "A" FACTOR in the S.P.A.C.E. model represents Authenticity. This dimension reveals how honest and sincere you are with people and with yourself, in any given situation. Do you befriend only those who can be of benefit to you somehow in the future—people who have something you want? Are you the type who collects business cards and phone numbers professionally—one who establishes many contacts but few real quality friendships and relationships? Do you manipulate others or allow others to manipulate you? Does your behavior focus on gaining others' approval, regardless of how you truly feel? Are you true to yourself?

87

To the extent that you feel—consciously or unconsciously—that others will not accept you, respect you, love you, or cooperate with you if you act according to your own needs and priorities, you are likely to behave in ways that others perceive as inauthentic. To the extent that you respect yourself, have faith in your personal values and beliefs, and "deal straight" with other people, you are likely to behave in ways that others perceive as authentic.

TAKE A TIP FROM POPEYE

The cartoon character Popeye has proven to be a remarkably durable icon of the American entertainment culture. Unlike CB radio, the Pet Rock, the Rubik's Cube, and henna tattoos, the spinach-eating Navy man has endured, in movie cartoons, TV cartoons, and even on the modern big screen, ever since his creation by E.C. Segar in 1929. Popeye says with his behavior, "I'm a man of the world, and a guy with certain principles. I have no hair, big feet, scratchy tattoos, small biceps, huge forearms, and a permanent right-eye squint. My voice sounds like I gargled with scouring powder, my use of English grammar is not that great, and I eat, sleep, and bathe with a pipe in my mouth. But I know who I am. I'm happy (just listen to me sing) and I'm comfortable in my own skin. You'll have to take me as I am."

In every one of the 109 Max Fleischer cartoon episodes, Popeye illustrated the concept of Authenticity as well as any popular icon might. He never bugged anybody, he tried his best to get along with others, and he stayed true to his principles. When attacked, he fought back—and usually won. He protected women and children. When provoked beyond endurance, he responded: out came the can of spinach, he flexed his muscles and went to work. Maybe this unsophisticated fellow symbolizes the best in all of us: being Authentic.

In other words, Popeye is the real deal—a straight-up guy, an archetype of playing fair, doing the right thing, and standing up for what he believes in. Beyond our North American slang terms, he exemplifies something we all admire, and to which we may secretly aspire. Australians, for example, would describe Popeye as "fair dinkum." In the Jewish culture, he's a "mensch."

That fair dinkum expression is an interesting one. If an Australian refers to you as fair dinkum, you're probably receiving a high compliment.[1] A "fair dinkum Aussie," also known as a "dinky-di Australian," is someone you can count on. It's a person of character, one who stands behind his or her word and who comes through, whatever the obstacles or hardships involved. Popeye is certainly a fair dinkum kind of a guy.

He's also a *mensch*. In the long, rich, and troubled history of the Jewish culture, many old-country words and phrases have managed to emigrate to the English-speaking cultures. Our Western lexicon is sprinkled with words that derived from some form of the Hebrew language or Yiddish dialects. Examples include now-common words like *kibbitz* (interrupt a conversation or offer unsolicited advice), *schlep* (walk yourself, or carry some awkward thing a long distance), or *chutzpah* (cheekiness, or "three sizes of gall"). And one of the most treasured terms in the Jewish popular lexicon is *mensch*.

To be a mensch is to be known by others as a "solid, trustworthy person with admirable characteristics." In short, being a mensch means being Authentic. And so Popeye, in addition to being "what he is" and fair dinkum too, is a mensch as well.

But here's a curiosity: while "fair dinkum" has no apparent gender restrictions (you can be a fair dinkum "bloke" (man) or a fair dinkum "sheila" (woman), the term mensch has always been attached only to males. Indeed, the root of the word may have come from the Old High German word "mennisco," which was yet another variation of the word for "man."

At the risk of drifting into deep cultural waters, we might ask: Why is there no word in the Hebrew/Yiddish/Jewish language for the *female* equivalent of a mensch? It's no surprise that the linguistic history of a patriarchal culture has a lot to do with how women are labeled, described, or referred to, alone or as a group. Linguists, sociologists, and other students of sociolinguistic behavior refer to terms like these as "gender-asymmetric" language forms.

Certainly much of the male-female asymmetry in the English language seems more idiosyncratic and historical than logical. Why do we have "actors and actresses," but not "doctors and doctresses"? We have "seamstresses," but one seldom hears about a "seamster." We have "teamsters," but not "teamstresses." Will the word "waiter" evolve to include both males and females, supplanting the diminutive female form "waitress?" Can the word "host" evolve to refer to both genders?

Why do we often hear "Stand up and take it like a man," but seldom hear "Stand up and take it like a woman"? And who will be the female cartoon counterpart of Popeye?

Language both signals culture and forms culture. Words are not mere lifeless symbols—they encode the beliefs, values, and priorities of the people who use them. As cultures evolve, we will probably see the terminology of male and female social roles and behaviors evolve with them. Shouldn't the SI dimension of Authenticity support a policy of inclusion—the ability and willingness to account for the interests and feelings of all parties?

IT'S A BEAUTIFUL DAY IN THE SI NEIGHBORHOOD

Authenticity is about the desire and ability to let yourself be real, not phony or contrived. It's how you connect with other people so you become worthy of their trust. It's the difference between being genuine and being counterfeit. It's a reliance on or belief in yourself, so you can take real authorship and ownership of your space or place.

One man in America who personified the idea of being comfortable in your own skin was Fred Rogers, or to most everybody who ever watched public television from 1967 to 2001, "Mr. Rogers" and his wonderful make-believe neighborhood.

The appeal of Mr. Rogers was simple: he always talked to children at their level, and he was neither sickly sweet nor condescending. His tone was always just right for whatever teaching moment presented itself. He breached the "fourth wall" of the TV screen all the time, talking *to* kids and not *at* them.

In terms of authenticity, Mr. Rogers was in the moment, from the time he came into his "house" and changed from his street shoes to his playtime tennis shoes. When he took off his suit jacket and replaced it with his friendly and comfy sweater, viewers knew that he was home. With his calmly spoken homilies about sharing and his lessons about taking care of each other, he offered peace and solace for at least thirty minutes every day. And when he passed away in 2003, it's likely that even the most jaded of Americans marveled that through his whole life, as a pastor and a teacher and a TV pioneer, he really was as he portrayed himself.

With his simple way of relating to children, Fred Rogers became an icon of goodness in the American culture, even to humorists. In the movie *Paternity,* Burt Reynolds appeared as a well-to-do bachelor who wanted to have a child by a surrogate mother. As he immersed himself in the project, he became fascinated with children and watching children's TV shows. In one scene, he walks into the room where his maid is working and, with no preamble whatsoever, says, "You know why I like Mr. Rogers? Because *he* likes *me,* just the way I am." His maid gives him a look that suggests that he has regressed to some infantile state; the scene works only because of Mr. Rogers' iconic appeal to so many viewers.

Do you have a Mr. (or Ms.) Rogers in your life? Could you be someone else's Mr. or Ms. Rogers? Think about the most nourishing people you know.

- Who is the most *positive* person in your life? And why is it that he or she can always see the best side, and never start out by looking at the worst side of any situation?
- Who is the most *generous* person in your life? Who would, if you asked him or her, in time of great personal need, help you or loan you money with no questions asked?

- Who is the most *reliable* person in your life? Who would go to the airport, buy a ticket, and fly across the country for you tomorrow, if you really needed him or her to do it?
- Who is the most *energetic* person in your life? Who has the sound of vibrancy in his or her voice and can't wait to get started, go somewhere, or do something?
- Who is the most *enthusiastic* person in your life? Who has an honest zest for life and all things in it?
- Who is the most *thoughtful* person in your life? Who is there with the little touches (a handshake, a card, a hug, a gift, a cup of coffee, a phone call) and all for no special reason?
- Who is the *kindest* person in your life? Who treats everyone with love and respect and can see the good in others?
- Who is the *smartest* person in your life? Who do you go to for answers, support, advice, and guidance?
- Who always shows the most *interest* in your life? Who always lets you know that your life, work, goals, and dreams are important?
- Who is the most *fun* person in your life? Who can you just hang out with and just be you, free from any judgments, negativity, fears, or criticism?
- Who is the *funniest* person in your life? Who gives you genuine, no-holding-back belly laughs?

If you are truly blessed, all of these adjectives may describe just one person: a best friend, a spouse, or someone who is as close (physically, emotionally, or both) to you as is humanly possible.

If you're just plain old lucky, this list may describe several people who, most likely, have been around you for many years. Whether they are friends or family or both, chances are good these people live absolutely in the moment, enjoying whatever and whoever is around them, and for no other reason than because they can. They exemplify the Mr. Rogers who lives in all of us. In a world sorely in need of empathy, compassion, and authenticity, he is certainly missed.

THE SNAP-ON SMILE: CAN
YOU FAKE SINCERITY?

In the context of social intelligence, authenticity involves more than simply being yourself; it's also about the ability to genuinely connect with other people, which demands a fair amount of empathy and compassion. It is possible, for example, to have well-developed "people skills" and yet lack the emotional depth to be considered truly socially intelligent.

Take the case of Ronald Reagan. Particularly while he served as President of the United States, Reagan engendered an unusual degree of affection in the hearts of many Americans, and even people in other countries. After he left office, and even during his declining health and eventual death, the sense of affection felt by many toward him only grew. His funeral ceremonies were accompanied by a remarkable outpouring of admiration; most of the American press and media coverage presented him as a lovable father-figure and compassionate leader. To the disgruntlement of many who disagreed with his politics, he was even elevated to the stature of a heroic leader.

Yet, even Reagan's most devoted associates readily acknowledged the paradoxical contradiction between his emotional and social personas. Skillful, on one hand, at charming and motivating people—individually and collectively—Reagan was a man whom very few people knew well or connected with on a deeply personal level. His relationships with close family members were generally distant and strained. People who worked closely with him on a daily basis reported that he showed very little interest in them as individuals. One of his biographers reported hearing exactly the same stories many times, told in exactly the same way—the same words, the same voice cadence, the same pauses, the same gestures and facial expressions.

Based on these observations, it seems reasonable to characterize Reagan as a man of remarkably high social intelligence—at least by any reasonable behavioral definition—and distinctly low emotional intelligence. Clearly, while EI and SI are closely interwoven, they do not seem to be the same thing.

In his book and many articles about Reagan and his life, biographer Edmund Morris made a sadly wistful comment on Dutch's public persona versus his private reality. It appears that, as great a statesman, politician, and leader as he was, the real-life Ronald Reagan was a painful contradiction—or at least a paradoxical version—of the SI dimension of Authenticity. Said Morris:

> "Sooner or later, every would-be intimate (including his four children, Maureen, Michael, Patti, and Ron) discovered that the only human being Reagan truly cared about (after his mother died) was [his wife] Nancy. For Michael Reagan, it was the high-school graduation day his father greeted him with, 'My name is Ronald Reagan. What's yours?'
>
> "Patti Davis, Reagan's younger daughter, writes in her 1992 autobiography:
>
> 'Often, I'd come into a room and he'd look up from his note cards as though he wasn't sure who I was. Ron would race up to him, small and brimming with a child's enthusiasm, and I'd see the same bewildered look in my father's eyes, like he had to remind himself who Ron was. . . . I sometimes felt like reminding him that Maureen was his daughter, too, not just someone with similar political philosophies.'
>
> "Reagan's scrupulously kept Presidential diary is remarkable for a near-total lack of interest in people as individuals. In all its half-million or so words, I did not find any affectionate remark about his children."[2]

LEFT-HANDED COMPLIMENTS

"Hey, that's a great tie. Keep that—it's bound to come back in style one of these days."

Some people just can't seem to bring themselves to compliment others freely and generously. They seem to think of compliments as a sort of zero-sum economy: by complimenting others they subconsciously believe they somehow devalue themselves.

People who are fiercely competitive, or hyper-achievers, sometimes display a kind of emotional stinginess. They are too preoccupied with shoring up their own shaky sense of self-worth to nourish and support others.

Some people with low self-esteem even figure out ways to use compliments to make others feel bad. They become masters of the left-handed compliment—arguably a more crazy-making social strategy than simply withholding compliments altogether. A really good left-handed compliment sounds like a genuine compliment at first, but as it soaks in the real intent becomes clear.

An expert LHC-er can even adjust the combination of sweet and sour so that the target person can't quite be sure whether he or she just received a compliment or a put-down. This is a useful skill: if the person being "complimented" calls attention to the toxic aspect of the statement, the LHC-er can always retreat to the safety of "Oh, you're just being too sensitive—I meant it as a compliment."

Here are a few classics:

"You've lost a lot of weight—you were really getting heavy there for a while."

"That's a nice dress—I used to wear that style."

"I see you're getting a lot of gray hair up there—makes you look distinguished."

"So, you finally broke up with that guy—I'm glad you came to your senses; I don't know what you ever saw in him."

"What's that book you're reading? Oh, that one. There's a much better one—I'll email you the title and author."

"Your face-lift looks good. Who did the surgery? Oh . . . I wish you'd called me—I could have referred you to the best guy in town."

"I see you got a new car. I looked at that model, but *Consumer Reports* didn't rate it very high."

What to do about the left-handed complimenter? Most of the coping strategies aren't very appealing. The first, of course, is just to let the put-down go by without comment; try to train yourself to spot it before you react angrily or take offense. This is what your mother meant when she advised you to learn to become a bit more "thick-skinned."

The second coping mechanism is to "call" such a person on the toxic behavior and to hold him or her accountable for it: "That sounded more like a put-down than a compliment. Which way did you mean it?" You'll seldom hear someone admit to the intention of making you feel bad; they'll almost invariably try to position themselves as innocent. However, if you make a regular practice of calling them on their behavior, you may find that they do it less often—at least to you. The effectiveness of the technique depends on ambiguity and the sense of confusion it induces in the victim; if you remove that, it's no fun for them anymore.

If you're skilled with words and quick on your feet, there's a third strategy: the ambiguous response. You respond to the supposed intent—the compliment portion of the statement that serves as the bait, and pretend you didn't hear the other part. Example:

LHC specialist: "It's good that your son is interested in sports. He's a little small for Little League, though, don't you think?"
You: "Oh, thanks for saying so. I'll pass on your encouragement— he'll be pleased to know you have confidence in him."

This strategy transfers the state of ambiguity into the other party's mind. It signals, on a meta-verbal level: "I recognize the real intention of your remark, hidden in the ambiguity of the statement. Instead of responding directly to your toxic behavior, I'm using the same channel of ambiguity to let you know that I'm on to you."

Strategy number three takes a bit of practice, and it can be very effective indeed. Perhaps its main drawback is the possibility that it may tempt you toward the use of sarcasm, veiled put-downs, and clever verbal retaliation. The result could be that you find yourself behaving inauthentically as well. In general, it's better to deal with low Authenticity by responding with high Authenticity. Overall, one needs to choose the strategy that fits the situation and works with one's own personal values.

THE PUPPY DOG SYNDROME

Another common variant of the inauthentic social pattern is the two-legged Puppy Dog. This person enjoys wearing a professionally-drawn "Kick Me. Now Do It Again, Please" sign. The person seems to enjoy getting other people to put them down, and then making them feel guilty for doing it. A sample conversation:

You: "From what you're telling me, it sounds like your relationship with Dave isn't going very well."

P. Dog: "No, it isn't. He treats me badly. Some of my money and jewelry is missing. I think he may even be cheating on me."

You: "Wow! That sounds serious. Why are you still together? I'd have broken up and left a long time ago."

P. Dog: "Well, I really don't want to go through a bad breakup again. I'm not ready to be alone, like I was last time for so long. He's not really that bad. Maybe we can still work things out."

You: "Work it out? You said you think he stole from you! What's to work out?"

P. Dog: "I'm just no good at this kind of thing. I don't know— maybe he'll break up with me. That way, I won't have to be the one who started it."

If you're on the listening end of this conversation, this apparent need for "puppy dog" likeability in some people is maddening and confusing. Because they are so afraid of conflict and confrontation, they're willing to be intentionally mistreated. What do they get from this? What is the emotional payoff from such a risky investment?

On top of the "kick me" factor, you can add another degree of difficulty: the guilt complex. Here, P. Dog is the master of having it both ways. They can *give* other people guilt trips: "How could you do this to me? After all I've been through, how can you hurt me like that?"

And they can *create* guilt trips, by twisting the words of the other person to support their need to stay in the puppy dog role: "That's fine. You go on without me. I'll be fine here. Don't you worry about it. If I fall and break my hip, I'll probably manage somehow." This tactic, coupled with the usual body language (heavy sighs, slumping shoulders, and the world-weariness that comes from being hurt, yet again) creates the perfect opportunity for the other person to feel the irrational need to reinsert himself or herself *back* into the situation and ride back to the rescue.

The main reason why Puppy Dog people lack Authenticity is because they make, have, and use hidden agendas. Their twist, unlike more overt, bullying, or confrontive players, is that they get their kicks internally. You're not sure why they do it because even they don't recognize their own motives.

NARCISSISM: IT'S REALLY ALL ABOUT ME

Narcissism and altruism stand at opposite poles of human motivation. Few of us are completely altruistic, and most of us are narcissistic to some degree. Our narcissism can become pathological if it renders us incapable of engaging in two-way relationships of mutuality, sharing, and support. The balance between our narcissism and our altruism expresses our emotional health, particularly our sense of self-worth.

Here's the real story on the origin of the term, as told by Latin poet Ovid:

"Narcissus was the son of Cephissus, the river god, and the nymph Leiriope. By the time he was sixteen everyone recognized his ravishing beauty, but he scorned all lovers—of both sexes—because of his pride. The nymph Echo was hopelessly in love but she was hindered by her inability to initiate a conversation. Eventually Narcissus rejected her. She wasted away in her grief to a mere voice. A young man, similarly spurned, prayed that he would love himself unremittingly. The goddess Nemesis answered this prayer by arranging that Narcissus would stop to drink at a spring on the heights of Mount Helicon. As he looked in the water he saw his own reflection and instantly fell in love with the image. He could not embrace his reflection in the pool. Unable to tear himself away he remained until he died of starvation. But no body remained—in its place was a flower."[3]

Mental health clinicians, who try to help notoriously hard-to-treat patients, describe the following characteristics of pathologically narcissistic people:

- An obvious self-focus during interpersonal communication
- Difficulty creating and maintaining relationships
- Lack of situational awareness
- Lack of empathy
- Difficulty seeing themselves as others see them
- Hypersensitivity to any real or imagined insults
- Vulnerability to shame over guilt

In the terminology of social intelligence, what some psychotherapists refer to as narcissism or "malignant self-love," we can simply call a lack of Authenticity.

In media-based cultures such as America, and increasingly in other Western cultures, we have a chance to study narcissism "writ large" in the personas of the celebrities our media minders promote to us. We're treated to the most mundane details of the marriages and divorces, spats and reconciliations, affairs, sex lives, and addictions of our cultural icons. Witness the number of times we see famous or rich people who appear to "have it all" end up in a drug rehab program, dead broke, or worse, just dead? And while it may be a somewhat notorious badge of honor in Hollywood to spend a few supervised months drying out, in the real world, it's much less glamorous when you lose your job, spouse, and career, all due to your self-destructive behavior.

The keepers of the American popular culture—the media minders—love both heroes and anti-heroes, although the anti-heroes seem to get the most exposure. We may see the narcissistic buffoonery of real-estate billionaire Donald Trump more often than we see the low-key wisdom and personal humility of financial genius Warren Buffett. We hear more from the "King of Crass" Howard Stern than from the soft-spoken, erudite, and articulate feature host Bill Moyers. We hear more about strident talk-show hosts like Chris Matthews or Bill O'Reilly than we hear about serious investigators like Jim Lehrer, Brian Lamb, Tim Russert, or Aaron Brown. We hear more about prima donna film directors like Stanley Kubrick—who once famously demanded 147 takes of a scene by the immensely talented actor Jack Nicholson in *The Shining*—than we hear about the quiet craftsmanship of Ken Burns, whose historical documentaries define the genre.

To be somewhat critical, we might say that for the Kubricks of the world, "It's all about me." For the Ken Burns's, Bill Moyers, and Jim Lehrers of the world, "It's all about the product." The Latin expression applies: *res ipsa loquitur,* or "the thing speaks for itself."

The Value of Humility

Two of the legends of comedy, actor and producer Mel Brooks and actor Zero Mostel, had a very contentious working relationship, yet each grudgingly respected the other's talents. During the filming of *The Producers* in 1968, Brooks reportedly flew into a rage when he wasn't getting what he wanted from his actors.

According to accounts of the incident, Zero Mostel walked off the set. Brooks demanded "Where are you going?"

Mostel fixed him with a withering stare and said, "I'm going to my dressing room. I'll be there until your tantrum is over."

> Brooks, aghast at the possibility of a production shutdown, demanded, "Do you mean to tell me that you're going to your dressing room and let this whole production come to a standstill, and waste thousands of dollars, until my tantrum is over?"
>
> "Yes," sniffed Mostel.
>
> With his characteristic half-smile, Brooks declared, "My tantrum is over."

Perhaps the only thing worse than blatant "dig me" narcissism in public idols or icons is when those same idols turn out to have feet of clay. For all his great feats on the baseball diamond, Joe DiMaggio was a cold and distant man who spent his last years worrying obsessively that people were making a profit (one that he should have) off of his name.

O.J. Simpson's skill on the college and professional football fields of his life will always stand in the shadows of his stormy relationship with his wife Nicole Brown Simpson. The level of his involvement in her murder, and that of Ronald Goldman, will probably never be known, regardless of what the courts have said. Simpson was a vain, narcissistically self-involved man. Whatever semblance of Authenticity he managed to display on camera seems highly contrived.

Ted Williams was a bona fide war hero and the greatest hitter for average in the history of baseball. He, too, was a difficult, diffident, and distant man. When he hit a home run in his last home at-bat for the Boston Red Sox, he disappeared into the dugout and refused to come out and tip his cap to the Fenway Park crowd. As John Updike observed in his famous column about the event in 1960, "Hub Fans Bid Kid Adieu":

> "Like a feather caught in a vortex, Williams ran around the square of bases at the center of our beseeching screaming. He ran as he always ran out home runs—hurriedly, unsmiling, head down, as if

our praise were a storm of rain to get out of. He didn't tip his cap. Though we thumped, wept, and chanted 'We want Ted' for minutes after he hid in the dugout, he did not come back. Our noise for some seconds passed beyond excitement into a kind of immense open anguish, a wailing, a cry to be saved. But immortality is non-transferable. The papers said that the other players, and even the umpires on the field, begged him to come out and acknowledge us in some way, but he refused. Gods do not answer letters."[4]

HEAD GAMES, POWER STRUGGLES, AND MANIPULATION

We all know a few people we think of as "game players." By this we usually mean that they seem to approach situations and relationships with the intention of tricking others or manipulating them into behaving in ways that meet their needs. The essence of inauthentic behavior is a pattern of trying to meet one's needs covertly rather than honestly and cooperatively. The term "head game" has crept into the popular vocabulary to describe the battle of wits inauthentic people drag us into.

Some years ago, psychologist Eric Berne made a thorough study of interpersonal manipulation in the form of what he called *transactional games*—a collection of repeatable, stereotyped interactions in which one party would win a miniature psychological victory over the other, usually by exploiting some unconscious vulnerability. His book *Games People Play* and his method of *transactional analysis,* or "TA," became fairly popular in business organizations, useful for training people how to deal with inauthentic people, and how to stay closer to authentic behavior in their own lives.[5]

Berne gave simple, vernacular names to the various games he identified. A simple example will illustrate what he meant by a transactional game. In the game he dubbed "Now I've Got You, You SOB," abbreviated to "NIGYYSOB," one party gets revenge on the other for some prior defeat.

Wife: "I'd sure like to redo the drapes in this room. They're really getting old."

Husband: "Well, why not? Let's go to the department store and see what they have."

Wife: "No, we can't afford it right now. That set of golf clubs you bought took a big chunk out of the budget."

According to Berne, the game consists of three parts:

1. The "set-up," or the offer to play, which is disguised as an innocent chunk of conversation.
2. The "acceptance," or the unwitting response by the other party, usually in the form of an attempt to rescue, comfort, or support the game-player who has made the offer.
3. The "sting," or the sudden turnabout, which causes the "mark"— the person who's been suckered into the game—to feel bad.

In essence, the transactional game has, as its covert objective, making the mark feel bad in some way. It might be anger, frustration, guilt, or any of a number of toxic emotions. According to Berne, game players are unable to meet their emotional needs by direct and honest interaction with others, so they opt for the negative emotional experience of revenge. Inveterate game players are typically people who did not succeed in building a strong sense of self-worth coming out of childhood—they may have been neglected, abused, intimidated, or unloved—and who have unconsciously decided: "I've been mistreated by the world, and somebody's going to pay for it." That somebody turns out to be everybody.

In extreme cases, game players game almost everyone they meet. Their thirst for revenge can never be satisfied. Usually, they have built very robust systems of rationalization to justify their game-playing behavior and to shift responsibility for their toxic behavior onto others.

Ultimately, according to Berne, the only way to win in dealing with a career game-player is simply not to play. One has to learn to spot the indicators of the set-up: complaining, whining, asking for sympathy, referring to situations or historical events that might serve as psychological weapons in making you feel bad. Once you can identify the game-player and get an idea of his or her repertoire of games, you can often spot most of the set-ups, and refuse to take the bait.

Authenticity Made Very Simple

In his 1986 bestseller, *All I Really Need to Know I Learned in Kindergarten,* pastor and essayist Robert Fulghum offered a list of "how to live, what to do, and how to be," that he learned while in kindergarten. It's elegantly simple, which makes it all the more compelling.

- Share everything.
- Play fair.
- Don't hit people.
- Put things back where you found them.
- Clean up your own mess.
- Don't take things that aren't yours.
- Say you're sorry when you hurt somebody.
- Wash your hands before you eat.
- Flush.
- Warm cookies and cold milk are good for you.
- Live a balanced life—learn some and think some and draw and paint and sing and dance and play and work every day some.
- Take a nap every afternoon.
- When you go out in the world, watch out for traffic, hold hands, and stick together.
- Be aware of wonder. Remember the little seed in the Styrofoam cup: the roots go down and the plant goes up and nobody really knows how or why, but we are all like that.
- Goldfish and hamsters and white mice and even the little seed in the Styrofoam cup—they all die. So do we.
- And then remember the Dick-and-Jane books and the first word you learned—the biggest word of all—LOOK.[6]

BUILDING THE SKILLS OF AUTHENTICITY

Things you can do to increase your skills in the dimension of Authenticity include:

- Keep track of situations in which others try to induce you to act in ways that contradict your personal values. How did you react? How did you assert your right to behave authentically?
- Keep track of any situations in which you acted a certain way and later may have felt uneasy about the choice you made. Did you give in when you felt you shouldn't? Did you take the easy route instead of living up to your personal code of conduct? Did you avoid disagreeing with someone or confronting someone because the idea of conflict made you uncomfortable?
- Make a list of your "emotional inputs"—the signals or behaviors you need from others to help you feel lovable, capable, and worthy of acceptance. Do some of these inputs or needs draw you into behaving in inauthentic ways— seeking approval, avoiding conflict, manipulating others, or being dishonest about your values or motives?
- Get a book about values and think through your primary values, the things you hold most dear. Are you behaving in ways that actualize those values?
- Write a personal mission statement that explains to yourself why you think you're on the planet, what your priorities are, and what you want to do to make your life meaningful. Keep revising it until it expresses what your life is all about. Then type it and print it out; put it up on your wall or on your refrigerator and read it every day. Ask yourself: Am I living the mission I want to live?

Notes

1. The etymology of the phrase depends on which Australian scholar, word-smith, or patriot you're speaking to. According to the best sources, "dinkum" was part of the British dialect imported "down under" by white settlers. It originally meant "work." From this came "fair dinkum," which originally meant "a fair day's work for a fair day's pay." Over time, the phrase evolved, as many others do, into its current definition, which is more about personality traits than toil.

2. Morris, Edmund. "The Unknowable." *The New Yorker,* June 28, 2004, p. 47.

3. Stevens, Bruce. Via World Wide Web:
www.psychotherapy.com.au/august00/featart1.html

4. Einstein, Charles. "Hub Fans Bid Kid Adieu." *The Baseball Reader.* New York: Bonanza Books, 1989, pp. 329–330

5. Berne, Eric. *Games People Play: The Psychology of Human Relationships.* New York: Ballantine, 1964.

6. Fulghum, Robert. All *I Really Need to Know I Learned in Kindergarten.* New York: Ballantine/Ivy Books, 1986, p. 4. Used by permission.

5

"C" STANDS FOR CLARITY

"The difference between the right word and the
almost-right word is like the difference between
lightning and the lightning bug."
—Mark Twain

THE "C" FACTOR in the S.P.A.C.E. model represents Clarity. This dimension measures your ability to express your thoughts, opinions, ideas, and intentions clearly.

Do you say what you mean and mean what you say? Do you speak too fast, too much, or not much at all? Does your voice production—pitch, rate, volume, and inflection—inspire confidence or lack of respect? Do you use language skillfully? Can you frame concepts and issues for others in an articulate, compelling way? Do you listen attentively and skillfully, so you can understand others' points of view?

Just improving your vocabulary can help you to better articulate your thoughts and intentions. Using metaphors effectively can help you get your ideas across to other people.

A WAY WITH WORDS

In an interview with a writer from *The New Yorker,* former Vice President Al Gore was explaining his views on the former Soviet Union. He provided a perfect example of how "sesquipedalianism obfuscates pellucidity" (translation: "hard words complicate the meaning of things").

Said ex-Veep Gore:

> "One consequence is that there is an emergent triumphalism among market fundamentalists that has assumed an attitude of infallibility and arrogance that has led its adherents to be dismissive and contemptuous of values that are not monetized if they don't fit into their ideology."[1]

Huh? One common criticism of Al Gore, both before and after the 2000 election, was his oratorical stiffness and his inability to communicate complex issues simply or, perhaps more telling, simple issues simply. There's no question he was a bright guy. But he had problems with his Clarity skills. Not knowing how to use the right language in the right situation may have cost him the presidency.

Here's a bit of text from an academic paper, published in a well-respected journal, and written by an intelligent and experienced professor of—ironically—communication:

> "Communication effectiveness is not an uncommon synonym for communication competence. As simple as this criterion seems, it masks several complicated issues. First, communicators may not be conscious of their objectives, and thus, may not be very cognizant of their own effectiveness. Second, being unaware of their objectives means preferred outcomes may be achieved by accident,

but attributed post hoc as indicators of ability and effort. Third, and related, effectiveness is akin to power, and thus is an extension of attribution principles of identifying oneself as the locus of cause."

Ditto the response to Mr. Gore: Huh? Is it possible to overanalyze something like how we communicate with and to each other? Isn't it a bit ironic that this treatise on effective communication is nearly incomprehensible?

Telling About Time

When I was a small boy, probably about five or six years old, my brother took it upon himself to help me learn to tell time. To this day, I can vividly recall my frustration as his attempt to explain it made it ever more incomprehensible. My brother's discursive strategy included drawing a picture of a clock face, drawing a bisecting line down through the center, and saying "Now, the left side of the clock is 'of,' and the right side is 'after.'" He went on talking about "of" and "after" until I called a halt to the conversation. I said the six-year-old equivalent of "What in the hell are you talking about?"

Actually, he had made a rather enlightened attempt to "find the end of the rope," that is, to establish a discursive jumping-off point from which he could lead me to understand the task of telling time as well as he did. Unfortunately, it didn't occur to him to start a few steps higher on the conceptual ladder, by pointing out that the two hands on the clock move around at two different speeds, and that the "little hand" made a complete circle in twelve hours, while the "big hand" moved much faster, going around once every hour. From there, he could have proceeded to show how the big hand marks out the time within the hour, and then introduce the idea of marking the time in terms of the number of minutes elapsed after the big hand passes twelve. The "of and after" business might have made more sense in that context. It made perfect sense to him; he couldn't understand my frustration and I couldn't understand his.

Many years later I came to realize that, having only spent one more year on the planet than I had, he had limited skill in teeing up a concept for another person. I've often met with adults who have never learned that skill.

Actor/comedian Rob Schneider once did a clever piece on language and tone as part of his stand-up act. He demonstrated, accurately, that the slang word "dude" could be said in a variety of different ways, with each meaning depending on the situation at hand:

- Said long form, with a knowing nod, "Duuuude!" (satisfaction)
- Said shortly, with a negative shake of the head, "Dude!" (disgust)
- Said as a question, "Dude?" (to a man hiding in the dark with a knife)

As adults, we live in a world of words. Yet surprisingly few of us seem to understand the power of language as a medium of thought and expression. More often than not, a conversation or the presentation of an argument or a point of view is little more than a "brain dump," a flow of words that come out as they come to mind. It is a relatively rare—and usually highly effective—person who has learned how to use language as a strategic asset.

HOOF-IN-MOUTH DISEASE: SOMETIMES SILENCE WORKS BEST

A standard feature of situation comedy has some form of the main character "talking trash" to someone about a husband, wife, girl friend, boy friend, boss, or acquaintance, only to see the listener's expression change in a telling way. "She's/He's standing right behind me, right?" is often the pained question of the speaker. (Loud canned laughter follows.)

Corny jokes about the hoof-in-mouth disease, and attempts to recover from it, abound:

A group of patrons in a local bar sits around watching a college football game on TV. Seeing the two teams line up, one man says to his friend, "Huh! Some college! The only people who go to that school are football players and cheap women."

Another very large man standing nearby overhears this remark and says, heatedly, "Hey pal! My wife went to that school!"

"Really?" says the startled man, "Uh . . . what position did she play?"

. . . . .

A man calls over the produce manager at the grocery store and asks him to have a large head of cabbage cut in half. "Why do you want it that way?" asks the produce manager. "I can't use that much cabbage. I only need half," says the man. The produce manager grabs the cabbage and goes off to the meat department. "Hey Larry! Some idiot wants to buy half a cabbage. Can you cut this for me?" Out of the corner of his eye, he sees that the customer has followed him over to the meat counter. "And this nice gentleman is willing to buy the other half!"

As you think about a number of social situations throughout your life, it's likely a few stand out as examples of people whom you recall as saying the perfectly wrong thing at the absolutely wrong time. We've all done it. Consider yourself lucky if it hasn't had a terminal effect on a relationship, career, friendship, or marriage.

Sometimes saying less accomplishes more. Skilled sales people know when to stop talking and let the customer finish the job of deciding to buy. Sometimes it's possible to persuade a person by offering the germ of an idea and allowing him or her to take ownership by inventing the rest of it. Sometimes letting the other person make the point, finish the sentence, or connect the dots wins their support for the idea.

That ubiquitous philosopher Anonymous gets credit for saying:

"Better to remain silent and be thought a fool than to open your mouth and remove all doubt."

Members of a U.S. Air Force fighter squadron adopted the motto:

"Never pass up an opportunity to keep your mouth shut."

And according to Laurence C. Coughlin (or Buddhist teaching or a number of other presumed sources):

"Don't talk unless you can improve on the silence."

Sometimes you can get into trouble no matter what you say. You just have to *sense* the right response, based on your overall understanding of both the context and the content of the encounter. Consider this painfully common example of when to say when:

Semi-Hysterical Friend: "I think my boyfriend is cheating on me! He's been acting strangely lately and I think he may be dating someone from work on the side!"

You: "Gee, that's too bad. You know, I never really liked that guy. I always thought he treated you badly. In fact, he's kind of a creep."

SH Friend: "You are so right! He's been terrible to me and I'm going to confront him about it when I see him tonight."

(One week later)

You: "So how did it go with your boyfriend?"

Now Angry Friend: "Well, we worked it out. By the way, I told him what you said about him and he says he never wants to see you again. In fact, I'm not too happy about it either. I love him, and he loves me. How could you say all those things about him?"

Let's replay the above episode with a more careful choice of words:

Semi-Hysterical Friend: "I think my boyfriend is cheating on me! He's been acting strangely lately and I think he may be dating someone from work on the side!"

You: "Gee, that's too bad. What are you going to do about it?"

SH Friend: "I'm going to confront him about it when I see him tonight."

You: "Well, good luck with that. I hope it goes well for you."

(One week later)

You: "So how did it go with your boyfriend?"

Seemingly Contented Friend: "Well, we worked it out. I really love him, and he loves me."

You: "Good for you. Shall we order lunch?"

Sometimes the art of skillfully saying nothing can be a very useful asset.

Political Hoof-in-Mouth Disease

During the 2004 U.S. Presidential election, Democratic candidate John Kerry's loyal wife, Teresa Heinz Kerry, frequently created problems for him with her injudicious comments and sparring with members of the press who'd figured out how to bait her into arguments. A wealthy heiress, familiar with the receiving end of courtesy from others, she seemed to have a short fuse when challenged on her prospects as America's First Lady, or on her husband's chances of winning.

In one breathtakingly incompetent encounter with the press, she demeaned the wife of the incumbent President, George W. Bush. Laura Bush, one of the least controversial and most-liked women to reside in the White House, had had a respectable career as a librarian and a teacher. She used that experience to advocate educational progress and a renewed focus on the special needs of children.

Teresa Heinz Kerry, displaying a remarkable capacity for wearing her foot in her mouth, said of the First Lady, "I don't believe she's ever had a real job—I mean, since she's been grown up. So her experience and her validation comes from important things, but different things."

She had managed to talk herself into a double bind: either she had to admit she didn't know—or had forgotten—about the First Lady's early career, or she had to face the outrage caused by news stories that cast her comments as demeaning the noble profession of teaching and denigrating the USA's millions of teachers.

A few days later she offered a lame attempt at recovery: "I had forgotten that Mrs. Bush had worked as a schoolteacher and a librarian, and there couldn't be a more important job."

To make matters worse, Laura Bush accepted her apology with uncommon grace: "She apologized, but she didn't even really need to apologize. I know how tough it is, and actually I know those trick questions."

ROLE-SPEAK AND REAL-SPEAK

Have you ever listened to the police officer on the news broadcast explaining what happened in the crime situation, how they caught the perpetrator, or the status of the investigation? Some of them give the explanation in simple, comprehensible language, using commonplace terminology. Others may lapse into "cop-speak"—a stilted, impersonal, mechanistic style of language. "The suspect was operating his vehicle westbound on 54th Street, at approximately 2:45 a.m. He was stopped by a patrol unit in response to a complaint by Mr. X. He was taken into custody and booked into the county detention facility." Apparently, that means "We arrested the guy and put him in jail."

Most likely, Officer Mechanical had just explained the situation to the news reporter before the cameras started rolling, and he probably used plain language. Why, then, did he snap into another, synthetic persona—one that communicated, nonverbally, a whole different set of implications about him as a person?

Police officers—and not all of them—represent a small sampling of the kinds of people who snap into "role-speak"—a depersonalized pattern of discourse—when they have to speak in an official capacity, either to a group of people or in a media interview. District attorneys, mayors, legislators, presidents and prime ministers, and a whole range of other public officials can slip into this default pattern of official language. Chief executives in press interviews, economists and other experts, attorneys for newsworthy figures—all have choices about not only what to say, but how to make themselves credible and attractive in the way they say it.

This role-speak phenomenon invites speculation about the subconscious choices the speaker makes, and the possible benefits he or she may have concluded will come from such a carefully constructed statement. Some may feel that the factual, impersonal language signals to listeners a certain precision of information—and of thinking. Some may find it a useful shield against the possibility of criticism by others who may have an axe to grind, such as the possibility of insinuations of police misconduct by the press. Others may simply feel more comfortable by limiting what they say to verifiable facts. In any case, however, the language itself may cause the listeners to assess the speaker as emotionally repressed, hyper-controlled, and lacking in intellectual courage.

Every day, in media interviews with all kinds of people speaking in an official capacity, and in business gatherings such as conferences, we see two different patterns of presentation. We could call them *role-speak* and *real-speak,* respectively. Real-speak seems to require some additional skills: the speaker has to turn a set of facts—and possibly choose which facts to share—into a story that engages the listeners and connects with their interests. This might involve choosing a simple metaphor around which to organize the explanation. It might involve dramatizing a situation into a coherent "morality play" or a story with a moral. Or it might involve building a compelling paradigm for the discussion and connecting the dots in a way that others might not, without the speaker's help.

Many of the famous figures in history have earned their places by their ability to make a case, build a story, or articulate a premise for action that others found appealing. In recent times the star communicators like Mohandas Gandhi, Franklin Roosevelt, John Kennedy, Martin Luther King, Ronald Reagan, and Bill Clinton have shown mastery of the skills of real-speak.

HELICOPTER LANGUAGE AND ELEVATOR SPEECHES

The helicopter provides an excellent metaphor for the ability to choose words and expressions for communicating ideas at various *levels of abstraction*. What's the unique feature of a helicopter? It can easily move up and down from one altitude to another. Sitting inside a helicopter, you can see the terrain clearly and in great detail when it's hovering at a low altitude, and at a higher altitude you can see much more terrain but with less detail.

By analogy—or metaphor—we can build and fly a "verbal helicopter," which can take us and our listeners down to the lowest level of detail or up to the highest level of generality. Using helicopter language to communicate ideas means choosing terms, figures of speech, expressions, analogies, and, of course, metaphors that position the listener's thinking process at the level where you want it to be. The helicopter is a near-perfect illustration of how changing altitude, or abstraction, can change the view and the thinking process.

The movement from "sky-high"—what we could call the abstract level—to ground-level—or what we could call the concrete level—is a skill that those with high SI Clarity have mastered. Because they're in charge of the helicopter—they're the pilots, so to speak—they can guide the flow of ideas in the listener's mind by moving to the right level at the right time.

People who lack this skill can't seem to control the throttle or the stick. They move too fast from the concrete to the abstract or they spend far too much time at one level or the other. In a business setting, when you hear an exasperated colleague say, "Don't ask that guy the time or he'll tell you how to make a watch," you're seeing an accusation of poor piloting. The listener's need for the exact time (concrete and finite) clashes with the speaker's need to go into great detail (abstract and infinite).

Similarly, when you hear someone say, in the same exasperated tone, "Just give me the *Reader's Digest* version," it means that the listener is losing patience, as the speaker goes into far too much detail for comfort. Some people seem constitutionally incapable of "editing" their story; they can't seem to summarize, they wander off into unrelated details, and they lose the thread of the basic idea.

Good "pilots" signal their moves, telling you where they're taking you. Two examples:

Pilot: "Okay, I just gave you the 'big picture' goals. Now I want to take you through the operational steps."

Pilot: "We've talked about what's taking place right now. Next, we can focus on where we want to be by the end of the project."

In the first example, we see the Helicopter Pilot move from the abstract (bird's-eye view) to the concrete (working view). In the latter example, he or she takes us from the concrete (focus on today) to the abstract (focus on the future).

Another useful metaphor for conveying ideas skillfully is the notion of the "elevator speech." Perhaps appropriate to today's hurry-up society, an elevator speech is a brief, compelling distillation of an important idea, proposition, proposed course of action, issue, or point of view. Figuratively, it's a message you could get across to someone if you were together in an elevator for about one minute.

Composing elevator speeches is becoming an ever more useful skill for Clarity in discourse. For business and professional people especially, more and more situations challenge a person to zero in on the essential elements of a message or a thought process and to express them in a compact and effective way.

A project manager might be invited to attend a board meeting and give a brief explanation of a new initiative in, say, five minutes or less. The discursive strategy and the choice of words can be all-important. In my profession, a chance meeting with a prospective client in an airport might present an opportunity to create interest in a possible business relationship. And, of course, such an opportunity might even arise while riding in an actual elevator.

Working with senior executives, I often find it helpful to invite them to test the clarity of their concept of their enterprise by composing an elevator speech of no more than three sentences. The litmus test of the clarity of the business concept is whether any of the leaders can explain it in three sentences to any employee, customer, board member, or news writer. A particular situation might allow for considerably more elaboration, or it might not. If one hasn't thought the concept through carefully, one might easily be caught off guard in a bumbled response.

Our sound-bite media culture also makes the skill of crafting an elevator speech ever more important. The executive who gets invited to participate in a telephone interview with the local news station may find that only ten seconds of his or her statement ever makes it to air. Getting your point across, as opposed to acting like a performing monkey for the interviewer, depends on packaging ideas skillfully and compactly.

Having appeared on countless radio and TV talk shows as part of my work, I discovered very early that on-air hosts appreciate the ability of an expert to package answers into convenient morsels that can stand alone and survive the editing process. Indeed, this is one of the key criteria interviewers use in deciding to invite an expert back, or to keep his or her contact information in the database of sources.

"CLEAN" LANGUAGE AND "DIRTY" LANGUAGE

What's the difference, if any, between the following two statements:

1. "That's a stupid idea."
2. "I disagree with your idea."

Or these two:

1. "You're dead wrong—you don't know what you're talking about."
2. "I have a completely different point of view."

Or these two:

1. "Boy, that's an ugly painting."
2. "I don't care for that painting."

Most of us would probably characterize the first of each of the pairs of statements as more forceful, edgy, and with an undertone of aggressiveness. They seem to leave little room for uncertainty or ambiguity. Each conveys a sense of finality, the implication that the statement is fundamentally "true for everyone" and that alternatives to its claim will simply not be considered. These implications are not expressed in the statements themselves. They're *meta-messages*—messages about the messages. The speaker's tone of voice, facial expression, and general demeanor can amplify or weaken the *affective content* that is conveyed by the particular choice of words.[2]

Studies in the psychology of language indicate that statements like the first of each of the three pairs tend to induce a subconscious feeling of anxiety in the listener, more so than the alternate statements. Some people—perhaps most—tend to feel somewhat "pushed" or pressured by the aggressive and dogmatic use of language. Although the speaker hasn't said anything of the kind, they tend to hear, on a subconscious channel, that the speaker insists they adopt the opinion or value judgment he or she is declaring. This subtle sense of a threat to one's personal autonomy tends to create a certain amount of resistance, even resentment, in the listener, which may well work against the purposes of the speaker.

Certain patterns of language, either aggressive, dogmatic, or restrictive in their implications, can alienate others, contaminating the process of understanding. We might refer to these corrupted linguistic forms as "dirty" language—not that they're obscene, but they muddy up the communication. Dirty language includes the kinds of statements and choices of words that can intimidate, offend, anger, alienate, or confuse others.

"Clean" language, by contrast, uses more neutral verbal patterns and choices of words that invite empathy, open-mindedness, and the free exchange of ideas.

One of the foundation skills of Clarity is awareness of these deeper-lying psychological phenomena of language, which involves the ability to monitor one's own use of language patterns and the language patterns of others, and to avoid certain verbal pathologies that can cause misunderstanding, conflict, and even psychological maladjustment, both individual and collective.

We can identify at least five primary categories, or variations of dirty language, and then learn to substitute more "semantically sane" versions. Exhibit 5.1 shows these primary types of semantic malfunctions, with some examples. Exhibit 5.2 shows the same malfunctions with antidotes, as well as some examples.

You may notice a key aspect of many of the clean-language forms: the speaker speaks for him- or herself, without presuming that what he or she says is true for everybody. The self-reference makes the sentence irrefutably true and not subject to argument or combat: "I don't think that approach will work" is a statement about the speaker, not about "the approach." The speaker provides information about his or her thinking or opinion with regard to the approach. The dirty-language alternative,

"That approach won't work," seems to telegraph a subconscious assault on the listener's autonomy. Semantic limiters, qualifiers, and other devices signal a respect for the listener and a willingness to acknowledge other possibilities or other points of view.

VERBAL BLUDGEONS

"Verbal bludgeons" are a specific—and especially troublesome—type of dirty language. A verbal bludgeon is one of those aggressive, dogmatic, take-it-or-leave-it statements that makes the listener feel that he or she is being figuratively hit over the head with somebody else's opinion, belief, or value judgment. Statements like "That's a stupid thing to say," "You're dead wrong," "That'll never work," "You don't know what you're talking about," "You're talking out of both sides of your mouth," and "You just contradicted yourself" tend to alienate people rather than invite them to consider the speaker's point of view.

If you'd like to make a moral commitment to eliminating verbal bludgeons from your conversation, you can start by becoming more aware of them, particularly by spotting them as others use them. Then you'll find yourself catching them before they come out, and you'll become skillful at rephrasing your statements into neutral language.

When you become keenly aware of the value and impact of a semantically flexible way of expressing ideas, it's possible to see how even the smallest and simplest of words can influence communication and understanding. Consider, for example, replacing "but" with "and" as an example of the way words can influence how someone feels:

Teacher says: "Johnny, you're doing a good job in English, *but* (then the other shoe drops) you need to work a little harder in math."

Johnny hears: "*yada yada yada* English, *yada yada yada* work harder in math."

Johnny's conclusion: "I'm no good in math."

Exhibit 5.1. Examples of Semantic Malfunctions

Semantic Malfunction	Examples
Opinionitis (aggressive value judgments)	"Mutual funds are a lousy investment"; "The best computer to buy is . . ."; "That's a rip-off. . . ."
All-speak (all-ness language; over-generalizing)	"All politicians lie. . ."; "Kids these days have no respect for their parents. . ."; "People are basically lazy" ("all" is implied)
Or-speak (either-or language)	"You're either with us or against us. . ."; "There are two sides to every argument. . ."; "Are you a liberal or a conservative?"
Should-speak (unwanted advice or directives)	"You should quit that job and get a better one. . ."; "Why don't you trade in that old car?"; "If you were smart, you'd. . . ."
Dogmatism (intolerance of other views)	"There's only one way to do it. . ."; "Anybody who would vote for him/her is stupid. . ."; "I've always voted for the 'X' party. . . ."
Labeling (categorizing with value-judging terms)	"That's just socialism. . ."; "The liberal elite media. . ."; "They're a bunch of troglodytes. . . ."
Sarcasm (caustic criticism)	"If you'd read the report, you wouldn't be asking such dumb questions. . ."; "I guess my opinion's not good enough for you. . ."; "You seem to think you're the only one who has problems. . . ."

Exhibit 5.2. Antidotes to Semantic Malfunctions

Semantic Malfunction	Antidote	Examples
Opinionitis	Self-reference; "owning" one's judgments ("I messages")	"I don't like mutual funds. . ."; "My favorite computer is. . ."; "I don't think that's a good investment. . . ."
All-speak	Limiters and qualifiers ("to some extent," "it seems to me," "so far as I know," etc.	"Some politicians lie. . ."; "It seems like more kids these days don't show respect for their parents. . ."; "Some people may not like to work hard. . . ."
Or-speak	"Gray-scale" language (spectrum of possibilities instead of two extremes)	"You might disagree with us on certain points. . ."; "There are lots of ways to look at this issue. . ."; "What are your views on Issue 'X'?"
Should-speak	Offering options and possibilities	"You might want to consider other jobs. . ."; "Maybe you could get a good trade-in allowance on a new car. . ."; "I suggest you consider. . . ."
Dogmatism	Limiters and qualifiers; "owning" one's conclusions	"I know one way that works. . ."; "I sure wouldn't vote for him/her, but. . ."; "I tend to favor the policies of the 'X' party. . . ."

Exhibit 5.2. (Continued)

Semantic Malfunction	Antidote	Examples
Labeling	Specifying ("de-generalizing")	"Could you explain that idea further?"; "Some media outlets seem to. . ."; "They seem to believe. . . ."
Sarcasm	Neutral language	"Maybe we can review the findings of the report. . ."; "I can give you my opinion, for what it may be worth. . ."; "I can see you've been having problems. . . ."

Suppose the teacher rephrases this statement in a small yet important way.

> **Teacher:** "Johnny, you're doing a good job in English. Please keep it up. *And* now we can go to work on the math."
> **Johnny hears:** "You're doing a good job in English, *and* (a transition) you can be good in math, too."
> **Johnny's conclusion:** "I want to work harder in math."

If you don't think this shift in perception is significant, try it for at least one week. Omit the word "but" from your vocabulary as often as possible, and substitute the word "and" whenever you find yourself in a typical "yes, but" situation.

Think back to how often you hear someone say (on talk radio or a cable news show): "I hate to disagree with you Ed, but. . . ." Notice that they *always* disagree, even though they just "promised" not to. The use of "but" after a neutral or positive clause almost always signals the start of a negative statement:

> "I hate to say you're wrong, but. . . ."
> "You could be right, but. . . ."
> "I usually agree, but. . . ."
> "For the most part what you said is true, but. . . ."
> "I believe you, but I have my own ideas. . . ."

The subtle effect of the "but" word in these contexts can make it somewhat more difficult to establish an effective connection with the other person. Try giving yourself a one-week trial run at replacing "but-speak" with "and-speak" in both your conversations and your written messages.

Here's another simple and easy suggestion for increasing your semantic sanity and cleaning up your language. Train yourself to say the following three things freely, appropriately, and without guilt:

- "I don't know."
- "I made a mistake."
- "I changed my mind."

There's lots more to learn about semantic sanity and clean language; for the moment, learning to apply the methods discussed here can cause a big improvement in your skills of Clarity. And, over time, a greater respect for the power of language can help you understand, be understood, persuade others, and win them to your points of view.

TAKING A BRAIN FOR A WALK

How do you get an idea, a concept, a conclusion, a proposal, or a point of view from your head into someone else's head—and get it to survive there? People who haven't acquired the skills of Clarity tend to say whatever comes to them, in whatever order it comes. Many of them don't understand the difference between an unformatted "brain dump" and a carefully chosen conversational strategy.

They may start explaining something to someone without having gotten that person's full attention. They may start in the middle of an idea rather than finding a logical stepping-off point. They may overload their listeners with too much information, with no logical order or arrangement of the ideas. They seem to assume that the listener's mind is processing the information in the same way that their minds process it.

If we want to influence other people with our ideas and get them to cooperate with us, it helps to present information in a way that makes it easy for their brains to process it. Think of it as getting inside your listener's mind and mentally "escorting" him or her to your truth—your conclusion, your belief, your point of view, or acceptance of the course of action you propose. Metaphorically speaking, you're taking the listener's brain for a walk. First you have to find out where it is—capture the full attention—and then you have to plan out a trip from where it is to where you want it to go.

Here are some conversational strategies and methods that can help you guide the thinking of others.

Route 350

The good news is that the human brain processes speech information at a rate of about 500 words per minute. The bad news is that you and most people can only speak at a rate of about 150 words per minute. Consequently the extra 350 words per minute is dead time, in which the listener's mind can process other, possibly competing or distracting inputs. If you want to keep their full attention, you need to capture that unused processing capacity—you need to keep them off of "Route 350." One way to do it is to pose a provocative question, which gets them thinking about the importance of the topic while you're present-ing the key points. Or you can refer to a topic of specific interest and promise to get to it, after you cover what you first want to say. They'll probably be more attentive because they expect to get something they really want to know. There are many conversational devices for keeping your listeners off of Route 350, and they all work by capturing that unused "bandwidth."

Dropping One Shoe

This method sets up a bold expectation of what will follow. You start with a provocative statement that captures attention, and then capitalize on the dramatic effect. At the beginning of a seminar, I asked the participants to introduce themselves. One woman said, "My name is Wilma, and I traffic in human misery." We sat, gaping, waiting for her to fill us in after that "grabber." Then she said, "I'm a social-work supervisor with the county department of social services. And when I retire shortly, I think I'm going to get a job in a shop that sells baby clothes, because I want to meet some happy people for a change." The one-shoe method also keeps the listener off of Route 350.

Telegraphing

A foreshadowing method, "This is about what happened yesterday . . ." or "I'm going to tell you three things. . . ." (Make sure you do discuss all three.) This method helps you frame the conversation; the listener has already begun to think about the topic and begins to form expectations for the conversation.

Pyramid

A quick snapshot of what you will say, followed by more and more information, building the facts as you go. It's a clarifying technique that's been used successfully in newspaper stories for many decades, and it works very well in conversation.

Marching Plan

"Here's what we're going to do, in three steps (ways, parts, phases, etc.)." In written form, this method uses agendas, bullet points, and outlines like I, II, III or A, B, C. This works especially well in communicating with people who have a high need for structure and order in their thought processes. They know where you plan to take them, and they feel comfortable following the sequence of topics.

Zooming In or Out
Use helicopter language to start with the big picture and move to the more detailed, or start with a very specific piece of information and go out to the broader view. "Let me zero in on something" or "Let me back up a bit. . . ." It's sort of like adjusting the zoom lens on your camera, according to what you want the listener to "see" in his or her mind's eye.

Diagramming
Draw it out, make a sketch, use a diagram (great for visual learners and those who need to "see it" before they can understand it). Consultants often refer to the "power of the pen," which means that the person who goes to the whiteboard or the easel pad and begins to write down the group's ideas takes on a temporary leadership role.

Metaphors
A metaphor substitutes a concrete image or a familiar experience for an abstract concept. One could say, "The proposed course of action offers several benefits, inasmuch as many of the problems we would otherwise face have already been solved, and several key issues are eliminated by this approach," or one could simply say, "This approach is a 'paved road'—we're already halfway there." Metaphors are economical; they incorporate the richness of a complete concept in a simple, shorthand phrase. They also stimulate lots of associations in the listener's mind, which enrich the conversation.

THE POWER OF METAPHOR
Metaphors in particular deserve special attention as tools for Clarity of thought and communication. Whether we realize it or not, we use metaphors in conversation all the time. They provide you with an

efficient way to write or talk to help "people get on the same page" (that's a metaphor, by the way). Men often tend to use metaphorical language based on sports themes or battlefield/war language. Women often tend to use metaphors of life, nature, and community. Some metaphors are cultural, gender-related, or age-related; others are simply goofy. A few examples:

- Barking up the wrong tree (pursuing a futile course of action)
- Painted ourselves into a corner (left ourselves without promising options)
- Connecting the dots (putting ideas together in a meaningful way)
- Like trying to herd cats (trying to get people to behave in uncharacteristic ways)
- Chasing too many rabbits (pursuing too many ventures at one time)
- Panning for gold in your bathtub (engaging in a pointless activity)
- Studying our navels (see panning for gold in the bathtub)
- Shot themselves in the foot (defeated their own purpose)
- Knows the words but doesn't know the music (superficial understanding)
- Career suicide (an action that destroys one's career)
- Circling the drain (going out of business)
- The organizational monkey bars (bureaucratic structure)
- Majoring in the minors (being good at something that doesn't count)
- Strategic radar (process of scanning the business environment)
- Palace war (feud between senior executives in an organization)

Spend a day listening for metaphors and you may be surprised how many you hear. Write down the ones you like best and add them to your vocabulary.

E-PRIME: THE LANGUAGE OF SANITY

In 1965, Dr. David Bourland, an expert in the psychology of language, made a strange proposal. He suggested that people in the English-speaking cultures learn to speak and write without using any form of the verb "to be." He believed that the habitual use of words like "is," "am," "are," "was," "were," and their variations could set up an unconscious tendency toward dogmatism and mental rigidity.[3] For example, a statement like "She *is* an attorney" assigns a person to a category. While categories may help our thinking, Bourland believed, they also invite us to think in stereotypes, substituting commonality for uniqueness. The thoughtless use of labels becomes more difficult with Bourland's method; one has to choose an *active verb* form, which transfers the emphasis to a behavior rather than an abstract category. Bourland might rephrase the example to say, "She *practices* law." He also believed that eliminating to-be forms makes it more difficult to criticize people and bludgeon them with value judgments. If one cannot say, "That *is* a stupid idea," one must find a totally different way to express one's opposition.

Bourland thought of English, minus all to-be forms, as an imaginary language, which he named "E-Prime," using the mathematical symbol E'. In the notation of algebra (or set theory), the concept became:

E-Prime equals [English] minus [to be].

As a quick English lesson, recall that the verb form "to be" includes the following conjugations: be, am, is, are, aren't, was, wasn't, were, weren't, been, and combinations like will be.

Bourland taught himself to speak and write entirely in E-Prime. He believed it forced the person using it to shift his or her conceptual process and to conceive of all reality as dynamic and evolving. Many years ago I incorporated E-Prime as a technique for training business people to write more effectively. It had the remarkable effect of quickly increasing the clarity and dynamism of the trainees' written products. Exhibit 5.3 shows some translations.

Exhibit 5.3. Translations from Regular English into E-Prime

"Regular" English	E-Prime Version
Tom is always late for work.	Tom comes to work late every day.
Sue is a team player.	Sue works well with others.
I am an architect.	I design homes and buildings.
A decision was made to. . . .	X (person) decided to. . . .
That's a good idea.	I like that idea.

E-Prime can also serve as a tool for conflict resolution. If two parties have become locked into a pattern of trading accusations, they might find it helpful to write down all of the provocative statements they've made about each other and then translate them into E-Prime. They may well find that the process of rephrasing their statements becomes a process of reframing their views and accusations.

Inasmuch as we've touched on the idea of using E-Prime to communicate more clearly in print, we might as well go a bit further—although skillful writing calls for an extensive dissertation that goes well beyond our objective here. One quick and simple formula for improving the quality of your writing involves three key principles. We can call it the "Triple-A" Rule. Not only can it lead to better, clearer writing, but it also helps you write in E-Prime.

The Triple-A Rule has the following components:

1. Average Sentence Length = 20 Words or Less

Shorter, snappier sentences make it easier for your reader to follow your thoughts. Studies of reading comprehension clearly show the highest levels of understanding when sentences range from 15 to 25 words each, peaking at an average of about 20. You can combine a few long sentences with very short ones; overall, shorter works better. Typically, you'll want to capture one idea per sentence, with about two to six sentences per paragraph.

2. Avoid Jargon

The overuse of jargon and acronyms, computer-speak, business-speak, and government-speak tends to confuse people who don't know it. Even for readers who know what various acronyms and "insider" expressions mean, substituting plain language can often make the message more compelling. While some jargon makes communication useful, it works best as a spice, not a main course.

3. Active Voice (E-Prime, If Possible)

E-Prime forces you to write in the active voice; in fact, it eliminates "passive voice" verb forms automatically. To review: passive voice language tends to hide or subordinate the "actor" in the sentence: "The office *was searched* and the file *was found* by Mary." In E-Prime the sentence becomes "Mary searched the office and found the file." E-Prime writing tends to make for shorter sentences. Count the words in the first, passive-voice example (11) versus the second, active voice sentence (8). Writing in the active voice, or E-Prime, forces you to choose your verbs (and their order) more carefully.

As an exercise, check the language of the section you've just read, to see if it uses E-Prime completely in explaining E-Prime (not counting to-be forms used as illustrations).

Speech by Chief Seattle, 1854 _____

The famous speech by Chief Seattle, of the Suquamish tribe in Washington, is considered an historical masterpiece of compelling language.

"The President in Washington sends word that he wishes to buy our land. But how can you buy or sell the sky? the land? The idea is strange to us. If we do not own the freshness of the air and the sparkle of the water, how can you buy them?

"Every part of the earth is sacred to my people. Every shining pine needle, every sandy shore, every mist in the dark woods, every meadow, every humming insect. All are holy in the memory and experience of my people.

"We know the sap which courses through the trees as we know the blood that courses through our veins. We are part of the earth and it is part of us. The perfumed flowers are our sisters. The bear, the deer, the great eagle, these are our brothers. The rocky crests, the dew in the meadow, the body heat of the pony, and man all belong to the same family.

"The shining water that moves in the streams and rivers is not just water, but the blood of our ancestors. If we sell you our land, you must remember that it is sacred. Each glossy reflection in the clear waters of the lakes tells of events and memories in the life of my people. The water's murmur is the voice of my father's father.

"The rivers are our brothers. They quench our thirst. They carry our canoes and feed our children. So you must give the rivers the kindness that you would give any brother.

"If we sell you our land, remember that the air is precious to us, that the air shares its spirit with all the life that it supports. The wind that gave our grandfather his first breath also received his last sigh. The wind also gives our children the spirit of life. So if we sell our land, you must keep it apart and sacred, as a place where man can go to taste the wind that is sweetened by the meadow flowers.

"Will you teach your children what we have taught our children? That the earth is our mother? What befalls the earth befalls all the sons of the earth.

"This we know: the earth does not belong to man, man belongs to the earth. All things are connected like the blood that unites us all. Man did not weave the web of life, he is merely a strand in it. Whatever he does to the web, he does to himself.

"One thing we know: our God is also your God. The earth is precious to him and to harm the earth is to heap contempt on its creator.

"Your destiny is a mystery to us. What will happen when the buffalo are all slaughtered? The wild horses tamed? What will happen when the secret corners of the forest are heavy with the scent of many men and the view of the ripe hills is blotted with talking wires? Where will the thicket be? Gone! Where will the eagle be? Gone! And what is it to say goodbye to the swift pony and the hunt? The end of living and the beginning of survival.

"When the last red man has vanished with this wilderness, and his memory is only the shadow of a cloud moving across the prairie, will these shores and forests still be here? Will there be any of the spirit of my people left?

"We love this earth as a newborn loves its mother's heartbeat. So, if we sell you our land, love it as we have loved it. Care for it, as we have cared for it. Hold in your mind the memory of the land as it is when you receive it. Preserve the land for all children, and love it, as God loves us.

"As we are part of the land, you too are part of the land. This earth is precious to us. It is also precious to you.

"One thing we know—there is only one God. No man, be he Red man or White man, can be apart. We are brothers after all."[4]

BUILDING THE SKILLS OF CLARITY

Things you can do to increase your skills in the dimension of Clarity include:

- Study the ways highly articulate people present ideas; watch interviews and listen to conversations to identify the methods they use: the flow of ideas, sequencing ideas, helicopter language, elevator messages, use of facts and figures, metaphors, word pictures, and the use of humor.
- Take a diagnostic vocabulary test to assess the size and breadth of your working vocabulary. If appropriate, get a book, an audio program, or a web-based vocabulary course to strengthen your use of words.
- Collect clever and powerful metaphors and introduce them into your conversation.
- Train yourself to illustrate your ideas with sketches, cartoons, or diagrams.
- Invent and practice "Route 350" methods to hold the attention of your listeners.

Notes

1. *New Yorker* Website, www.newyorker.com/fact/content/?040913fa_fact. Issue: Sep 13, 2004.
2. Parts of this chapter are adapted from "The Power Thinking Course," a training seminar created by Karl Albrecht International, 2004. Used with permission. For further information, visit KarlAlbrecht.com.
3. D. David Bourland, Jr., "A linguistic note: Write in E-prime," *General Semantics Bulletin,* 1965/1966, 32 and 33, 60–61. Psychiatrist Albert Ellis wrote a whole book in E-Prime: Ellis, Albert. *Sex and the Liberated Man.* Secaucus, NJ: Lyle Stuart, 1976.
4. The speech given by Chief Seattle in January of 1854 is the subject of a great deal of historical debate. Several versions contend for validity, and the history of the speech is clouded. The version given here is one of the most poetic and compelling, but not necessarily the most widely accepted by scholars.

6

"E" STANDS FOR EMPATHY

"When I left the dining room after sitting next to Mr.
Gladstone, I thought he was the cleverest man in
England. But after sitting next to Mr. Disraeli, I
thought I was the cleverest woman in England."
—A woman when asked her impression of
English statesmen Benjamin Disraeli
and William Gladstone.

THE "E" FACTOR in the S.P.A.C.E. model represents Empathy. This
dimension invites you to look at how truly aware and considerate you
are of others' feelings. Are you able to tune in to other people as
unique individuals? Do you show that you're willing and able to accept
them as they are, for what they are? The usual connotation of being
empathetic means to identify with another person and appreciate or
share his or her feeling. However, in the context of social intelligence,

there is an additional level of depth—the sense of *connectedness*—which inspires people to cooperate. In this discussion, empathy is defined as a state of positive feeling *between* two people, commonly referred to as a condition of rapport.

Common sense tells us that people are more likely to cooperate with, agree with, support, and help you if they like you and share a sense of mutual respect and affection with you. To achieve empathy with another person means to get him or her to share a feeling of connectedness with you, which leads the person to move *with and toward* you rather than *away and against* you.

The opposite state, of course, is antipathy, a feeling that causes a person to move away and against you. Toxic behavior, obviously, destroys empathy. Nourishing behavior restores and builds empathy. Psychologists and human relations experts sometimes refer to the "abrasive personality" to describe people who habitually alienate others. The old expression "He/she rubs me the wrong way" is a metaphor for interpersonal abrasion.

If we want to gain the personal and practical benefits that come with building empathy with others and maintaining quality relationships, we have to do two things: (1) avoid or abandon toxic behaviors; and (2) adopt or increase the use of nourishing behaviors. It's not realistic to think that we can abuse people, insult them, make them feel insignificant or unloved or unworthy, or praise them when we need something and ignore them when we don't, and then expect them to feel a sense of connectedness with us. Empathy requires a long-tem investment, not an episodic application of "charm."

First let's be sure we know how *not* to treat people, and then we can explore ways to build on the respect and affection we've earned.

WHAT DESTROYS EMPATHY?

"Hey, man! How's it going, buddy? How's the wife?"

"Well, actually, she's in the hospital. I'm kind of. . . ."

"Great! Glad to hear it. See you around, pal!"

To repeat: toxic behavior destroys empathy. Nourishing behavior builds empathy. As Jack Nicholson's character the Marine colonel in *A Few Good Men* says: "It's that simple."

In Chapter 1 we touched on the basic idea of toxic and nourishing behavior. Now it's time to get much more specific. Exhibit 6.1 provides a fairly extensive inventory of toxic behaviors and their nourishing alternatives. As you read the list, slowly and thoughtfully, picture each behavior in action. Can you visualize someone, or various people, acting out the toxic behaviors? Can you visualize yourself acting out the nourishing behaviors?

Let's remember that being nourishing requires more than just not being toxic. Eliminating toxic behaviors only gets you to the zero-point on the empathy scale. Avoiding antipathy only gets you to apathy. Getting to empathy calls for a proactive commitment. You need to "add value" as other people perceive you.

As you read the two lists of contrasting behaviors, did you identify any toxic behaviors that you detect in yourself, to a smaller or greater extent? Did you identify any nourishing behaviors that seem utterly foreign to you, behaviors you clearly don't engage in? Does this thinking process add to the possibilities you've been accumulating while reading this book? You may not have experienced a personal epiphany while reading the list, but it could still be helpful to you in various ways. And I certainly hope you didn't experience an attack of anxiety, guilt, or self-condemnation. This is supposed to be a positive experience of discovery and growth, not an exercise in self-flagellation.

One particularly toxic form of verbal behavior, which is especially destructive in business situations and organizations, is *killing other people's ideas.* Idea killing involves saying things like:

- It won't work here.
- We tried it before.
- It costs too much.

Exhibit 6.1. Toxic vs. Nourishing Behaviors

"Toxic" Behaviors	"Nourishing" Behaviors
Withholding "strokes"	Giving positive strokes
Throwing verbal barbs, "zingers"	Kidding positively
Giving nonverbal put-downs	Giving positive strokes
Patronizing or "parenting" a person	Treating a person as an equal
Seeking approval excessively	Speaking and acting assertively
Flattering others insincerely	Giving honest compliments
Losing one's temper easily	Deferring one's automatic reactions
Playing "games" with people	Cooperating; giving positive strokes
Disagreeing routinely	Agreeing where possible
Speaking dogmatically, inflexibly	Using "semantic flexibility"
Bragging, scoring "status points"	Sharing another person's successes
Violating confidences	Keeping confidences
Breaking promises and agreements	Making only promises one will keep
Joking at inappropriate times	Joking constructively
Monopolizing the conversation	Sharing "air time"
Interrupting others frequently	Hearing others out
Changing the subject capriciously	Sticking to the subject
Complaining excessively	Giving constructive suggestions
Giving someone the "hard sell"	Suggesting, advising, negotiating
Insisting on having one's way	Compromising, helping others
Attacking or criticizing others	Confronting constructively
Inducing guilt in others	Persuading honestly; negotiating
Ridiculing others	Supporting others; sympathizing
Shooting down ideas	Deferring judgment; listening
Giving unwanted advice	Offering information and ideas

- It's too complicated.
- It's not practical.
- We don't have time.
- They won't go for it.
- We're different here.
- We've never done it.
- It's not in the budget.
- Let's stick with what we know.
- Our system isn't set up for that.
- Good idea, BUT. . . .
- Not our bailiwick.
- It's too risky.
- It's probably illegal.
- Maybe next year.

The antidote, or defense, against idea killing, which seems to be so prevalent, is the practice of "idea selling." This technique involves using certain key statements to put the other person into a mental state of greater receptiveness to your thoughts or ideas.

You can often get people to listen and respond more open-mindedly if you use the following kinds of *idea-selling* statements in your conversations:

- May I ask a question?
- Before we make our final decision, let's review our options.
- I suggest we not eliminate any options at this point.
- Are we ready to decide? Are we sure we've considered all the key factors?
- Let's discuss the way we're approaching this problem.
- I'd like to back up a step and clear up a certain point.
- I hope we're not developing a case of "groupthink" here.
- I've been hearing about X. Do you have any information on it?

- I don't know much about that. How about you?
- Were you aware that. . . ?
- There are a couple of new factors you might not know about.
- Maybe we should reconsider that point.
- Maybe you'd like to reconsider your opinion, since. . . .
- I've changed my mind on that, since I found out that. . . .
- This idea might sound far-fetched, so let me explain it before you react.
- You might not want to make a decision on this yet, but. . . .
- I have an idea I'd like to share with you some time.
- I'd like to get your help on an idea I'm trying to work out.
- I'd like to have your take on. . . .
- Here's a half-baked idea: how does this strike you. . . ?
- Here's a partly baked idea; maybe you can add to it.
- We'd better start thinking about how we're going to. . . .
- What options do you see at this point?
- What are some of the ways we can. . . ?
- Have you considered doing it by the X method?

Perhaps the simplest message emerging from this discussion would be: Empathy, like God and the Devil, is in the details.

WHAT BUILDS EMPATHY?

Let's think in terms of two opportunities to build empathy: (1) the moment-to-moment experience of connecting with people; and (2) the "maintenance" process, by which you keep a relationship healthy over time. First, the momentary part.

In a specific situation, you can usually establish a strong empathic connection with one person or a group of persons by concentrating on three specific kinds of behavior. In this case, like the case of communicating clearly, as discussed in Chapter 5, we can think in terms of another "three A's"—Attentiveness, Appreciation, and Affirmation.

Attentiveness

First we need to make a practice of getting outside of our own mental bubbles and tuning in to other people as unique individuals. All normal human beings like to be noticed, listened to, and taken seriously. Those who feign interest in others often give themselves away with nonverbal cues that contradict the story. The best way to show interest in someone is to be interested in that someone. A genuine intention to listen, and possibly learn from someone, comes through in your conscious and unconscious behavior. In addition, certain voluntary nonverbal cues can signal to the other person that you do consider him or her a valuable and worthy individual.

For example, orienting your body toward the other person, making eye contact, pausing and listening attentively as he or she speaks, and nodding or otherwise signaling that you're following what is said, all help to strengthen the sense of attentiveness. If you're a reasonably expressive person, you probably don't have to think very much about these cues; they typically come naturally. If you're more shy or reserved, consider voluntarily increasing your use of these cues, to add energy to your interactions with others.

A less well-known but very effective form of attentiveness is *nonverbal pacing,* which means matching your body posture, general physical orientation, and gestures to those of the other person. You can also sense these same kinds of cues to determine whether the other person feels an empathic connection with you. You've probably noticed that, when two people are having an amicable conversation, their body postures, gestures, voice cadence, facial expressions, and even their breathing, tend to fall into alignment. If you detect a significant mismatch between their "nonverbals," you might be seeing evidence of alienation, conflict, or disagreement. To establish an initial rapport, you can begin by pacing the other person's nonverbal cues with your own—not in an obvious way, or out of a sense of manipulation, but in a natural way. This just adds to the set of natural signals of empathy and connectedness that you convey with your nonverbal cues—provided you really are paying attention and not faking.

Verbal pacing, which also helps to build empathy, is a habit of reflecting the other person's words, expressions, and figures of speech back to him or her. If the other person uses a particular metaphor, using that metaphor in your reply serves as an endorsement of the idea, and a nonverbal confirmation of connectedness. You can also pace the style of language. For example, some people like to use mild forms of profanity to spice up their conversation and to emphasize certain points. This kind of behavior has become much more acceptable in recent years. However, it may be advisable to refrain from strong language until or unless the other person's language drifts in that direction. Then you can verbally pace that pattern of speech.

The microstructure of human conversation is remarkably complex and diverse; in this brief discussion we can only touch on some of the more interesting dynamics. As previously mentioned, attentiveness tends to come naturally if you choose to really pay attention to others as individuals. And it won't hurt to know a few specific methods or techniques to help make the connection.

Appreciation

Do you show other people that you're willing and able to accept them as they are, for what they are? You may disagree with their political or religious views, and your personal world of values and experiences might be quite different from theirs; at the same time you can acknowledge their right to a place on the planet. On a nonverbal level, this means that your cues signal acceptance, or at least the absence of rejection or animosity. If you tell yourself that you can probably co-exist peacefully with them even if you disagree on some things, you'll probably signal acceptance and appreciation naturally.

In addition to the natural signals that cue people that you accept them and appreciate their right to be who and what they are, you can do quite a few other things to strengthen the bond of mutual respect.

One important skill for reinforcing the perception of respect, accept-ance, and appreciation is the use of "clean language," as explained in Chapter 5. By adopting a semantically flexible and considerate pattern of language, free from dogmatism, sarcasm, opinionitis, all-ness, polar-izing, and dichotomizing, and making good use of semantic limiters and qualifiers, you can avoid building resistance in others to your ideas. When they truly believe that you respect them and their ideas, they are more likely to listen to yours.

Affirmation

It's admittedly easier to like, respect, and feel close to someone whose values and ideas you share than to someone with whom you strongly disagree on significant matters. At the same time, it's possible to affirm that person, as a person, in the ways you interact with him or her. As child-rearing experts say, "You can love the child and dislike the child's behavior." The same applies to adults: you can disagree with a person and yet treat him in a way that invites him to respect you and possibly even like you. It would be a bit of a stretch to claim that this philosophy extends all the way to hardened criminals and other despicable people, but thankfully most of us don't have to deal with people like that very often. Most of us get to interact with fairly "normal" people, even though some of them might not be easy to deal with.

As human beings, we typically need, want—and often seek—affirmation of ourselves on at least three levels: (1) lovability, (2) capabil-ity, and (3) worthiness. Each of us needs to know that we are deserving of affection. Each of us needs to feel that we are respected for what we're capable of. And each of us needs to feel that we are acknowledged as a worthwhile person. In all three respects, honest and genuine compli-ments go a long way. The legendary motivational expert Dale Carnegie pointed out that most human beings are hungry for "emotional input"—the kind of recognition, acceptance, praise, and affirmation that's actually very easy to give. The principle is deceptively simple: if you help people feel good about themselves, they'll feel good toward you.

At this point in the discussion, some people—possibly many—may protest: "What about us introverts? All of these empathy-building behaviors might come easily to extraverted people who are highly sociable. But not everybody is so outgoing and inclined to connect easily with people. What about those of us who are not 'networkers' by instinct?"

Actually, the world might not be so full of extraverts as many introverts seem to think. In fact, many people who seem friendly, outgoing, and sociable are actually closet introverts. Many skilled seminar trainers, for example, are actually more introverted than the audiences they're facing might assume. They have the learned ability to connect to a group with stories, humor, and a humanistic approach to their subject. They're "on" when they need to be "on," using a light touch and good SI presence.

When these people are finished training for the day, they're often tired and in need of downtime to recharge their intellectual and social batteries. "Let's go out for a drink and some dinner," suggests someone in the seminar group after a long day of group work. "Thanks, but I have some work to catch up on," is the reply for the fatigued trainer, eager to get back to his or her room, rest, eat, and sleep long enough to be able to do it again the next day or in the next city.

And with regard to the highly touted "networking" skill, here's a secret I discovered a long time ago: You don't have to be a skilled networker to get the benefits of networking; you just have to have one or more friends who are networkers. They'll do your networking for you. In fact, people who are highly motivated networkers *must* network—it's part of their psychic make-up. Actually, they can't help themselves. They love being allowed to network for you. If you need to find a pediatric ophthalmologist or an expert in tree care, just contact your friendly neighborhood networker; he or she will be grateful you called. Once I discovered that I could "outsource" my networking, I no longer felt handicapped by being the adapted introvert that I am.

THE PLATINUM RULE

The oft-repeated "Golden Rule"—"do unto others as you would have them do unto you"—may be a fatally flawed piece of advice. George Bernard Shaw said, "Do not do unto others as you would have them do unto you—their tastes may not be the same." Shaw's suggestion may be more than a wisecrack; it suggests a different angle of view on empathy.

It makes more sense to recast the advice—let's call it the Platinum Rule: "Do unto others as others prefer to be done unto."[1]

Once we move outside the bounds of our selfish preoccupation with our own needs and priorities, we can better understand how to get what we want by ensuring that others get what they want. In fact, we might even argue that trying to treat people the way we *think* they want to be treated can cause even more problems.

For example, healthcare professionals—doctors, nurses, and allied practitioners—tend to like dealing with "compliant" patients, a euphemism for docile people who don't cause trouble by questioning their decisions, asking for information, or wanting special attention. Yet patient research studies clearly indicate several important variations in patient preference for the way they interact with caregivers—a psychosocial "patient style," if you will.

Certainly there are compliant patients, those meek souls who put their health—and sometimes their lives—into the hands of medical people. But there are also assertive patients, who expect medical people to treat them like customers, not like obedient children. There are other patients who consider themselves responsible for their medical outcomes, and expect medical practitioners to explain things to them.

The flawed "Golden Rule" approach in healthcare, for example, seems to imply that "we" would like to be treated with condescension, given very little information other than what we specifically ask for, and "managed" like so many sheep. The alternative Platinum Rule suggests that we discover the particular needs of individual people in particular situations, and care for them as individuals, with those needs in mind.

Case in point: my ophthalmologist, who has performed several surgeries on my eyes, understands me as a human being as well as a pair of eyes. When we first came to the point of considering surgery, he adapted his explanatory approach to what he knew. He knew I had been trained as a scientist and had worked as a physicist, and that I have an investigative sort of a mind. He also knew that I had relatively little fear of surgery and that I appreciated knowing as much about my medical condition as a lay person could reasonably know.

So when we sat down in his office to discuss the surgery, he immediately produced a plastic anatomical model of the human eye and began to explain in some detail how he planned to do the surgery. Although some other patients might have been horrified and apprehensive at hearing such a graphic explanation, it my case it was just the right approach. Some others would "rather not know." But thinking as a trained scientist, I found the procedure and its logic fascinating. I later acquired a copy of a videotaped eye surgery of the type we were considering and, after watching it, I felt quite confident of the outcome.

I then became a "good patient." He had met my particular platinum-rule needs for information and a sense of mastery through knowledge. I'm certain that in other cases he might approach such a discussion quite differently, according to the needs of the individual.

This is one of the key principles of empathy, in the SI context: making an effective connection with another person, based on where he is, what he needs, how he views the situation, and how he sets priorities. Some people are huggers; some aren't. Some like to touch and be touched; some don't. Some like to use strong language and profanity; some don't. Some people share their feelings and their personal lives with others; some don't. A key part of Empathy is a conscientious effort to understand and acknowledge the life positions of others, and to work from that knowledge in forming effective relationships with them.

THE IRONY OF EMPATHIC PROFESSIONS

Psychologists, psychiatrists, and other licensed mental health clinicians are over-represented as suicide cases. They rank near the top of professional people who kill themselves, and certainly near the top of all medical specialties. Many medical schools can report students who have killed themselves, perhaps from the stress of the schoolwork, perhaps from the stress of their profession, or because they are clinically depressed upon entrance at school.

How can people in helping professions hit bottom in their own lives? Do they run out of emotional steam by giving all they have to others? Or do they enter their profession with demons already in tow?

Idealism, when it turns into jaded weariness, can be a dangerous thing in some helping professions. Several paramedics, firefighters, and police officers who responded to serious trauma incidents—like the September 11 attacks on the World Trade Center, the Oklahoma City Federal Building bombing, and the Columbine High School shootings—later took their own lives. For reasons that may have made sense to them at the time, they could no longer cope with what they saw or had to do.

Is it possible that some of those people were in the wrong jobs? The irony of empathic professions is that the wrong people can end up practicing them. Consider this list of people who chose the wrong professions:

- Doctors who are bright and should be in a lab, researching cancer or other diseases, not standing at a hospital bedside talking to patients with whom they feel no empathy.
- Doctors who spend more time talking into their tape recorders instead of looking into the eyes of their patients. (Spare us the "HMOs only give us so much time" diatribe. Medicine is about giving scared people comfort and help for people whose pain level is matched only by their anxiety level.)
- Teachers who don't like being around kids (or speaking to groups of adults).

- Police officers who stay on patrol too long and start dodging radio calls and sitting in their cars for the entire shift.
- Mental health clinicians who have a bushel basket of their own problems, and who should turn their laser beam acumen onto themselves first, before they start helping others.
- Child protective service workers who don't like kids or having to deal with abused kids.
- Social workers who don't really like the poor, the miserable, and the bewildered.
- Nursing home nurses who don't like being around elderly patients.
- Lawyers who don't like to battle, don't like the law, and don't feel good about creating or participating in conflicts.
- Customer service people who say, "This would be a great place to work if it weren't for all those damned customers."

The Stone-Face Syndrome

One of the clues that a person is having difficulty finding the energy to build and sustain empathy is the "stone-face syndrome." Someone who falls victim to this disorder simply stops smiling, adopts a visage and demeanor that sends out "stay away" signals, and simply plods through the day's experiences. People begin to avoid them, brief and pleasant conversations tend to disappear, and they may find themselves wondering why people use labels like "grim" or "unapproachable" in talking about them.

As you review the previous list of less-than-empathic people, stuck in their empathy-oriented professions, consider how many of them have unconsciously adopted the stone face as their look of choice. The hard question is why? The easy answer is: because they are starting to lose their sense of humanity and their work is taking its toll on their idealism and emotional connections with others.

"But," counter the Stonefaces, "we have to act this way; otherwise people will think we're weak, silly, or not serious." This is especially prevalent with police officers, military people, paramedics, doctors, and other male-dominated professions where showing too much humanity (like smiling at other people) can seem effeminate, unprofessional (especially among peers), or vulnerable. Doctors and police officers aren't supposed to cry when death and pain is all around them, so they may adopt the stone-faced persona as a coping mechanism. Best to keep a stiff upper lip, just in case someone catches you having real emotions or being outwardly human.

In the best cases, professionals who find themselves stuck at these career crossroads make changes. They retire, quit, or move into new positions that emphasize what they like to do rather than what they have to do (or were trained to do). It's not uncommon to see people who have had long and difficult careers retire and do something that is completely unrelated to their previous professions.

Laughter Is the Best Medicine

If you believe, as I do, that one's sense of humor is a reliable barometer of stress, then the stone-faced clan look like they're straining under the weight of their personal and professional stress. If you can't laugh at what is truly funny, then you're overstressed. If it's a chronic affliction, then you're suffering with the "Stone Face Syndrome."

The treatment for this disorder is simpler than you might expect: laugh more and smile more. Remind yourself, several times a day, that life is either a tragedy or a comedy depending on how you choose to view it.

The late Dale Carnegie advised us to always "keep an emerging smile on your face," no matter what the circumstances. Your facial expression can actually influence your feelings. So can your posture. Just changing from a slumped position to a more upright stance, and from a sour puss to the edge of a smile can immediately change the way you feel.

Imagine the facial expression you might have when you walk around after you've just heard a piece of really great news. That's the "Dale Carnegie face" in action. It's not about convincing the world you're tough; it's about letting the world know you're not tough *all the time.*

> The German philosopher Wolfgang von Goethe said, "One should, each day, try to hear a little song, read a good poem, see a fine picture, and if it is possible, speak a few reasonable words."
>
> He might also have added, "And have a good belly laugh."

L.E.A.P.S.: EMPATHY BY DESIGN

Dr. George Thompson is a bit of a Renaissance Man. He created several books, a series of training seminars, an institute based in New Mexico, all based on his communication concept called "Verbal Judo."[2] His ideas have been taught to police officers, teachers, medical and mental health professionals, and other regular or high-risk service providers to help them better deal with angry, irrational, or even dangerous people.

One of Dr. Thompson's models—L.E.A.P.S.—references the need to listen on many levels, provide support for the person on the other side, and solve whatever problem exists to his or her satisfaction, not necessarily yours. While the steps seem obvious in some respects, witness how few people actually follow them. It's one thing to understand the behaviors and another to operationalize them. L.E.A.P.S. stands for: Listen, Empathize, Ask, Paraphrase, and Summarize.

- *Listen.* Demonstrate active listening skills by nodding, leaning forward, making appropriate eye contact, and really listening. Active listening starts by trying to make a human connection with the other person. The biggest obstacle to this is the human need for multitasking. In our nonstop society, it's easy and likely that most working people feel the need to do more, even when they need to stay in the moment. Multitasking in business includes talking on the phone while trying to carry on a face-to-face conversation, checking email (a passion bordering on the obsessive for some), or trying to read, think, and talk at the same time. It's no wonder that angry people will get even angrier if they feel you're not paying attention to them. Sometimes, they will raise the stakes (and their voices) to get your full attention. It says a lot to someone when you stop what you're doing, turn to face the person, and demonstrate, verbally and non-verbally, that he or she is your highest priority at that moment. If you don't believe this, recall your own childhood, when either of your parents was too busy to look up from the TV, the paper, chopping the carrots, or fixing the car to listen to your concerns. Too many people half-listen, waiting for you to stop talking before they can start again.

- *Empathize.* This happens when you can see the problem from the other person's side, and feel it too.

- *Ask.* Start with opened-ended questions, get more information, and allow the other person to vent if he or she needs to. Questions and answers create a dialogue for angry people and allow them to burn some energy while talking to you. It also creates some control for you, by modeling what it is you want them to do, which is stay in control and use the back-and-forth method of communication to hear and be heard.

- *Paraphrase.* Re-state the other person's ideas, using his or her words as much as practically possible. People who are angry rarely listen to your words, but they often will when you para-phrase what they have said back to them. Paraphrasing gives you some time, demonstrates empathy on your part, and—more importantly—tests to make sure you really understand their concerns, and that they believe you understand.

- *Summarize.* Find the answer together, create solutions that are good for all parties, and help the person discover what will solve the presenting problem. If either or both of you have promised to take certain actions—or to stop acting in certain ways—it's advisable to itemize the terms of agreement.

EMPATHY IN FOUR MINUTES

We might have significantly fewer divorces in modern countries if more husbands and wives would see fit to adopt a simple but very effective behavioral strategy. We could call it the "creative contact" strategy.

In his timeless book *Contact: The First Four Minutes,* Leonard Zunin presents a compelling proposition: that most people who meet a stranger in a social setting will decide within approximately four minutes whether they would like to continue to engage that person and, if so, whether the idea of some continuing interaction or involvement would appeal to them.[3]

Before we stereotype and file away this proposition under the cliché of "the first impression," consider an interesting extension of Zunin's proposition: that people in close friendships or intimate relationships recapitulate the event of their first meeting every single time they come into contact with each other after any period of separation.

If the person you meet at a social function sets up an unconscious score card and grades the interaction in terms of the desirability of continuing, then clearly your behavior in those crucial four minutes or so deserves some creative thought. Aside from the value of incredibly good looks, your behavior toward the other person can make a "sale" or it can sink all chances for development. Stand-up comics make a staple out of the "pick-up line" syndrome, the idea that saying just the right thing—or just the wrong thing—determines a person's success with the opposite gender. But rather than hoping to discover that magic "line," we would do better to focus on the other person, and consider the basic principles of establishing rapport and connectedness—the macro-skill of Empathy.

Returning to Zunin's second key proposition, that people figuratively "restart" their relationships every time they meet, we can find specific ways to make every restart a positive one.

Hypothetical Case: in a fairly traditional husband and wife relationship, John comes home from work feeling tired, stressed, and preoccupied with a problem that arose shortly before he left the office. Mary has had a hectic day of running errands, dealing with the trades people working on their house, and looking after the children's needs. They come into contact in a very perfunctory, almost businesslike way, each still preoccupied with his or her day's distractions.

"Hi," she says.

"Hi," he says. "Did the landscape guy get finished?"

"Not yet," she says. "Probably tomorrow."

"Okay. Where are the kids?"

"Down the street. I called to tell them to come home."

After dealing with the immediate business, the conversation winds down. He turns on the TV news and she begins preparing dinner.

Substitute any number of alternative scenarios—a two-career couple, a couple who don't live together but date on a regular basis, a couple who run a business together and work together all day—and we often see the same thing. The mundane trumps the personal. Many personal relationships, whether between men and women, parents and children, best friends, bosses and employees, or business partners, lack a single very powerful ingredient: *relationship maintenance.*

Consider an alternate scenario for John and Mary. John walks into the house, puts aside his briefcase or other personal items and greets her in a cordial, affectionate way.

"Hi, baby-doll. How's it going?"

Mary puts aside her project of the moment and walks out of the kitchen to meet him half-way.

"Hi, sweetie. Welcome home. Gimme a kiss."

They hug, kiss, and share small talk for a few minutes. Both of them consciously and deliberately refrain from any mention of the day's activities, problems, or preoccupations. They do not resume any previously unfinished conversation. *They talk only about each other, or about their relationship.*

"Let's go sit for a few minutes, before the kids come home."

In this four-minute episode, they have figuratively restarted their relationship. They have recapitulated the basis for their affection,

mutual respect, and shared experience. And they have created a positive state of mind between them that will carry over into any later discussion of life's logistical problems. And if they make this four-minute
method an everyday habit—*an unbreakable rule and policy*—they create
a permanent emotional bias for both of them, which can serve to
relieve the stresses imposed by the mundane problems of life.

Zunin's four-minute method may seem too simple-minded, and
not all that necessary for people with ongoing relationships. A
married person might say, "Oh, we've been married too long for that
sort of thing. We get along OK." Someone might say, "That wouldn't
work with my mother." Or "My boyfriend knows I love him. We don't
have to go through that kind of thing every time." But the person who
says that may wake up one day and realize that the relationship has
become stale, that the other party no longer seems interested or committed, or that the "magic" has died. The next phase may be a long
period of emotional détente, and possibly a separation leading to
divorce.

Any person who has lived through a divorce will attest that an
emotional divorce usually precedes the legal divorce. When you ask
such a person, "At what point do you think the relationship began to
die?" he or she may not have a definite answer. "Oh, I don't know—it
just gradually went downhill, I guess. I can't think of any one thing that
really killed it. We just 'grew apart,' I suppose."

A poignant line from Edna St. Vincent Millay's poem "The Spring
and the Fall" tells the story:

"Tis not love's going hurt my days;
But that it went in little ways."[4]

BUILDING THE SKILLS OF EMPATHY

Things you can do to increase your skills in the dimension of Empathy
include:

- Study a person who seems unable to connect with others easily; make a list of specific behaviors you observe that seem to alienate others. Make a list of behaviors he or she could adopt that could enable him or her to connect more skillfully.

- Study a person who seems to connect with others easily; make a list of specific behaviors you observe that seem to attract others and invite them to connect on a personal level.

- Imagine that you meet Mr. or Ms. Stoneface at a social function. Write down five things you can say or do to "loosen him/her up," that is, to invite the person to share more freely and to express more energy in the way he or she interacts (without clumsily instructing the person to "Smile!").

- The next time you witness—or participate in—an argument or dispute between two or more people, make a list afterward of the toxic, empathy-destroying things any of the participants said or did that might have aggravated the situation, or might have made it more difficult to resolve.

- If you have a close friend or a "SOSO" ("spouse or significant other"), offer to make a deal with that person to use the four-minute rule every time you meet for the next week. Spend the first one to four minutes talking only about one another, and not doing any of the day's "business" until you've re-established your personal bond.

Notes

1. See "The Platinum Rule." Albrecht, Karl. *Quality Digest,* April 1994. See also *The Platinum Rule.* Tony Alessandra and Michael J. O'Connor. New York: Time-Warner Books, 1996.
2. See, for example, *Verbal Judo: The Gentle Art of Persuasion.* New York: Morrow, 1993.
3. Zunin, Leonard. Contact: *The First Four Minutes.* New York: Nash, 1972.
4. Edna St. Vincent Millay, "The Spring and the Fall," 1923. See *Collected Lyrics of Edna St. Vincent Millay.* New York: Harper Brothers, 1943.

7

ASSESSING AND DEVELOPING SI

"I who am blind can give one hint to those who see—one admonition to those who would make full use of the gift of sight: Use your eyes as if tomorrow you would be stricken blind. And the same method can be applied to the other senses. Hear the music of voices, the song of a bird, the mighty strains of an orchestra, as if you would be stricken deaf tomorrow. Touch each object you want to touch as if tomorrow your tactile sense would fail. Smell the perfume of flowers, taste with relish each morsel, as if tomorrow you could never smell and taste again."

—Helen Keller

As RESEARCH CONTINUES within the academic community to find technically rigorous measures of the multiple intelligences, and to scientifically characterize component intelligences such as SI, those of us who labor in the vineyards of professional development and organizational culture continue to need practical models and tools we can use on an everyday basis. We must rely on the science of common sense, hoping that our subjective attempts to define and measure these important competencies can serve adequately under the circumstances.

This chapter provides some simple assessment procedures you can use to paint a clearer picture of your SI skills and preferences. It invites you to compare your perceptions of yourself with those of others and to reflect on and plan the areas of social intelligence that you would like to improve. These self-assessment tools, adapted with permission from the *Social Intelligence Profile,* a published self-assessment questionnaire,[1] will give you a start on the process. Please keep in mind that a thorough and deeper assessment requires a more comprehensive process, going beyond the scope of this discussion.

ASSESSING YOUR INTERACTION SKILLS
Step 1

Begin by conducting a mental inventory of a large number of people you know, have known, or have interacted with fairly extensively. Using the worksheet in Exhibit 7.1, write down in the left-hand column the names of five people whose general pattern of behavior you consider particularly toxic. Think carefully about how they have acted toward you or others. Beside each name, write a few key "S.P.A.C.E." behaviors you've observed that you find especially troublesome. The more accurately you consider their behaviors, the more useful information you'll have for your own self-review.

Does the person you've identified make a habit of treating people rudely? Insulting people? Ridiculing or humiliating others? Gossiping or character assassination? Complaining, whining, and criticizing? Lying, manipulating others, or breaking promises? Monopolizing conversations?

Exhibit 7.1. Examining Toxic People You Have Known

Toxic People I Know:	
Name of Toxic Person	**S.P.A.C.E. Violations**
1	
2	
3	
4	
5	

Battering others with dogmatic opinions and intolerant views? Imposing on others or abusing relationships with them?

By thinking about various people you've known, you can probably easily itemize a range of toxic behaviors.

Step 2

On the worksheet provided in Exhibit 7.2, write down the names of five "nourishing" people, those you consider especially wise about people and especially skillful in getting along with others and getting others to cooperate with them. Write down as many specific S.P.A.C.E. behaviors of these "magnetic" people as you can call to mind.

Does the person you've identified make a habit of affirming people, complimenting them, listening to them, and congratulating them on their successes? Including them in the conversation? Showing respect for their views, values, and opinions? Acknowledging their rights to make their own life decisions? Offering advice sparingly and only when asked?

Now, think carefully about each of the five primary SI skill factors—Situational Awareness, Presence, Authenticity, Clarity, and Empathy—as you review the behavior of each person on your toxic and nourishing lists.

Do certain people on the toxic list exhibit toxic behaviors in one or more particular S.P.A.C.E. categories? Do certain people on the nourishing list excel in certain dimensions?

If a particular individual excels—or fails—on one particular dimension, write the initial—"S," "P," "A," "C," or "E"—of that factor beside his or her name. The objective here is to identify specific behaviors or patterns of behavior in each dimension that these people exemplify for you.

Step 3

Now mentally combine all of the toxic people you identified into one imaginary person. Give this hypothetical person a hypothetical name. If

Exhibit 7.2. Examining Nourishing People You Know

Nourishing People I Know:	
Name of Nourishing Person	**S.P.A.C.E. Skills**
1	
2	
3	
4	
5	

one of the people on your list outranks all the others in toxicity, you might want to use his or her name as a shorthand identity for the composite "toxic person" you've assembled. Write this name on the line labeled "Toxic Role Model" on the rating form in Exhibit 7.3.

Do the same for the nourishing people you identified. Take the best and most noticeable behaviors you've observed in these people and construct a highly nourishing super-model. Give this imaginary nourishing person a hypothetical name as well, or use the name of one of the role models who seems to incorporate most of the positive behaviors. Write this name in Exhibit 7.3 on the line labeled "Nourishing Role Model."

Step 4

Now comes the challenging part. In this step you compare your own pattern of behavior, as you perceive it, with the behavior patterns you've observed in both the toxic and nourishing role models. The value of this process for you will depend entirely on your honesty and willingness to engage in a candid, non-defensive self-evaluation. You have the right to delude yourself; if you do, you also have the responsibility to live with the consequences of your self-deception.

For each of the five primary SI skill factors, circle a number on the ten-point scale to indicate where you believe your overall behavior

Exhibit 7.3. Toxic and Nourishing Role Models

Toxic Role Model: **Nourishing Role Model:**

Situational Awareness	1	2	3	4	5	6	7	8	9	10
Presence	1	2	3	4	5	6	7	8	9	10
Authenticity	1	2	3	4	5	6	7	8	9	10
Clarity	1	2	3	4	5	6	7	8	9	10
Empathy	1	2	3	4	5	6	7	8	9	10

pattern—the way you typically interact with others—falls on the spectrum between your composite Toxic Role Model and your composite Nourishing Role Model. A "1" on the scale means you see yourself as just as toxic as your toxic role model. A "10" means you see yourself as just as nourishing as your nourishing role model.

Step 5

Once you've figured out your "T/N" scores, plot them as dots on the five matching axes of the "radar chart" shown in Figure 7.1.

To make sense of your chart and start moving from a self-assessment focus to self-development, consider some of these questions: Which, if any, of the five key SI skill dimensions seems to stand out as a particular area of strength for you? Do one or more of the dimensions present a developmental need or opportunity for you? How much would you need to shift your behavior in each of the five skill dimensions to closely approach your Nourishing Role Model?

Do you actually *want* to make any changes? Do you see a need, or an opportunity for change? Do you believe that shifting your habitual patterns further toward the nourishing end of the spectrum would bring positive benefits for your life, your relationships, or your career?

What if your scores on some or all of the five SI skill dimensions fall in the middle of the scale? Not "good" and not "bad"? How do you interpret such a result? Does a mid-point score say you have nothing to worry about, or do you hold yourself to a higher standard? Does this self-review appeal to your sense of achievement?

Bear in mind that changing habitual behaviors requires time, attention, and diligence, so before you launch yourself on a total "social makeover," you might want to select a few key areas to start with. You will have an opportunity to identify priorities for improvement later. For now, you might want to jot your preliminary thoughts beside your radar chart.

Figure 7.1. S.P.A.C.E. Radar Chart

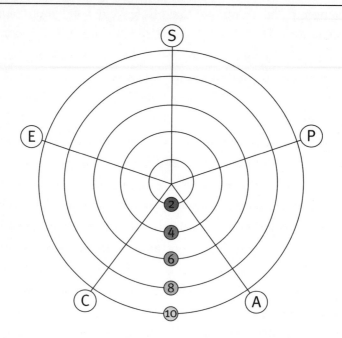

SELF-AWARENESS: SEEING YOURSELF
AS OTHERS SEE YOU

Having assessed your social skills in terms of specific behaviors and their effectiveness, you might like to go a step further and try to test the accuracy of your self-perceptions. You may have friends, acquaintances, coworkers, or colleagues who will give you feedback about how they perceive you. If so, you may get some very valuable insights and suggestions. Don't be surprised, however, to find most of the people you know reluctant to provide candid observations, and to find yourself reluctant or apprehensive about asking them. Personal feedback can serve a very valuable purpose—if you can get it, and if you can take it.

If you don't have an adequate supply of helpful feedback from others, or if you don't feel quite ready to solicit it, you can take the intermediate step of speculating about how they perceive you. One simple method for this uses simple adjective descriptions. Do you think people who know you well would describe you as "articulate"? "Cooperative"? "Considerate"? "Rude"? "Insensitive"? "Bossy"? "Talkative"? "Caring"? "Ethical"?

The Adjective Pairs exercise gives you an opportunity to guess how others see you. Whether or not you go further and solicit their feedback and compare their perceptions of you with your perceptions of their perceptions, you may still find this a helpful step in your personal examination. As with all self-assessments, the value of the results will depend on your personal honesty. You can easily delude yourself with these kinds of evaluations if you like.

For each of the pairs of opposing adjectives shown in Exhibit 7.4, circle a number on the scale between them, to indicate the extent to which you believe people tend to see you as one or the other. When you've finished, glance at the whole list of pairs and see if a general pattern emerges. You might like to draw a zigzag line down through all of the scores, to create a visual profile of your answers.

To begin to make sense of your results, reflect on these questions: Do your answers tell a story? Have you succumbed to the temptation to make yourself "look good"? Do certain adjectives cluster together to indicate a pattern? Do your highest-rated adjectives seem to indicate a particular dimension of strength? Do certain adjectives appeal to you as aspects of your interactions you'd like to develop, even if you may not have scored them low?

As a self-development exercise, you might like to pick out one or two of these adjective dimensions for special attention. For example, suppose you rated yourself more long-winded than concise (related to the Clarity dimension of SI). You might choose to experiment with it over the next few days or weeks, to see whether it offers particular promise for improving your interactions with the kinds of people and situations you typically encounter.

Exhibit 7.4. Adjective Pairs Exercise

ToxicNourishing

Argumentative	1	2	3	4	5	Diplomatic
Boring	1	2	3	4	5	Interesting
Bossy	1	2	3	4	5	Cooperative
Cold	1	2	3	4	5	Warm
Critical	1	2	3	4	5	Affirming
Inarticulate	1	2	3	4	5	Articulate
Inconsiderate	1	2	3	4	5	Considerate
Long-winded	1	2	3	4	5	Concise
Manipulative	1	2	3	4	5	Honest
Moody	1	2	3	4	5	Even-tempered
Opinionated	1	2	3	4	5	Open-minded
Rude	1	2	3	4	5	Courteous
Self-important	1	2	3	4	5	Humble
Short-tempered	1	2	3	4	5	Tolerant
Timid	1	2	3	4	5	Outgoing

ASSESSING YOUR INTERACTION STYLE: DRIVERS, ENERGIZERS, DIPLOMATS, AND LONERS

Once you've assessed your skills on the five S.P.A.C.E. dimensions and considered the ways you believe others might perceive you, the next step is to consider those skills as they relate to your preferred pattern of influencing others and getting things done. In this regard, you can think about your *interaction style*.

Various models and assessment methods have been introduced over the past several decades, most of which characterize interactive style in approximately the same ways. We will use one of the more familiar of these models. These kinds of assessments, and the assessment we will use here, are best thought of not as "personality" assessments, but rather as simple ways to characterize personal preferences. For our purposes, we will characterize interactive styles with a relatively basic framework that involves two distinct dimensions of your interactions with people: Social Energy and Results Focus.

Are You Drawn Toward People?

Social energy refers to the impulse or tendency to engage, interact with, or influence people. A person with high social energy usually finds it easy and desirable to get involved with other people, to interact with them, to spend time with them, and to get things done with and through other people. These people tend to feel drawn to group situations, social situations involving strangers, and occupations that involve interacting with others. A person with low social energy, while typically able to interact successfully with others, does not lean toward others as his or her first preference. These people tend to be more individualistic, preferring more limited interactions, and preferably with people they know and feel comfortable with. Some theories and models of interactive style refer to this dimension as *introversion* versus *extraversion*,[2] but for our purposes we will use the somewhat broader concept of social energy.

How Do You Get Things Done?

Results focus refers to whether you see yourself as more *task focused* or more *people focused* when you try to achieve a goal or get something done. Task-focused people may tend to rely more on themselves than on others—the "do it myself" mode. They sometimes view the "human factor" as a distraction: "Why do I have to worry about everybody's 'feelings'? I just want to get the job done." People-focused people tend to place a much higher priority on interacting with others, recruiting them to the common cause, getting them to collaborate, and keeping them involved and motivated.

All of us mix both of these orientations, so no one uses only one mode or pattern. However, many people gravitate early in life toward one or the other primary orientation, and many people develop a preference for one of the two extremes of each orientation. Without trying to represent these distinctions as any kind of theory of "personality," nevertheless we can gain some interesting insights into our own patterns of interactions, and we can better understand the choices others make.

How Do You Prefer to Interact?

By organizing these two dimensions, *social energy* on one axis and *results focus* on the other axis, we have four primary combinations, or *interaction styles,* represented by the four "window panes" in the grid diagram shown in Figure 7.2.

For convenience, we can give these four patterns metaphorical names: the Driver, the Energizer, the Diplomat, and the Loner.

The *Driver* pattern combines high social energy with a strong task focus. A person with this preference tends to take charge in many situations and to assert his or her view of how to get things done. While they may have highly developed social skills, Drivers usually work by directing the attention of others to the agreed task at hand, and do not

Figure 7.2. Interaction Styles

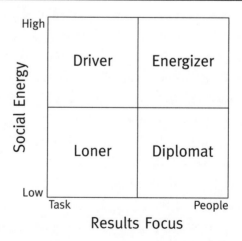

particularly emphasize personal relationships or team spirit. A person with the Driver preference generally tends to use a directive style of leadership when in a position of formal authority. In sales roles, they tend to take charge of the selling situation. Action-adventure films and TV shows often characterize the main hero as a Driver pattern.

The *Energizer* pattern also displays high social energy, but tends to influence people through personal relationships. The Energizer typically seeks to bring people together, and may try to motivate the group to work toward common goals. Energizers tend to value personal relationships with those they deal with and they tend to emphasize cooperation, involvement, and team spirit. As managers, they often tend toward an inclusive, team-based approach to getting things done. In sales roles, they tend to "sell themselves" in order to make the case for the product or service they represent.

The *Diplomat* pattern displays somewhat less social energy, but nevertheless prefers a people focus in getting things done. Somewhat less directive or assertive, Diplomats place a high value on cooperation and collaboration, and they often seek to help others come to agreement. They may serve as "go-betweens" in situations involving conflict or controversy. As managers, they tend to build and capitalize on close working relationships with their people, although they may not use meetings and team activities as frequently as those with higher social energy might. In sales roles, Diplomats tend to build long-term relationships with their customers or clients when possible, and to use the strength of their relationships to help them do business.

The *Loner* pattern combines both low social energy and a primary task orientation. While many Loners have well-developed social skills and can often deal with others effectively, they tend strongly to rely on themselves. Loners tend to experience "contact fatigue" more than others, and to seek privacy after intensive social activity. As managers, they tend to focus attention on the work itself, often viewing "people" issues as distractions. They tend to prefer working with individuals on a one-to-one basis, solving problems as they arise. In sales roles, they tend to emphasize the practical considerations of the selling situation, such as product benefits, various ways to add value, and competitive advantages of their products.

No Judgments, Please

Please note that your interaction style, as defined here, has no connotation of good or bad, right or wrong. While interaction *skill*—the S.P.A.C.E. formula—represents your assessment of your relative *effectiveness* in dealing with people, your interaction *style* represents your individual *preference*. A person with a particular interaction style can function effectively or ineffectively in various situations, depending on how his or her skills go together with the primary style. The style assessment contributes to self-insight; the skill assessment invites self-development.

Most of us have some sense of our primary interactive tendencies, but reviewing our behavior more carefully can sometimes clarify aspects of our preferences we have not fully appreciated. Realistic and typical social scenarios can provide useful insights for better self-perception.

If you would like to consider your interactive preferences more carefully, you can take the short quiz in Exhibit 7.5, which presents several scenarios and some typical behavioral choices. For each of the scenarios, circle the letter beside the behavioral option that you consider closest to your primary tendency. Note: for this analysis, please set aside various considerations about how you feel you *should* behave, or the choices you might make according to the nature of the situation. Simply choose the option that feels most like what you would *prefer* to do. Be sure to read all four choices before deciding.

Once you've selected your preferences for the six scenarios, count the number of "A" options you selected, count the number of "B" selections, and the number of "C" and "D" selections. Note that the "A" options favored the Driver pattern, the "B" options favored the Energizer pattern, the "C" options favored the Diplomat pattern, and the "D" options favored the Loner pattern. Write the counts for the four patterns in the right-hand column of Exhibit 7.6.

Exhibit 7.5. Social Scenarios

1. *Reception:* You're attending a cocktail reception party at the end of a convention or conference. During this reception, your tendency is to:

    a. Keep your conversations brief and try to spot people who seem like potential customers or good business contacts.

    b. Circulate as widely as possible, looking for people who might be interesting to talk with.

    c. Circulate in the reception area briefly, chatting with a few people whom you know or feel comfortable with.

    d. Have a drink, eat some hors d'oeuvres, make a circuit of the room, and leave—unless you happen to connect with someone who seems interesting.

2. *Diagnosis:* You're meeting with your doctor to review your test results and decide on a course of treatment for a complicated medical condition. Your tendency is to:

    a. Take the initiative in the conversation, making it clear that you want a full explanation of the problem and the potential solutions.

    b. Try to start the conversation on a personal level, knowing that you'll be working with this doctor often in the course of your treatment.

    c. Treat the doctor with respect and deference, allowing him or her to guide the conversation.

    d. Read up on your medical condition ahead of time, listen carefully, take notes, and ask questions so you fully understand your options.

3. *Doing Business:* You're representing your firm in a negotiating meeting with representatives from another firm. Your tendency is to:

    a. Take control of the meeting, present your offer, and prepare to answer their objections or counteroffers.

    b. Make an effort to get the meeting started on a positive, cooperative basis.

    c. Invite the other team members to explain their interests and objectives, so both sides can cooperatively search for a good solution.

    d. Wait to hear what they have to say first, and then go from there.

Exhibit 7.5. (Continued)

4. *The Problem Employee:* As a supervisor, you have the responsibility of dealing with a "problem employee"—someone whose work habits are unsatisfactory and who is not contributing adequately. Your tendency is to:

   a. Call the person into your office and discuss his or her inadequate performance.

   b. Use staff meetings to remind everyone—including the problem employee—about the work standards and hope he or she gets the message.

   c. Work more closely with the employee, encouraging him or her to pay more attention to the quality of the work.

   d. Point out the unsatisfactory work performance on a case-by-case basis, instructing the employee how to do the job better.

5. *Dating Game:* Let's assume you're single. During a family gathering, your cousin has just informed you that the friend she brought to the gathering is very attracted to you. You also find this person attractive and would like to meet him or her. Your tendency is to:

   a. Personally approach that person, introduce yourself, and take the opportunity to get to know him or her.

   b. Try to start a conversation with several people, including the other person, and then focus your attention on him or her; then develop it into a personal conversation.

   c. Ask your cousin to introduce you to this person you're attracted to.

   d. Take no action, hoping that the other person will take the initiative or that an opportunity for a conversation will somehow materialize.

6. *Making the Sale:* You're considering buying a new car, which is rather expensive by your standards. You have an appointment with a salesman to discuss the car. Your tendency is to:

   a. Take charge of the discussion; let the salesman know that you're considering other dealers; get an exact specification for the car; and get a written price offer.

Exhibit 7.5. (Continued)

b. Take a friend with you and ask the salesman to explain the options and prices for the model of car you are interested in; make it a three-way conversation, and have your friend help you negotiate a firm price.

c. Allow the salesman to steer the discussion, but make sure you get answers to all of your questions and get a firm price quote.

d. Decide exactly the make, model, and options for the car you want to buy; then send letters to five dealers in your area asking for a firm price and delivery date. Take the best offer.

Exhibit 7.6. Scores for the Social Scenarios

Interaction Style	Score
Driver Pattern ("A" selections):	_____
Energizer Pattern ("B" selections):	_____
Diplomat Pattern ("C" selections):	_____
Loner Pattern ("D" selections):	_____

Did you find yourself leaning strongly toward the same type of option in each case—all "A's," all "B's," all "C's," or all "D's"? Or did several options in each case have a similar appeal for you? Did your preference vary from one scenario to another?

If you'd like to make a somewhat more thorough assessment and comparison of your preferences for the four primary interaction styles, you can plot your perceptions on the chart shown in Figure 7.3. Considering the choices you made in the social scenarios above, and thinking about the wide variety of situations you encounter in real life, distribute 100 points across the four primary interaction styles—Driver, Energizer, Diplomat, and Loner. Try to avoid "tie" scores; if possible, emphasize your preferences to the extent that it seems reasonable to do so.

Once you've assigned preference points to the four primary styles—admittedly a fairly subjective process—write your numbers into the corresponding squares on the grid chart in Figure 7.3. Reflect on these questions: Do your scores pass the "common sense" test? Does this profile seem to represent you reasonably well? Would people who know you well tend to agree with your scores?

Over the next few days and weeks, try to stay alert to the actual social scenarios that you encounter and sense your tendency to behave in various ways. Consider the possible merits and drawbacks of different ways of behaving. Does it make sense to act in a highly directive manner in certain situations? Does the Energizer pattern seem advisable sometimes? Do you find times when you feel you need to take action without overdoing the diplomacy factor? Do some situations call for collaboration, team building, or peacemaking?

Bear in mind that this model for social interaction represents your own perceptions of your own preferences. It cannot categorize your "personality" and it cannot tell you how you "should" behave in various situations. It can, however, potentially illuminate your choices for dealing with various situations.

Figure 7.3. Scoring Grid

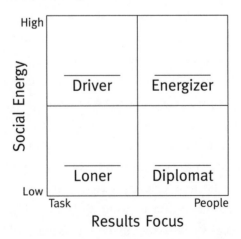

THE STRENGTH-WEAKNESS IRONY

Sometimes, too much of a good thing can become a bad thing. I observed a situation during my service as an Army officer, in which an idealistic young enlisted man carried his idealism and self-assertiveness to a self-destructive extreme.

Specialist Carter (not his real name) prided himself in not going along with the crowd. Fiercely individualistic, he seldom passed up an opportunity to demonstrate that he thought for himself. One has to admire that in a military person, especially because it presents some special challenges in a highly structured environment. Carter, however, seemed determined to lead a one-man mutiny against the world.

Although he performed well and behaved acceptably as a member of the staff unit I supervised, Carter often found himself at odds with the senior noncommissioned officers on the Army post that housed the command headquarters we worked in. My authority over his actions began and ended with the work day, and outside of the office he had certain responsibilities as an occupant of the post—even though he lived off-post with his wife and family. Never completely insubordinate, nevertheless he enjoyed pointing out any evidence of hypocrisy, bureaucracy, or institutional injustice he could find.

He finally came to a near-terminal collision with a group of the "old salts"—the senior non-coms who ran the infrastructure of the base. These long-serving career sergeants had known one another and worked together for many years, and they decided he needed a lesson in conformity. Their opportunity came when he kicked up some dust over a base-wide fundraising campaign for one of the national charities. The base commander wanted to achieve a 100 percent contribution rate for all enlisted personnel assigned to the base.

After an intensive motivational campaign, led by the non-coms at various levels, they had achieved a 99.9 percent participation, with Carter the lone hold-out. He made it clear that he did not believe in the particular charity supported by the brass, that he made donations to the charities of his own choice, and that he had no intention of contributing—not even a dollar. One of the non-coms approached me informally and asked me to try to prevail on Carter to make a donation so the whole base could achieve the goal. Although my authority did not extend to forcing him to comply, I agreed to counsel him and appeal to his better nature. He refused.

Already the subject of considerable anger from the non-coms, he decided to compound the offense with another finger in the eye. When one of the non-coms told him he intended to donate a dollar in Carter's name and add his name to the list of donors, Carter threatened to file a formal complaint—of what sort, I couldn't imagine. He ranted at length, to anyone who would listen, about the hypocrisy and injustice of coercing everyone into donating to a charity just so the top brass could claim a 100 percent participation rate.

A week later, Carter received official orders transferring him to Vietnam. His comfortable desk job had suddenly turned into a combat-zone assignment.

He registered an appeal with his Congressional representative, largely without success. Congressional contacts did, however, open up the possibility of a hardship discharge, based on the claim that he needed to return to his home state to care for his terminally ill father. As part of his discharge process, he signed a form that affirmed his agreement never to enlist in the U.S. Armed Forces again. This maneuver amounted to the moral equivalent—in the eyes of the non-coms—of a dishonorable discharge, although he left the Army on "honorable" terms.

Psychologists and experts in aptitude assessment refer to Carter's syndrome as the *strength-weakness irony:*

> *Any strength, when taken to an unreasonable extreme,*
> *can become a weakness.*

This applies to many traits we normally consider valuable assets: determination can become stubbornness; cooperativeness can become wishy-washiness; cautious analysis can become paralysis; spontaneity and risk taking can become recklessness.

Certainly we must acknowledge that some of history's most famous and admired individuals showed more than a trace of extremism. Some have faced death, or the prospect of it, for their beliefs. On the other hand, we'll never know how many talented but obscure people might have succeeded grandly, had they not picked the wrong hill to die on.

The important skill, it seems, involves deploying one's strengths with a sense of strategy and an understanding of the tradeoffs involved. The macro-skill of situational awareness comes into play, and one must ultimately acknowledge the potential consequences of any particular behavioral choice.

How to Connect with People

Excerpt from the *Social Intelligence Profile. Used with Permission.*[3]

1. Train yourself to "read" social situations. What's going on here? What are the interests, needs, feelings, and possible intentions of those involved?
2. Respect, affirm, and appreciate people and you'll find that most of them will reply in kind. Putting people down seldom gains you anything.
3. Listen—attentively, respectfully, and with the intention of learning.
4. Pause for one heartbeat before you respond to what someone says; it gives your brain extra time to choose your words well.
5. Remember that arguing is one of the least effective ways of changing one's mind; you don't always have to fight to win.
6. When you disagree with others, first acknowledge their right to think the way they do—then offer your views respectfully.
7. Try using questions rather than confrontation, to invite others to change their minds.

8. Stay out of conflicts with toxic people; work around them.

9. Get the "cats and dogs" out of your conversation—minimize dogmatic and categorical declarations.

10. Accentuate the positive—and that's what you'll mostly get in return.

PRIORITIES FOR IMPROVEMENT

If you would like to improve certain social skills, a good way to begin is to select a few key areas to concentrate on first. Use the "Keep, Stop, Start" formula to help you.

Review the key behaviors described in this chapter, as well as the adjective pairs and your scores on the interaction style grid. Go back to Chapters 2 through 6 and review the "Building the Skills of . . ." section at the end of each. Reflect on the ideas outlined in the sidebar How to Connect with People and on the preliminary targets for improvement that you jotted down earlier on your radar chart (Figure 7.1).

Now choose three skills you definitely want to *keep*—and possibly increase. Then identify three things you want to *stop* doing, and three things you want to *start* doing. Write them in the form shown in Exhibit 7.7 and keep this list handy so you can review it every day.

The examples, suggestions, and self-assessment and development methods to this point can give you a good start on the process of raising your SI quotient if you so desire. They are offered in the spirit of food for thought, to stimulate the deep reflection that leads to the heightened awareness and understanding that underpins effective action. Your own development as a more socially intelligent human being is only one application of the S.P.A.C.E. formula, though. In the following chapters, we shift the spotlight to focus on everyday issues associated with low SI at work and at home—and on ways to deal with them.

Exhibit 7.7. Keep, Stop, Start

I want to keep doing, or do more of:

1.

2.

3.

I want to stop doing, or do less of:

1.

2.

3.

I want to start doing:

1.

2.

3.

Notes

1. *Social Intelligence Profile.* Self-assessment instrument created by Karl Albrecht. San Diego, Albrecht Publishing Company, 2004. Excerpt used with permission. For further information, contact www.KarlAlbrecht.com.

2. Although lay people tend to use the spelling and pronunciation of "extroverted," the original term, as made popular by psychologist Carl Jung, was "extraverted." Why Jung chose the form "introverted" instead of "intraverted," no one seems to know.

3. Excerpt from the *Social Intelligence Profile.* Self-assessment instrument created by Karl Albrecht. San Diego, Albrecht Publishing Company, 2004. Excerpt used with permission.

8

SI IN THE WORLD OF WORK
Some Reflections

"The first efficiency expert was Simon Legree."
—H.L. Mencken

WHERE DOES THE CONCEPT OF SOCIAL INTELLIGENCE fit into the world of business? How does it apply on the job? How does it apply to the way people work together? Does it apply to the way teams accomplish their missions? Does it apply to the way employees serve customers? Does it apply to the ways in which bosses and employees interact? Does it apply more broadly, across the miniature society that exists in every established organization?

The answers to some of these questions are still evolving and it will doubtless be quite some time before we reach convincing conclusions on all of these issues. In the meantime, however, there is plenty of food for thought for those of us whose heads and hearts long for more socially intelligent workplaces. We begin with the idea that we can better understand the role of SI in the workplace partly by studying the absence of it—organizations and organizational cultures mired in social incompetence. Then perhaps we can better imagine what high-SI organizations might look like.

THE REAL AND LEGAL CONSEQUENCES OF SOCIAL INCOMPETENCE

Robert Mack walked into the Human Resource Department conference room at San Diego's General Dynamics plant to meet his fate: the company had decided to fire him. After an increasingly heated conversation, Mack pulled out a gun, shot and killed the HR representative handling his termination, and then shot his boss, permanently paralyzing him. He walked out of the conference room, still brandishing the gun. Although the terrified employees in the area believed he intended to kill himself—which typically happens in most workplace homicides—he eventually put down the gun and surrendered to police.

Mack's experience became one in a long series of news stories about disgruntled employees who resorted to murder when they could not cope with their circumstances. According to employee violence expert Dr. Steven Albrecht, who conducted an exclusive interview with Mack in his prison cell, "Robert Mack was clearly a disturbed— and disturbing—individual. Obviously, not everyone who gets fired deals with the news by killing the boss or coworkers. However, later investigations determined that Mack and most of his coworkers had been subject to a toxic workplace environment. Draconian work rules, oppressive supervisory practices, and intense pressures to meet production requirements certainly seemed to have increased his stress level, and possibly aggravated his disturbed emotional state."

While no credible expert has argued that General Dynamics' management should bear full responsibility for the episode, one could certainly postulate that a more humane working environment, which included adequate access to mental-health assistance for troubled employees, might possibly have prevented the deaths.

For his part, Robert Mack admitted that he should have used the Employee Assistance Program (EAP), provided by GD as part of his medical benefits, but did not. When Steve Albrecht asked him why, he replied that he didn't know the program existed. Robert Mack had worked at the company for twenty-five years; General Dynamics had an EAP program in place for seventeen of those years.

Industrial organizations vary considerably in the extent to which they maintain work environments that support mental health and quality of work life. Some have invested heavily in programs, services, facilities, and expert resources to help employees; some have shamefully neglected and exploited their workers. Every organization has its own distinctive work culture—the psychological environment within which people work and interact.

Modern businesses and government agencies, particularly in the United States, have for years served as a legal and political battleground for issues of workplace justice. Some of them have implemented very farsighted practices; others have gone along kicking and screaming against the force of litigation and pressure from government agencies. Some executives view the investment in maintaining a psychologically healthy workplace and high quality of work life as not only decent and reasonable, but also as economically sensible. Others seem to view it as a nuisance cost, which comes due only in adverse circumstances.

Toxic Management

Human resources experts have understood for years the impact of managerial behavior—social intelligence of the tactical leaders—on employee morale and perception of quality of work life. Yet relatively few organizations have any kind of comprehensive program for ensuring quality of supervision at all levels. In far too many organizations, people get dropped into supervisory and managerial jobs for the wrong reasons: longevity, expertise in the technical specialty practiced by a particular workgroup, friendship with higher managers, political maneuvering—almost everything except the ability to lead. Every toxic manager in an organization represents a preventable cost, measurable in employee morale and effectiveness, work productivity, and retention of valuable employees.

Tom Puffer, an experienced labor consultant known for his strong anti-union views, related a thought-provoking experience to me:

> "I found myself sitting on an airplane beside a guy who identified himself as a union organizer for one of the big-name industrial unions. We got to swapping war stories, and each of us described the world from our own particular point of view. He said something that struck me like a lightning bolt, and I knew right away what he said was correct.
>
> "He said 'You know, there's one thing company executives could do that would make my job infinitely harder; one thing that would actually reduce our win rate in unionizing their companies. If they would *fire all the supervisors* who bully and oppress their employees, we'd have an uphill battle. That's what we capitalize on—an alienated workforce of people who feel they're not being treated like human beings.'
>
> "But he said something even more provocative than that," Puffer recalled. "He said 'I have no hesitation about telling you this, because *I know they won't do it*. The blockheads that run the companies we go after just don't get it. Apparently, it's too simple for them.'"

Puffer—and the union rep—may have overstated the case somewhat, but probably not by much. Looking at management and leadership through the lens of SI invites a very practical approach. Before we try to apply the various sophisticated theories of leadership that have come and gone over the decades, maybe we need to ask the simple question: Do our managers know how to treat people as human beings?

In recent years, researchers and experts in business performance have begun to consider factors such as emotional intelligence as fundamental to leadership.[1] As this constructive trend continues, it only makes sense to consider the obvious component of social intelligence as well, and indeed to link both EI and SI together with the known and accepted principles of leadership and the methods of management. Still, for every organization that is consciously evolving a multiple-intelligent culture, there are dozens that are mired in conflict and craziness.

CULTURES OF CONFLICT AND CRAZINESS

Over the course of about thirty years working as an organizational consultant, I've observed a wide range of social pathologies that can defeat an enterprise from within. In fact, I would say I've seen more organizations defeat themselves than get beaten fair and square by worthy competitors. Psychiatrists and psychologists have a handbook, titled the *Diagnostic and Statistical Manual,* which exhaustively lists and explains the full inventory of human maladjustments. In the consulting business, we also have a "DSM," although a somewhat less formal and rigorous one. We recognize the same kinds of organizational disorders recurring across all industries, all types of organizations, and indeed all national cultures.

While collective sanity tends to involve relatively simple and consistent patterns, craziness is entertainingly diverse. The range of primary organizational disorders is both broad and varied. I've identified some seventeen primary patterns, or syndromes, of organizational dysfunction. Some organizations have more than one; some have many. Each imposes significant entropic costs on the resources of the enterprise and contributes to its tendency toward ballistic podiatry—shooting itself in the foot.

1. ADD: Attention Deficit Disorder. Senior management cannot seem to focus on any one primary goal, strategy, or problem long enough to gain momentum in solving it. Typically, the CEO or the top team will hop around from one new preoccupation to another, often reacting to some recent event, such as a hot new trend, a key move by a competitor, or a change in the marketplace. A variation—the "too many irons in the fire" syndrome—involves a whole raft of programs, or "initiatives," most of which squander resources and dilute the focus of attention.

2. Anarchy: When the Bosses Won't Lead. A weak, divided, or distracted executive team fails to provide the clear sense of direction, momentum, and goal focus needed by the extended management team. A war between the CEO and the board or a major battle among the members of the top team can leave the organization without a rudder. Lacking a clear focus and a set of meaningful priorities, people begin to scatter their efforts into activities of their own choosing. Without a sense of higher purpose, unit leaders put their own priorities and political agendas above the success of the enterprise.

3. Anemia: Only the Deadwood Survives. After a series of economic shocks, downsizings, layoffs, palace wars, and purges, the talented people have long since left for better pastures, leaving the losers and misfits lodged in the woodwork. They have more at stake in staying put, so they outlast the more talented employees. When conditions start to improve, the organization typically lacks the talent, energy, and dynamism needed to capitalize on better times.

4. Caste System: The Anointed and the Untouchables. Some organizations have an informal, "shadow" structure based on certain aspects of social or professional status, which everybody knows about and most people avoid talking about. Military headquarters organizations, for example, tend to have three distinct camps: officers, enlisted people (or, as the British call them, "other ranks"), and civilian staff. Hospitals tend to have very rigid caste systems, with doctors at the top of the heap, nurses in the next lower caste, and non-medical people toward the bottom. Universities and other academic or research organizations tend to have very clearly defined categories of status, usually based on tenure or standing in one's field. These castes never appear on the organization chart, but they dominate collective behavior every day. Caste categories usually set up de facto boundaries, promote factionalism, and tempt the in-group members to serve their own social and political needs at the expense of the organization and to the detriment of the lower castes.

5. Civil War: The Contest of Ideologies. The organization disintegrates into two or more mega-camps, each promoting a particular proposition, value system, business ideology, or local hero. The split can originate from the very top level, or it can express profound differences between subcultures, for example, engineering and marketing, nursing and administration, or the editorial culture and the business offices. In some cases, the dynamic tension between ideologies can work to the benefit of the enterprise; in other cases it can cripple the whole operation.

6. Despotism: Fear and Trembling. A tyrannical CEO or an overall ideology of oppression coming from the top causes people to engage in avoidance behavior at the expense of goal-seeking behavior. A few episodes in which people get axed for disagreeing with the chief or for questioning the lack of ethics and leadership, and everybody soon learns: keep your head down and don't draw attention to yourself.

7. Fat, Dumb, and Happy: If It Ain't Broke. . .   Management guru Peter Drucker once observed, "Whom the gods would destroy, they first grant forty years of business success." Even in the face of an imminent threat to the basic business model, the executives cannot muster a sense of concern, and cannot come to consensus on the need to reinvent the business.

8. General Depression: Nothing to Believe In.   Sometimes things get really bad, such as during an economic downturn or a rough period for the enterprise, and senior management utterly fails to create and maintain any kind of empathic contact with the rank and file. Feeling abandoned and vulnerable, the front-line people sink into a state of discouragement, low morale, and diminished commitment.

9. Geriatric Leadership: Retired on the Job.   When a CEO has had his or her day, either for reasons of physical health, psychological arthritis, or personal obsolescence, he or she may hang on to the helm too long, refusing to bring in new blood, new ideas, and new talent. This syndrome can extend to the whole top team, whose members may have grown old together, committed to an obsolete ideology that once made the enterprise successful, but that now threatens to sink it.

10. The Looney CEO: Crazy Makes Crazy.   When the chief's behavior goes beyond the merely colorful and verges on the maladjusted, the people in the inner circle start behaving in their own crazy ways, in reaction to the lack of an integrated personality at the top. This begins to look like a kind of syndicated craziness to the people down through the ranks, who find themselves perpetually baffled, bemused, and frustrated by the increasing lack of coherence in executive decisions and actions.

11. Malorganization: Structural Arthritis. A defective organizational architecture works passively and unremittingly against the achievement of the mission. Departmental boundaries that don't align with the natural processes of the operation or its work flow, conflicting responsibilities and competitive missions, and unnatural subdivisions of critical mission areas impose high communication costs, inhibit collaboration, and foster internal competition.

12. The Monopoly Mentality: Our Divine Right. When an organization has long enjoyed a dominant position in its environment, either because of a natural monopoly or a circumstantial upper hand, its leaders tend to think like monopolists. Unable or unwilling to think in competitive terms, and unable to innovate or even reinvent the business model, they become sitting ducks for invading competitors who want their piece of the pie.

13. The One-Man Band: Clint Eastwood Rules. A "cowboy" type of CEO, who feels no need or responsibility to share his or her master plan with subordinates, keeps everybody in the organization guessing about the next move. This creates dependency and learned incapacity on the part of virtually all leaders down through the hierarchy, and renders them reactive rather than potentially proactive.

14. The Rat Race: They Keep Moving the Cheese. The culture of the enterprise, either by design or by the style of a particular industry or business sector, burns out its most talented people. A prevailing notion that one must sacrifice his or her personal well-being in order to get ahead, possibly in pursuit of big financial rewards, definitely creates a goal focus, but at the expense of cooperation, *esprit de corps,* and individual humanity. A reduction in the commissions or other elements of the financial cheese creates a sense of victimization and resentment, not a sense of shared fate.

15. Silos: Cultural and Structural. The organization disintegrates into a group of isolated camps, each defined by the desire of its chieftains to achieve a favored position with the royal court, that is, senior management and the king makers at the top. With little incentive to cooperate, collaborate, share information, or team up to pursue mission-critical outcomes, the various silos develop impervious boundaries. Local warlords tend to serve their individual, parochial agendas, and evolve patterns of operating that favor their units' suboptimal interests at the expense of the interests of the enterprise. These silo patterns tend to create fracture lines down through the organization, polarizing the people who have to interact across them.

16. Testosterone Poisoning: Men Will Be Boys. In male-dominated industries or organizational cultures such as military units, law enforcement agencies, and primary industries, the rewards for aggressive, competitive, and domineering behaviors far outweigh the rewards for collaboration, creativity, and sensitivity to abstract social values. In non-"co-ed" organizations, that is, those with fewer than about 40 percent females in key roles, executives, managers, and male coworkers tend to assign females to culturally stereotyped roles with little power, influence, or access to opportunity. This gender-caste system wastes talent and often stifles innovation and creativity.

17. The Welfare State: Why Work Hard?. Organizations that have no natural threats to their existence, such as government agencies, universities, and publicly funded operations, typically evolve into cultures of complacency. In a typical government agency, it's more important not to be wrong than it is to be right. Lots of people have "no-go" power, that is, the power to veto or passively oppose innovation, but very few people have "go" power, or the capacity to originate and champion initiatives. Welfare cultures tend to syndicate blame and accountability just as they syndicate authority: you can't take risks, but if anything goes wrong you get to blame the system.[2]

HIERARCHIES, TESTOSTERONE, AND GENDER POLITICS

The hierarchy—the "pyramid," the "ladder," the "pecking order," the "totem pole," the "command structure"—is so commonplace and so dominant in organizational structures that we typically take it completely for granted and seldom pay much attention to it. It may seem self-evident that human beings need hierarchies in order to function in large numbers, but in the modern era we are beginning to question whether the hierarchy is always the appropriate structure for getting things done. In particular, hierarchies seem to appeal to males considerably more than to females, and some female workers, professionals, managers, and executives do not always feel that stacking people up in pyramids is the best solution.

It seems clear that hierarchies are more about males than about females, and that females tend to accommodate them perforce, not by choice. Social scientist Geert Hofstede, who has pioneered the comparative study of values between cultures, identifies several dimensions that relate to hierarchy and to male values. One is "power distance," which is the degree to which people in a culture recognize and accept formal and authoritarian relationships between leaders and followers. Another is "individualism" (contrasted to collectivism). Another dimension he specifically identifies as "masculinity," meaning the extent to which certain key roles are assigned to males rather than to females. He defines the relationship between organizational masculinity and femininity in terms of the distribution of roles.[3]

Some sociologists and anthropologists believe that any society, if it is ever to achieve a degree of stability that might lead to economic development, must first solve the problem of controlling and channeling male aggression. Whether one considers violence an innately human impulse, or simply the evidence of failed socialization, clearly males are—taken as a whole—more physically aggressive and violent than females, by any imaginable standard of comparison. One of the most important functions of a hierarchical power structure is to keep males from attacking one another, and from attacking others *ad lib*—at least others whom their leaders don't want to have attacked. Hierarchies apparently provide sufficient control and predictability of male behavior to allow social codes to develop and take hold, thereby creating the conditions for more complex social structures and eventually large, extended societies.

This becomes evident when we observe failed societies—those in which the political structure and social order have broken down. In failed states such as Afghanistan, Iraq, Somalia, and various other African countries, East Timor and others, armed groups of young men run wild, robbing innocent people, murdering and raping, destroying property, and killing one another. According to one anthropologist, "The most dangerous animal on the planet is an unmated human male between the ages of sixteen and twenty-four."

The only semblance of order in those disastrous cases lies in the miniature hierarchies formed around local gang leaders—"warlords," as news writers are fond of calling them—who are tough enough or smart enough to dominate or intimidate the others, usually through sheer force. Many contemporary totalitarian societies have evolved under the control of powerful warriors who have used violence to subdue their opponents and impose their will on whole societies. As they have consolidated their control, they have invariably built hierarchies to control and direct the aggressive energy of males.

In fact, many totalitarian leaders have discovered that having a large standing army provides multiple benefits. While they may publicly rationalize the need for a large army in terms of the need to defend the country, social group, or political faction from outside enemies, its greatest value lies in getting most or all of the aggressive young males into a single, controllable group, under the power of military leaders who can keep them in line. The extra, added bonus lies in the implied threat posed by a formally recognized military force to any citizen who would presume to violate the dictator's law, or—worse—who would presume to organize a political faction to oppose the dictator. Hierarchies are very handy things.

In the organizational context of modern business enterprises, we can see the cultural holdover of hierarchical structures. Of course, a company doesn't usually have an army—just a security guard force. Authority is divided up and parceled out—and down—to various chieftains, sub-chieftains, clan leaders, and work groups, all reporting upward to a single, powerful leader, or to a council of powerful leaders.

It is interesting to see the interplay of male-female social dynamics within the context of organizational hierarchies. Until only a few decades ago, female workers were systematically excluded from rising through the hierarchical levels of most business organizations, in the developed nations in North America, Europe, and Asia, and most certainly in underdeveloped or developing nations in Latin America, Africa, the Mediterranean region, and in Asia. As this has changed, organizational cultures have changed.

While an exploration of socio-biological differences between males and females in the world of work is well beyond the scope of this discussion, nevertheless it is instructive to consider some of the ways in which interactions between the two can shape, and be shaped by, their different proclivities for working in and with hierarchies. From the standpoint of social intelligence, it seems clear that the ability to "read" these dynamics, and to interpret them in the context of organizational culture, can be a useful skill.

Most organizational sociologists seem to agree that, with some exceptions, males in general tend to lean toward hierarchical structures based on subdivided authority in order to organize themselves for some undertaking, while females tend toward more multi-dimensional network-like arrangements. A number of scholarly investigations have shown that women tend to view personal relationships as more important and more meaningful than the formal relationships defined by structure. Males, in contrast, seem to view structure and function—the formal organization—as taking precedence over personal relationships.

Some studies indicate that males and females tend to employ somewhat different vocabularies, different figures of speech, and different metaphors in operationalizing their ideas. While men tend to use metaphors of warfare, sport, mechanics, and procedure, women tend to use metaphors of procreation, life, growth, and affiliation. A male manager might ask, "How do we get that going?" or "How do we get that train moving down the track?" A female manager might ask, "How can we bring that to life?" or "Who has to be involved in this?"

While male leaders seldom adopt the metaphors used by females, one commonly finds in hierarchical organizations that female leaders appropriate male metaphors in order to sell their ideas and get agreement. And while males tend to be only vaguely aware of the dominant roles they hold, by historical default, females tend to be acutely aware of the differences.

One can also see changes in behavior—and language—when males and females interact, based on the relative numbers of each involved in a particular situation. Consider a meeting in a conference room, attended by fifteen males and one female. Typically, although certainly not always, the males will unconsciously "fence off" the female, through use of language, body posture, eye contact, and allocation of air time. In that instance, it is typically a "male" group, that is, the males act as if a lone female has entered their space. This is particularly likely if the female's position or formal rank is in any way ambiguously defined.

Add one female manager and the situation changes somewhat. The males may tend to accommodate the two females somewhat more, perhaps by censoring their language, acknowledging the contributions of the females more frequently, and possibly shifting their use of metaphors.

Add another female, and another, and another, and the social dynamic of the group steadily shifts. As you approach a ratio of females to males of about 40 percent, at some point it becomes a "co-ed" group. It's no longer a meeting of males attended by a few females; it turns into a group of males and females. One can easily observe a change in male behavior under these circumstances. Some would say that the males tend to act in a more "civilized" way, paying more attention to social courtesy, using less aggressive language, and using fewer metaphors of warfare and sport.

In a number of business cultures, in more and more of the developed countries, educated males have accepted women in leadership roles and as professionals, to a much greater degree than in the past. This trend will probably continue, particularly as more and more females attain higher educational levels and higher levels of professional recognition.

Arguments will surely continue about whether male-female differences are innate, biological, "hard-wired," or genetically determined. The "Mars-Venus" conversation will probably never go away. In any case, the ability to observe and account for the dynamics of gender interaction will remain an important skill of social intelligence, and will possibly become more important over time.

Hierarchies Have Been Around a Long Time

Hierarchies originated very far back in ancient history, particularly with military organizations and nomadic warrior tribes.

Moses' father-in-law Jethro may have been the earliest management consultant on record. He observed that Moses had become overwhelmed trying to solve the problems and settle the disputes of the many thousands of Israelites who sought his help. Jethro advised Moses to divide them up into groups of tens, fifties, hundreds, and thousands, each of which would be headed by a strong leader. He recommended that each group choose its own leader.

According to the Biblical account:

"The hard cases they brought to Moses, but every small matter they judged themselves." (Exodus 18:26)

Some historians believe that the modern-day use of formal hierarchies in human organizations traces back to Moses and the Mosaic law he developed. Sculptures decorating the U.S. Capitol and Supreme Court portray Moses, together with other legendary lawgivers, as iconic references to law, order, and social structure.

There appears to be no historical evidence to indicate whether Jethro received a fee for his management consulting services.

GETTING IT RIGHT AT WORK AND WRONG AT HOME

Bob, who's a senior Air Force Master Sergeant, gets excellent ratings from his superiors on his job performance. He runs an electronics repair unit on a large air base, which operates on a demanding production schedule and a stressful workload. Bob keeps the operation rolling. He makes sure all of the military specialists and civilian contractors show up on time, keep focused on the work, and do the right things at the right time. As a highly involved, "hands-on" leader, he frequently reassigns tasks and priorities according to the changing demands of the workload. If anything, he may run things a bit too tightly. The workers in his unit perceive him as tense, humorless, and overly preoccupied with minutiae. They'd like to see him loosen up a bit.

At the end of the day, Bob goes home and takes charge of his other key mission: raising a family and keeping everything "in line" at home. He walks in the front door, assembles his wife and three children in the living room, and conducts an inspection. He questions each of them about their assigned responsibilities, inquires about any pressing problems or issues needing his attention, and then dismisses the formation. No hugs, no kisses, no maudlin expressions of affection—Bob runs his family like he runs his shop. He decides everything. He's given his wife a budget, and each of the children gets a precise allowance, with no exceptions. He makes the same mistake at home that he makes at the shop: demanding and criticizing, but seldom praising.

On this particular day, however, Nancy has some news for Bob. After dinner, the kids have gone outside to play. She asks for a meeting, and she tells him she wants a divorce. The news hits Bob like a thunderbolt. He would never, ever, have imagined that she would want to leave him. "I've worked hard," he thinks, his mind spinning and trying to grab onto this perverse reality. "I've always thought of myself as a good provider. I've given her and the kids everything I possibly could. What more could she want?"

Nancy struggles to explain her feelings and her reasons for deciding to leave, ultimately with little success. Bob replies with a quick rebuttal to everything she says. Point for point, he either refutes or bypasses each of her concerns. The careful explanation she's rehearsed many times falls apart. She can't seem to get a message from her planet to his planet. The conversation ends, for now, with Nancy feeling frustrated and impotent and Bob feeling confused and betrayed. As typically happens in this oft-repeated scenario, Bob never saw it coming.

Bob has several SI deficits, the most destructive of which prevents him from adapting his behavior to the varying contexts he encounters. He tries to manage all of his work-crew members with the same authoritarian, hands-on methods, regardless of differences in their ages, skills, know-how, and social maturity. He tries to run his home like he runs his shop. His wife and children need love, respect, care, and companionship, not "management." Bob's preoccupation with his own neurotic needs for structure and order, together with his relatively low emotional intelligence, prevent him from navigating successfully through the various cultural bubbles he encounters.

We could almost christen this kind of situation the "master sergeant syndrome"—the inability of a person accustomed to authority to set aside the rank and rules and to relate to people on a direct, personal level. It probably accounts for millions of failed marriages and romantic relationships. People in other occupations sometimes get stuck in this syndrome as well—police officers, for example, and others whose daily activities center on controlling situations.

THE DIVERSITY PUZZLE

As a favorite training seminar subject for most American managers, supervisors, and employees, "diversity" ranks just below having their roofs fixed and just above having teeth pulled. Once considered a distinctly American business issue, the diversity challenge is finding its way into more and more multicultural settings. One of the reasons that this subject makes many people in the workplace so uncomfortable is that they don't really understand what it's all about.

Is it about better communication between people of different races, ages, or genders? Is it about respecting differences between people of color or other cultures? Is it about women getting along with men or men understanding the work issues of women? Is it about understanding people with disabilities? Does it cover homosexuality, AIDS/HIV, or employees with transgender issues? How about height and weight differences? Is that covered? Does it cover religious or political differences?

Yes to all of the above and then some. Diversity is about helping people in organizations better understand each other at a multitude of levels. It's about either teaching or reminding employees to treat each other with dignity and respect. It's about getting departments, teams, and groups to work toward common goals, by asking employees to refocus on each others' outputs and not on differing personalities.

Now that we've defined the complexity to a confusing degree, let's focus on two troublesome parts of the diversity concern that gives many people so much grief: communication between employees and the use of native languages in the workplace.

Respecting diversity is a key aspect of social intelligence in the workplace. It calls for using many of the skills in the S.P.A.C.E. model and relies on people understanding and supporting each other. But the literal way in which employees speak to each other can become a "political" dividing line, especially when native foreign language speakers use their own languages in the presence of native English speakers who do not speak those languages. Everything in the following discussion could easily apply in any language culture, although the examples offered are rooted in English-speaking cultures.

If you're a native of an English-speaking country, something like this may have happened to you, possibly as a customer: you're standing at the hostess' station at a restaurant, waiting for a table. Two employees who work at the restaurant are standing nearby and begin a conversation in an other-than-English language, which you don't speak. They look at you, say more to each other, and then burst out laughing. As your imagination works overtime, you may get the uneasy feeling that they've just made a joke at your expense.

In another vignette, the employees may quickly switch back and forth between talking to you in English and then to themselves in their native language. Why don't they use English entirely during the exchange? This game of verbal Ping-Pong can help create tension and animosity between them and the other party. It's as if they're trying, perhaps intentionally, to distance themselves and stay within the confines of their own linguistic comfort zone, regardless of the situation.

In the behind-the-scenes workplace, away from the paying customers, this language issue manifests itself in many ways: in the working space of a team, all employees speak the local "official" language and some speak other languages as well. When the native local speakers are out of the room, the remaining members may revert to their home language. When the native local speakers return to the room, the others continue in their tongues, possibly creating the perception that they're talking about something they don't want to share with the others.

Because equal employment opportunity—"EEO"—and affirmative action—"AA"—violations are a significant concern in American workplaces, companies as well as state and federal labor and employment agencies are careful not to impose restrictions that stifle diversity or ethnic expression. On the communications dimension, most government labor boards and equal opportunity commissions advise organizations thusly:

- You can require that all employees speak English while working in public or customer-contact areas (over the telephone, a hotel lobby, at the cash register of a retail store, at the "front of the house" of a restaurant, as opposed to in the kitchen, etc.).
- However, in many states, because of a number of legal challenges, a business cannot prevent any employees from speaking in their native languages when they are not in public/customer-contact locales or interacting with the public/customers. So therefore this issue of "they're talking or laughing at us" is not being addressed.

It's not uncommon to hear native English-speaking employees complain privately and bitterly to their bosses about this social separation behavior. When it continues unabated or gets more frequent, we can sometimes see real dividing lines forming in the workplace, where employee groups don't speak to each other at all.

All this becomes more than just a diversity problem and more than just an employee communication problem. It becomes a business impact issue that can affect employee morale, retention, performance, and, in a worst case, lead to transfers, fistfights, or terminations.

So what can be done to raise the collective social intelligence of the work group? What can a manager do to stay within the appropriate confines of respecting diversity, yet keep his or her employees from dividing in a hostile way? The answer to each question lies in the root of the problem: the need to communicate, honestly and openly and yet tactfully, in the workplace.

Many conflict resolution sessions between groups center around the presenting problem of, "Why can't we all just get along? Why can't things go back to the way they used to be?"

Whether they bring in an outside facilitator or they tackle it themselves, department managers must bring every member together into a room and say, "We owe it to ourselves to set some communication ground rules that will make it easier for us all to talk and work together. We are going to spend this time hearing each other's concerns and complaints, without judgment or criticism. We are going to find a middle ground, where people can use their own language when it's both comfortable and appropriate. We are going to talk about how we can satisfy the needs of our customers and our co-workers, with respect. This isn't about setting a bunch of rules and taking people out of their comfort zones. It's about meeting each other in the middle."

This boundary-setting and air-clearing process, while not always pleasant, can start the group down the road to better understanding and raise the organization's intelligence.

RITUAL, CEREMONY, AND CELEBRATION

Some leaders understand the value of drama in human life; many do not. All cultures have—and need—stereotyped patterns of collective behavior; rituals, ceremonies, and celebrations that play an important part in maintaining a sense of community. Organizations with healthy cultures tend to acknowledge and support these needs. Conversely, the lack of meaningful patterns of community is one of the key indicators of a toxic, psychologically destructive organizational culture. And leaders who succeed in building healthy, high-performing cultures capitalize on the sense of community to advance the aims of the enterprise.

Many managers and executives only vaguely grasp the power and impact of ceremonial experience. Males in particular may tend to act on the unvoiced premise: "I'll let you know if you've done anything wrong (that is, anything to displease me); if you don't hear from me, you can assume you've done a good job." In highly "macho" work cultures, the conversations tend to focus on things and actions, while in more feminized cultures the conversations tend to also signal a significant interest in people, relationships, and community. The use of ceremony serves to shift the attention, or at least to balance the attention between people and things.

One can hardly overstate the appeal of—and appetite for—ritual and ceremony in all reaches of human culture, and this includes organizational experience as well as civil interaction. Consider the functional value of all three social dynamics:

- *Ritual,* according to many social psychologists and anthropologists, serves to relieve *existential anxiety*—the primal fear all human beings have of ceasing to exist. By repeating simple, familiar patterns of interaction—greeting rituals, departure rituals, conversational rituals, family meals, religious activities—countless experiences enable human beings to confirm their connections to one another and to distract themselves from the threats of an uncertain world.
- *Ceremony,* according to many of those same psychologists and anthropologists, serves to help people accept and confirm significant changes in their lives. While common discourse tends to use the terms ritual and ceremony interchangeably, for this discussion it may help to distinguish them. *Ritual* confirms that certain valuable things don't change. *Ceremony* acknowledges and integrates those things that have changed.
- *Celebrations,* as contrasted to rituals and ceremonies, serve to formally mark emotionally significant events in the lives of individuals, families, clans, extended communities, and even nations. To the extent that they follow well-established rules and customs, we can also think of them as rituals or ceremonies—the terms become interchangeable at some point.

Consider how widely pervasive ritual, ceremony, and celebration are in human life. The Jewish culture ceremonializes the arrival at puberty with the *bar mitzvah* for males and the *bat mitzvah* for females; in Latino cultures in Mexico and the southwestern United States, the passage for females is marked by the *quinceañera.*

In America and many other Western cultures, we ceremonialize birth. Almost all cultures have marriage ceremonies (although very few have divorce ceremonies), and virtually all cultures ceremonialize death. Some cultures, such as the Japanese, continue to honor their dead with special rituals such as the *bon-odori,* or "dance for the dead."

People throughout the world observe holidays that mark important events, or ritualize important meanings in their lives. Religious holidays dominate life in some cultures, such as the Jewish culture and many Islamic cultures. The Catholic Church, over the centuries, has raised religious ritual to a scale of grandeur unmatched even by the historical monarchies.

The occasion of the coronation of a king or queen, the inauguration of a president or prime minister, and the death of a head of state give cause for nationwide, culture-wide, or even worldwide ceremonies. National celebrations, such as those commemorating the founding of a republic or its achievement of independence from a colonial power, have enduring value and meaning, spanning across generations.

Local and cultural celebrations abound. Most families think of a wedding as both celebration and ceremony. People in some rural areas still celebrate the final payment on a farm or home with the ceremony of "burning the mortgage." Many, many celebrations, as experienced locally, involve food—another important source of psychological assurance. The American feast of Thanksgiving, and similar rituals in other cultures, serve to confirm the survival and longevity of a community of people under difficult circumstances. All developed cultures have elaborate customs for preparing special foods for celebrations.

In organizational life, managers and executives ignore or diminish the importance of ritual, ceremony, and celebration at their risk. Both national-cultural rituals and ceremonies as well as idiosyncratic organizational rituals and ceremonies all help to shape the unique culture of any enterprise. As a manifestation of organizational SI, virtually all "strong-culture" businesses have highly developed habit patterns that ritualize important experiences, ceremonialize important changes and transitions, and celebrate successes.

But certainly not all managers and executives use ritual, ceremony, and celebration as extensively as they might. An unpublished study conducted by my firm, which compared self-perceptions of leadership behavior on the part of managers in various organizations, detected a significant difference in self-ratings between Australian managers and their counterparts. While both groups scored themselves approximately equal on some forty-one leadership behaviors, Australian managers rated themselves a full point lower, on average, than their American counterparts on a standard five-point scale, in the "use of ritual, celebration, and ceremony."

A Change-of-Command Ceremony

I discovered a remarkable—to me—ceremony while visiting a museum that displayed a traveling collection of papal artifacts and historical items on loan from the Vatican. One particularly interesting display explained a very specialized ceremony, designed for performance whenever one Pope died and another took his place in the long succession of Catholic leadership. The highly unusual nature of the ceremony made me wonder how such a procedure could arise, who might have invented it, and how it became generally accepted.

The museum display consisted of a small gold hammer, elaborately decorated and placed in its own special carrying case. According to the tutorial material accompanying the display, the incoming Pope—along with a whole entourage of Catholic nobles—would visit the casket or sarcophagus containing the corpse of the recently deceased Pope. They would open the casket and the incoming Pope would ceremonially strike the dead Pope on the head with the little gold hammer. This procedure would officially acknowledge the death of the outgoing Pope. One might wonder about the choice of that particular gesture: perhaps it might also serve to make sure he had passed on.

POSITIVE POLITICS: GETTING AHEAD WITH YOUR VALUE SYSTEM INTACT

I've often heard people who work in large organizations say, "I don't play politics. I just do my job" or "You have to play politics to get ahead around here." Those kinds of statements, often made with a somewhat resentful tone of voice, usually indicate that the speaker feels disadvantaged in career competition with others and rationalizes his or her inability to get along with the people in power by condemning "politics" as some kind of a despicable activity beneath his or her moral standards. They reflect a naïve view of work cultures and organizational dynamics.

The person who scorns organizational politics usually does not understand that he or she continually participates in a political context, willingly or unwillingly, consciously or unconsciously. If you work for an organization or participate in any kind of organized human activity, you've involved yourself in its politics. Declaring yourself out of the game doesn't get you out of the game. You can't "not play"—you can only play competently or incompetently.

If you don't mind lying, cheating, assassinating the character of others, and placing your own selfish interests above those of the enterprise, then you have more options for "playing politics." On the other hand, just because you insist on living to a higher moral code than those who engage in those kinds of political activities, you don't have to lose out in the competition for position, influence, and reward. One can often acquire and deploy a considerable level of political skill and not violate one's personal code of ethics.

The first step on the road to becoming an "honest politician," organizationally speaking, is to give up on the fiction that you can avoid the political process—it goes on all around you constantly, every day. You might as well engage the opportunities for acquiring influence with others, rather than passively accept the fate others decide for you.

The second step in your salvation is to rid yourself of the negative associations you may have had with the very concept of politics. If we define politics simply as a set of interactions by which human beings seek to influence one another, we open up a whole range of behavioral strategies for getting ahead honestly and honorably. One can get used to the idea of "positive politics"—the strategies for getting ahead with your value system intact.

For many years I've coached managers, executives, and other professional people about ways to advance their careers at the same time they serve the interests of the enterprise. I've argued that the most successful political strategies, over the long term, involve creating real value, helping others, and contributing to the achievement of the organization's mission. I've also maintained that people who engage in self-serving, destructive political behavior that works against the interests of the enterprise, or behavior intended solely to disadvantage others without creating value, tend to do less well in the long run than those who compete through contribution and achievement. Although I cannot say that "dirty" politicians never succeed and never rise to the top, I continue to bet my money on those who skillfully apply the positive strategies.

Our tour of social intelligence issues for organizations is incomplete, and barely scratches the surface, to be sure. Organizational behavior is confoundingly complex, and in this book we have just begun to explore the meaning and implications of social intelligence in individuals. Still, I believe there is value in shifting our gaze outward, to the places where we live our work lives. If nothing more, these observations on organizational structure, cultures, and politics serve as an invitation to engage in a thinking process that might start to raise the intelligence of our workplaces and other organizations.

Ten Skills of Positive Politics _____

In my book *Personal Power: Knowing What You Want, Getting What You Want,* I devoted a considerable discussion to specific strategies and guidelines for positive politics.[4] After the passage of quite a few years, I find that I wouldn't change a single one of them. I offer them again here:

1. Do something well; get recognized as an achiever.
2. Form alliances and service them regularly.
3. Get visibility.
4. Get credit for your achievements.
5. Relieve pain when possible.
6. Contribute to the big picture.
7. Keep developing yourself.
8. Have a plan for your progress in the organization.
9. Have options to your current job—especially in good times.
10. Know when to leave.

Notes

1. See, for example, Goleman, Boyatzis, and McKee, *Primal Leadership: Learning to Lead with Emotional Intelligence* for an exploration of the role of EI in leadership.
2. Albrecht, Karl. *The Power of Minds at Work: Organizational Intelligence in Action.* New York: Amacom, 2003, p. 21. Used with permission.
3. See Hofstede, Geert. *Culture's Consequences: Comparing Values, Behaviors, Institutions and Organizations Across Nations.* New York: Sage, 2003.
4. From Albrecht, Karl. *Personal Power: Know What You Want, Get What You Want.* Englewood Cliffs NJ: Prentice-Hall, 1986, p. 192 (Out of print). Used with permission.

9

SI IN CHARGE
Thoughts on Developing Socially Intelligent Leaders

> "FLOGGINGS WILL CONTINUE UNTIL
> MORALE IMPROVES."
> —Sign in Australian factory

FORMER FBI DIRECTOR LOUIS B. FREEH reportedly told his senior executives on his first day in his new position, "My idea of teamwork is a whole lot of people doing exactly what I tell them."

You know the type: "It's my way or the highway." "If I want your opinion, I'll give it to you." "I'm not here to win a popularity contest; my job is to get results." "If you don't show people who's boss, they'll walk all over you."

Does a manager have to "kick butts" in order to succeed? Does making people hate you or fear you come with the job? Does the performance of a work team, a department, a division, or a whole enterprise depend on a policy of "law and order"? Can a manager combine authority and empathy?

These questions have occupied the minds of countless people who have found themselves in leadership and management jobs in all kinds of organizations. Military commands, government agencies, nonprofit enterprises, corporations—all place unique demands on those charged with getting things done. Each manager has to work out, either consciously or unconsciously, his or her attitudes and beliefs about the use of authority and the use of personal influence.

THE S.O.B FACTOR

Trying to function in an authority role challenges a person's emotional intelligence and social intelligence at the same time. Many leadership experts contend that people with relatively low emotional intelligence—as characterized by low self-confidence and diminished feelings of self-worth—tend to "hide behind the badge." Lacking the necessary confidence or skills to explain their views, persuade others of the soundness of their decisions, and solve problems collaboratively, they may use their authority to intimidate others. The fearful or insecure manager may suppress dissent, reject the ideas of team members, scold and criticize them, and maintain a distant relationship with them, primarily out of a fear of loss of control.

Working for, or dealing with, an SOB in charge of a situation also requires a combination of SI skills.

Case in point: I learned something about the need to understand the rules of context in situations, and the value of thinking tactically about how to deal with them, during my early military training as an officer candidate in the U.S. Army's Reserve Officers Training Corps during college.

I participated in a six-week summer training camp during the break between my junior and senior years at the university. As prospective Army officers, but having no official rank as yet, our superiors referred to us as "Cadet so-and-so" or simply "Mr. so-and-so." Our treatment at the hands of our superiors and trainers ranged somewhat above the level of harassment reserved for enlisted people but well below the level considered appropriate for real officers. When the time came to collect our—exceedingly modest—pay, I went with my fellow cadets to the barracks office where the paymaster had set up a desk. One by one, we walked up to the desk, behind which sat a young Army captain—a man of modest rank by U.S. military standards. At my turn, I presented myself to the captain, saluted, and said "Cadet Albrecht, sir."

He refused to return my salute and demanded, "Give me a *full* report." I drew myself up higher, snapped a more formal salute and said "Sir—Cadet Albrecht, First Platoon, Foxtrot Company, reporting for pay—*sir*!" In identifying my unit, I had used the customary military "phonetic alphabet"—"F" company became "Foxtrot" company.

Perhaps a bit flustered himself, and possibly new at his job, the captain said, "That's better. Now sign here for your pay, Mr. Foxtrot."

Here we had a rare moment in the psychology of authority. Technically, I had him. After reinforcing my subordinate status, he'd just made a verbal blunder that contradicted the implied sense of infallibility conferred on him by the context. But my instinctive situational awareness told me that preserving the authority relationship came at the top of the list of contextual priorities. I could have exploited his blunder, finding a subtle way to intensify his embarrassment, but at some potential cost to myself. Passing up the opportunity, I simply signed the pay voucher, thanked him, and saluted out.

The lore of leadership, particularly in military organizations, has long reflected this ambivalence about humanity and power. Western military organizations have typically discouraged "fraternizing" between officers and "enlisted" people—or officers and "other ranks," as the British call them. The underlying proposition seems to be that two people who have a personal relationship of some kind cannot function effectively in a boss-subordinate relationship. For some people, this is probably true; the never-answered question remains: "Is it always, or almost always, true?"

Add to this ambivalent social doctrine the commonly experienced sense of uncertainty and self-doubt experienced by people in authority roles—particularly newcomers to those roles—and we have a formula for dysfunctional cultures.

Many business journalists and authors of business books love to conjure up the image of the SOB-CEO. It makes for entertaining reading: the ruthless competitor who defeats all enemies, punishes those who displease him, and eliminates those who question him or challenge his authority. (It's even more fun to find a female executive who does the same things.) Human brain structure being what it is, a journalist can always cook up a more interesting story about a double-dyed SOB leader than about a likeable one. If you're writing about a likable person, then you have to find some quirk or some character flaw to make the story interesting.

One such SOB-hero was the legendary Al Dunlap, dubbed by venture capitalists and business journalists as "Chainsaw Al." According to *slate.com*'s editor David Plotz:

> "A holy terror of a CEO, Dunlap has emerged as the mascot of a new kind of capitalism. Dunlapism begins and ends at Wall Street. Its *sole* credo is: 'How can we make our stock worth more?' Nothing that is valued by less steely businessmen—loyalty to workers, responsibility to the community, relationships with suppliers, generosity in corporate philanthropy—matters to Dunlap. Business ethics professors tout 'stakeholder capitalism.' Dunlap sneers at the phrase.
>
> "Other executives share his creed, but none matches Dunlap's methods. In the past two decades, the sixty-year-old executive has

run nine companies in the United States, Australia, and England. He served as right-hand man/enforcer for both Australian media magnate Kerry Packer and recently deceased British billionaire Sir James Goldsmith. In the process, he has earned a reputation as the most merciless turnaround artist in the world.

"To wit: As CEO of struggling cup manufacturer Lily Tulip Corp. in the '80s, Dunlap fired most of the senior managers, sold the corporate jet, closed the headquarters and two factories, dumped half the headquarters staff, and laid off a bunch of other workers. The stock price rose from $1.77 to $18.55 in his two-and-a-half-year tenure. At Scott Paper—his pre-Sunbeam tour of duty—he fired 11,000 employees (including half the managers and 20 percent of the company's hourly workers), eliminated the corporation's $3-million philanthropy budget, slashed R&D spending, and closed factories. Scott's market value stood at about $3 billion when Dunlap arrived in mid-1994. In late 1995, he sold Scott to Kimberly-Clark for $9.4 billion, pocketing $100 million for himself—a modest payoff, he says, for the $6 billion in increased shareholder value."[1]

Dunlap publicly excoriated AT&T CEO Robert Allen for not firing enough people. He posed as Rambo on the cover of *USA Today*. And he laid out his fundamental belief system and methods in his best-selling book *Mean Business: How I Save Bad Companies and Make Good Companies Great*.[2]

Contrast Dunlapism with the philosophy and management methods of "Ben and Jerry," the founders of Ben & Jerry's Ice Cream. Two unreconstructed '60s liberals, Ben Cohen and Jerry Greenfield founded a successful consumer products company on the ideas of social responsibility, micro-capitalism, profit sharing, and support to the disadvantaged. After twenty years of admirable business performance, they wrote their counter-cultural manifesto *Ben & Jerry's Double Dip: How to Run a Values Led Business and Make Money Too*.[3]

In 2001 Ben & Jerry's was acquired by Anglo-Dutch food giant Unilever, yet the company has continued its commitment to its values.[4] A number of Ben & Jerry's shops are still owned and operated by non-profit groups, and all the profits from those businesses benefit the sponsoring organizations. The company is unfailingly recognized as a leader in corporate social responsibility, and through its employee-led corporate philanthropy and the Ben & Jerry's Foundation contributes some $2.5 million annually to support its founding values: to aid Vermont communities and to foster economic and social justice, environmental restoration, and peace through understanding. As Cohen put it, speaking to a group of college students in Rhode Island, "The last remaining superpower on Earth needs to learn to measure its strength by how many people it can feed and clothe, not how many people it can kill."

Dunlapism or Ben-and-Jerry-ism—two radically different world-views and radically different definitions of the social proposition of business. The contradiction between the two will probably never be resolved.

EXECUTIVE HUBRIS: ITS COSTS
AND CONSEQUENCES

While some executives govern and lead with considerable humility, others do so with an air of grandeur, almost as if they consider themselves modern-day royalty. Some of them have ruled almost as if by divine right, building power images and lifestyles for themselves to rival the wealthiest monarchs.

In recent years, six men, all corporate CEOs, deserve most of the credit for destroying the confidence of the American public in corporate leadership and executive ethics. They also deserve considerable credit for the destruction of billions of dollars of investor wealth, and an unprecedented phase of investor cynicism and distrust of Wall Street.

- Michael Ovitz, who spent a year as president of Walt Disney Company, had a compensation deal that made him better off for being fired than had he kept his job. He joined the firm with a million-dollar salary—lavish even by Hollywood standards— plus an annual bonus of $7.5 million, plus stock options worth over $100 million. He also had a $10 million termination package that would kick in if he was fired without cause before his contract expired. After being forced out by his former friend, Disney Chairman Michael Eisner, Ovitz walked away with over $140 million. His ill-fated reign and contentious departure triggered a palace war in the company that raged for several years and permanently tarnished the image of Walt Disney's commercial legacy.

- Bernie Ebbers, the financial mastermind who grew Worldcom from an obscure telecom firm to a high-flying Wall Street darling, was caught with both hands in the till. The discovery of over $9 billion in "accounting errors" forced the $180 billion company into bankruptcy, but not before Ebbers "borrowed" over $400 million from the treasury to support his opulent lifestyle. Ebbers was convicted of orchestrating the largest corporate accounting fraud in history, yet walked away with a $1.5 million annual pension.

- Dennis Kozlowski, CEO of conglomerate Tyco International, set records for spending the shareholders' money on lavish offices, Manhattan apartments, art, furniture, and splashy parties. Kozlowski and several other insiders were accused of siphoning $600 million in shareholder funds from the treasury, using the money to pay for luxury apartments, villas, yachts, and million-dollar birthday parties. Tyco's board finally fired him when he was indicted for income tax fraud.

- John J. Rigas, founder and CEO of Adelphia Communications, reportedly conspired with four other executives to drain the corporate coffers of the fast-growing cable TV company.

Prosecutors asked the court to force Rigas and his cohorts to return some $2.5 billion to the shareholders. For Rigas, taking the investors for a ride was a family affair. He and his three sons were indicted for fraudulently excluding billions of dollars in liabilities from the firm's consolidated financial statements, by hiding them on the books of off-balance-sheet affiliates. Prosecutors charged that they also falsified operations numbers and inflated earnings to meet Wall Street's expectations. This, on top of reported self-dealing by the whole Rigas family, including the undisclosed use of corporate funds for Rigas family stock purchases and the acquisition of luxury condominiums in New York and elsewhere, led to his ouster and prosecution.

- Kenneth Lay, a good ole boy from Texas, presided over the implosion of the legendary Enron Corporation, a financial house of cards built on clever energy trading and financial manipulation. As the firm reeled toward bankruptcy, Lay and other insiders concealed mountains of debt, faked profits, and looted the treasury. Lay alone received more than $150 million in payments and stock before the company cratered, throwing 6,000 people out of their jobs and ruining most of them financially, as they watched the Enron shares in their retirement funds go into free-fall. While Lay had been quietly selling his stock and investing in lawsuit-proof variable annuities, he was vigorously encouraging Enron employees to keep buying the stock for their 401(k) investment plans. His annuities gave him and his wife a lifetime income of nearly $1 million per year, which was untouchable by litigation or legal penalties regardless of any conviction he might face.

- Richard Grasso, one of the financial heroes of Wall Street, finally had to resign as chairman of the New York Stock Exchange, under mounting investor criticism and political pressure related to his $140 million pay package. In his eight-year reign, he managed to pack the NYSE's board of directors with cronies who approved his unconscionable compensation. Virtually all reputable financial experts agreed the package amounted to an unmitigated rip-off of NYSE's shareholders. Grasso generously relinquished claim to another $50 million in previously undisclosed entitlements— once New York State's Attorney General Eliot Spitzer began to scrutinize the Big Board's financial practices, and the practices of quite a few other financial firms.

All of these corporate monarchs, consumed with their own grandiose self-images, became poster boys for all that's wrong with Wall Street and Corporate America. They ruined their companies, they ruined the lives of their workers, they ruined many of their investors, and they ruined the confidence of Main Street in Wall Street.

And the consequences ripple out farther: In the summer of 2002, the U.S. Congress passed a landmark bill that imposed very stringent requirements on corporate governance, largely as a result of the excesses of the Wall Street royalty. Created by Maryland Senator Paul Sarbanes and Ohio Representative Michael Oxley, "Sarbanes-Oxley" came in the aftermath of the spectacular crashes the robber barons engineered. The bill passed the Senate 99–0, and cleared the House with only three dissenting votes. Most financial analysts agreed that the new measures would impose additional operating costs on corporations amounting to at least $5 billion per year, with particularly severe impact on smaller corporations.

BEST BOSS, WORST BOSS

As part of a team building, leadership, or organizational development seminar, I often ask the participants to break into small groups and go to a nearby easel pad with their marker pens in hand. Once there, I ask each group to come up with a list of attributes for two distinct people: the best boss they ever worked for and the worst boss they ever worked for. I ask for adjectives, descriptors, behaviors, and the styles of the people who have led them.

I ask them to cover the span of their entire working lives, even starting at their first jobs: delivering papers, working at a fast-food restaurant, mowing lawns, working on their college campus, in the military, or during their first jobs out of school. Not surprisingly, the groups get into some spirited discussions at their pads about who was great, who was awful, and why.

On the best boss list, the groups often come up with traits similar to these:

- Supportive
- Teacher
- Good delegator
- Communicates frequently
- Gives rewards and praise
- Takes care of us
- Good sense of humor
- Goes to bat for us with senior management
- Criticizes in private, not in front of others
- Smart
- Helps you get ahead
- Knows his or her job very well

On the worst boss inventory, the list is often longer and filled with emotionally laden terminology:

- Backstabber
- Mean
- Absent, too hands-off
- Cruel to others
- Sour personality, complains
- Weak, won't take action
- Avoids conflicts or problems
- Game player

- Keeps us in the dark
- Doesn't support us with his/her boss
- Sexually harasses others
- Loud and argumentative
- Alcoholic
- Micromanager, too hands-on

To make this exercise even more productive, at about the halfway point, I ask the group members to shift to another easel pad, going from bad to good or good to bad. This adds even more color and flavor to the lists, until we have about thirty or so traits and behaviors on each sheet.

I ask the group members to go around to all the easel pads and look at the total outputs. Then we discuss the results, who said what, and why. There are some fond memories of early bosses who took the time and trouble to teach their young employees how to work hard and smart. And there are plenty of reminders of terrible bosses, whose behavior was so rotten that some of the employees actually quit good or well-paying jobs.

The end of this exercise leads to some questions: Do the people who make the Good Boss list have high SI scores in the areas covered by the S.P.A.C.E. Model? The answer is an unqualified "yes"; they have what it takes to lead, motivate, and challenge their people, both to get good results and to have a bit of fun while doing it.

And do the problem supervisors, who make the Worst Boss list, score high on the important S.P.A.C.E. criteria? The answer there is certainly "no." Their inability to manage with situational awareness, presence, authenticity, clarity, and empathy—never mind compassion, direction, energy, honesty, etc.—makes them hard to work for.

For the management or supervisory group discussing this issue, the burning question becomes: Do *your* employees rate you in this same way? Do the people who work for you keep their own "report cards" in their heads when they evaluate your leadership and management styles?

Of course they do, on a regular updated basis. From Day One, all employees begin to evaluate and compare their current boss with the best and the worst they've ever encountered. They compare their answers with each other, and they may change their perceptions in one direction (feeling more or less favorably toward you) or they may never change their minds, once they feel they've worked for you long enough to decide.

So if you're a boss, or play a leadership role in any type of organization, think about how you want to be perceived. Which list do you want to make: the Hall of Fame or the Wall of Shame?

P.O.W.E.R.: WHERE IT COMES FROM, HOW TO GET IT

If social intelligence generally is the capacity to get along with others and to get them to cooperate with you, then power and influence have to be part of the equation. Some people seem to understand, almost innately, how power and influence work, and many others seem baffled by it. Getting into a position of power and control involves more than sheer accident: one has to know how to accumulate power and when to use it to get more of it. Some of the most evil people on the planet have, unfortunately, learned how to acquire power and how to hold on to it.

Power—the entitlement to influence others—comes in various forms. We can characterize the various sources of influence using the acronym P.O.W.E.R.:

P = Position
O = Opportunity
W = Wealth
E = Expertise
R = Relationship

Position power rests on formal authority. A military rank, an elected office, the formal appointment as an executive of an organization, or a position of acknowledged authority such as head of a rebel faction, enable a person to direct others as he or she sees fit, within certain limits.

Opportunity power involves a special set of circumstances—unique access to a business opportunity, a special reputation that confers entitlement of some type, or having custody of some valuable asset— figuratively, showing up at the right place at the right time.

Wealth confers power by dint of the entitlement to deploy resources in some way needed by others. A deep-pocket investor, an executive in control of a large source of funds, or a political figure in a position to parcel out public funds, all have the power of wealth. As the somewhat cynical redefinition of the Golden Rule goes: the person who has the gold makes the rules.

Expertise, in the form of special skills, unique knowledge, necessary know-how, or access to critical information can confer a unique form of influence. As a bluntly stated example: If we're lost in the woods and you know the way out of the woods, then you're my leader—at least until we get out of the woods.

Relationship power can accrue to a person who, by diligence or good fortune, enjoys access and acceptance with people who possess any of the other kinds of power. The son or daughter of a highly placed political figure may bargain access in exchange for material or circumstantial rewards. A person of modest rank who happens to have a personal relationship with an important client, benefactor, political figure, or other person of influence may wield influence far beyond that considered typical of his or her station.

People who know how to accumulate power methodically and strategically clearly have some degree of social intelligence, at least in certain dimensions. Some of the worst despots in history have had this special know-how, although most of them have had severe deficits in emotional intelligence. Reporters, commentators, and other onlookers often seek to demean the mental capacity of such people, sometimes dismissing them as merely "crazy" in order to avoid the ego-threatening avenue of giving them credit for the warped set of skills they actually have.

How the Worst Bastards on the Planet Get and Keep Power

Totalitarian leaders like Genghis Khan, Attila, Lenin, Hitler, Mussolini, Stalin, Mao Tze-Tung, Pol Pot, Idi Amin, and Saddam Hussein certainly could not kill thousands or millions of human beings single-handedly. They had to find ways to leverage the violence of others by acquiring power and projecting that power through various levels of their dynastic structures.

Typically, power accumulators—even those who have little or no evil intent—operate in approximately the same ways. They generally follow a stage-wise process of building their power and influence over time. Studying some of the worst despots in history, we can readily observe four key phases:

Phase 1: Networking. The prospective dictator shows up, gets to know people, gets into social circulation, and begins forming relationships with a core population of people who have the intentions or potential aspirations of asserting power. In the early stages, this population might represent little more than a group of coffee-house intellectuals; in other cases they might have already begun forming a political identity.

Phase 2: Coalition Building. Using various social skills, subtle forms of influence, political persuasion, an appealing political ideology, and the proposition of bettering their circumstances through collective action, the organizer gets into the center of a developing subculture. In the early stages, he or she might have to accommodate other would-be leaders and may have to settle for a place within a miniature oligarchy at the center of the coalition. He or she may have to wait patiently for the opportunity to knock off the other contenders and make a play for the key role.

Phase 3: Taking Over. Many people forget—or never knew—that Adolph Hitler came to power as a result of free and open elections. But once he got to the center of the ruling coalition, the National Socialist party, he moved quickly and ruthlessly to consolidate his power. The take-over phase usually involves a significant risk and requires that the would-be ruler act aggressively in order to acquire position power in the minds of the other members of the coalition. Many aspiring despots fail at this phase, either because their rivals manage to dilute their influence, because the followers see an evil side of them that they don't like, or because the timing and circumstances don't offer the right set of imperatives to get behind an aggressive leader. The aspiring despot who succeeds in the take-over phase reaches a tipping point of influence, after which he has a more or less official entitlement in the eyes of others to decide, direct, control, reward, and punish.

Phase 4: Unrelenting Consolidation. The successful despot, once having arrived at the stage of general control, spends the rest of his life, or tenure, eliminating or disabling his political opponents, installing loyalists into the various subordinate layers of power, building mechanisms for instilling fear into them and into the general population, and extending his control to all parts of the realm.

Disturbingly, perhaps, these same four stages generally apply to anyone's rise to power, with occasional exceptions. A strong corporate CEO may well have made the last few career moves using the power-accumulation model, even if he or she lives to very honorable values. A person who seeks to achieve a position of influence, especially in a fluid or unstructured political situation, could readily use these four stages as his or her road map to that goal.

Certainly, having the road map doesn't guarantee that anyone who wants to can reach the goal. A mistake in timing anywhere along the way, an unforeseen turn of events, the presence of other talented and determined power-seekers, or any of a number of other uncontrolled factors could derail one's progress to power. And, of course, not everyone who rises to a position of significant stature and influence has a craving for power. Some of the most effective leaders derive their primary motivation from their need for achievement. In general, however, those who consciously value and seek positions of power will tend to get them more often than those who do not. The achievement motivated individual tends to see a position of authority as merely a particular opportunity for achievement, whereas a more power motivated person achieves satisfaction from the direct experience of having power.

THE ALGEBRA OF INFLUENCE

How does one influence others in a situation where one has no P.O.W.E.R., no formal authority? As an aspiring executive, political leader, or organizer—or an aspiring despot—how can you acquire influence in human affairs? The secret lies in understanding the difference between *formal authority* and *earned authority*.

Formal authority, obviously, comes with position power—someone or some entity, such as a president or prime minister, a governor, a mayor, a board of directors, or an electorate—has anointed you formally and has granted you a certain range of authority. Earned authority, on the other hand, does not come from others in power positions; you get it from other people, one at a time.

You can earn authority by behaving in ways that cause others to consider you worthy of the right to influence them. Your ideas, your practical skills, your situational know-how, your concern for the well-being of others, and your willingness to give direction in leaderless situations all add up on an unconscious scorecard in the mind of each of the people involved. The more that people as individuals respond to you as a prospective leader, the more they tend to look to you collectively for leadership. And if the situation involves conscious choices, they may tend to "elect" you their leader, either formally or informally.

There's a sort of algebra of influence at work here. In any situation involving power or influence, your total usable authority consists of a combination of your formal authority, if any, and your earned authority, if any. Any of the players contending for influence in a power-oriented situation can have either high or low formal authority and high or low earned authority. A person with relatively high formal authority, who has failed to win the trust and respect of those under his or her control, may actually have a low total authority score. Indeed, if one has somehow acquired a negative earned authority score, the net authority score—formal authority plus the negative earned authority score—might add up to a net negative total score.

Conversely, a person with little or no formal authority might have earned a high level of personal authority with others, and might enjoy a higher score on net authority than the one with the formal position.

S.P.I.C.E.: LEADING WHEN YOU'RE NOT IN CHARGE

Many people, including those with a strong desire for influence and control, have no clear idea of how to go about earning authority. They don't understand the strategies for acquiring influence without having formal power. Those who know how can generally explain the specific methods they use. We can even find a formula, of sorts, which works as a general strategy for earning influence.

A person can emerge as the *de facto* leader in an unstructured situation, or can earn a significant measure of informal authority, even in a group that has a formally appointed leader, by providing any or all of five distinct forms of assistance to the group, when—and only when—needed. You can easily recall these five types of leadership behavior by remembering the acronym S.P.I.C.E., which stands for:

1. Skills. If you know how to do the orbital calculations to get the space ship back to Earth, and no one else in the group does, then you can assist the group with your skills. Other people perceive, consciously or unconsciously, the helpful use of expertise as a leading behavior. Do it often enough—and only when it serves as a constructive contribution— and they begin to rely on it. Specialized knowledge, manual skills, organizing skills, technical skills, and social skills can all serve to earn influence in the minds of others.

2. Procedures. Sometimes, perhaps often, a group of people will get stuck in their own processes. Skillful consultants often muse about how frequently groups just can't seem to get off the ground. The community action meeting starts with everybody putting in his views, opinions, and recommendations. Disagreement sets in quickly, and the process grinds to a halt as people argue for their favorite course of action. You politely inquire as to the actual objective of the meeting and invite the participants to decide what they hope to accomplish before they leave. Invoke the "power of the pen"—pick up the felt marker and begin to write their outputs on the newsprint pad—and you've become the group's leader, at least temporarily.

3. Information. Most group decisions or problem-solving discussions depend heavily on having the right information and using it effectively. Yet it seldom occurs to people in a meeting to ask, "What information do we need to solve this problem?" "Do we have it?" and "If we don't, how or where can we get it?" The person who provides critical information, or who helps the group use its information effectively, gets "leader points" in the minds of the others.

4. Consensus. Sometimes a group just needs to have someone summarize the discussion or the thinking process, propose or confirm the favored option for action, or guide the members through some humane process for deciding what to do. Many unskilled group participants have no idea how to navigate to a conclusion or decision. The person who can provide this service gets leader points here as well.

5. *Empathy*.   Also known as the group climate or sense of team spirit, empathy supports the process of thinking collaboratively, without animosity or undue conflict. The group may have a norm for debate and even heated argument, but if the controversy crosses over into the domain of personal rancor, then the group has an empathy problem. At any time during the group's process, a person who acts to move the group back toward a positive and constructive climate can earn leader points for this service. Restoring empathy does not mean squelching disagreement or painting over conflict; it means helping people relate to one another humanely while working out their differences.

The key to using the S.P.I.C.E. formula for earning authority is using it selectively, sparingly and—above all—helpfully. A skilled group may need very little in the way of intervention. A floundering group, or one in a state of conflict, may benefit significantly from one or more assists from someone who knows how to fit the intervention to the need.

A Final Thought

There is much left unsaid in this discussion about leadership, power, and social intelligence. The enormous body of literature and scholarship devoted to the topic testifies to its complexity as well as its lingering fascination for those who think about such things.

Indeed, the discussion creates more questions than it answers: Can we—and if so, how—educate and develop a generation of socially intelligent and socially responsible leaders? How can a business enterprise, a government, or other institution—indeed a whole society—safeguard the seats of power from those who would exploit them for personal gain? How do we encourage those with the necessary combination of ability and ethics to give their services as leaders?

Perhaps one small but important step in the direction of those answers is in a process of raising expectations through discussion and dialog. As the concept of social intelligence finds its way into the public consciousness, and into the public discourse about our leaders and the leadership they offer, we may increasingly hold our leaders in all sectors of society to a higher standard.

Executive Hoof-in-Mouth Disease

We all occasionally say things the wrong way or say things we later wish we hadn't. For some reason, these bloopers become more significant—and often comical—when said by powerful or famous people.

Some ill-considered statements attributed (not always accurately, perhaps) to some famous figures:

- "When more and more people are thrown out of work, unemployment results." —U.S. President Calvin Coolidge.
- "I haven't committed a crime. What I did was fail to comply with the law." —New York City Mayor Donald Dinkins, accused of not paying his income tax.
- "He didn't say that. He was reading what was given to him in a speech." —U.S. President George Bush's budget director, explaining why Bush didn't keep his campaign promise that there would be no loss of wetlands.
- "I was a pilot flying an airplane and it just so happened that where I was flying made what I was doing spying." —Francis Gary Powers, pilot of the U-2 reconnaissance plane shot down over the Soviet Union.
- "It is necessary for me to establish a winner image. Therefore, I have to beat somebody." —Richard M. Nixon, early in his political career.
- "A billion here, a billion there—pretty soon it adds up to real money." —U.S. Senator Everett Dirksen.

- "We pray for MacArthur's erection." —Sign displayed by Japanese citizens in Tokyo, when Douglas MacArthur was considering running for U.S. President.
- "My fellow Americans, I've signed legislation that will outlaw Russia forever. We begin bombing in five minutes." —U.S. President Ronald Reagan, before a radio broadcast, unaware that his microphone was already live.
- "The President has kept all of the promises he intended to keep." —George Stephanopolous, aide to U.S. President Bill Clinton.
- "The streets are safe in Philadelphia; it's only the people who make them unsafe." —Frank Rizzo, ex-police chief and mayor of Philadelphia.
- "The police are not there to create disorder; they're there to preserve disorder." —Mayor Frank Daley of Chicago.
- "Oh, goddammit! We forgot the silent prayer!" —President Dwight Eisenhower, after a cabinet meeting.
- "Outside of the killings, Washington has one of the lowest crime rates in the country." —Mayor Marion Barry, Washington, D.C.
- "Smoking kills. If you're killed, you've lost a very important part of your life." —Actress Brooke Shields, during an interview to become spokesperson for a federal anti-smoking campaign.
- Question: If you could live forever, would you and why? Answer: "I would not live forever, because we should not live forever, because if we were supposed to live forever, then we would live forever, but we cannot live forever, which is why I would not live forever." —Miss Alabama in the 1994 Miss Universe contest.
- "They couldn't hit an elephant at this dist—" —Last words of General John Sedgwick, a Union army commander in the U.S. Civil War, commenting on the legendary skills of Confederate snipers.

Notes

1. "Al Dunlap: The Chainsaw Capitalist." *slate.com,* posted by David Plotz, Sunday, August 31, 1997.

2. Dunlap, Albert J. *Mean Business: How I Save Bad Companies and Make Good Companies Great.* New York: Crown, 1996.

3. Cohen, Ben, and Greenfield, Jerry. *Ben and Jerry's Double Dip: How to Run a Values Led Business and Make Money Too.* New York: Simon & Schuster, 1998.

4. Chrystie Heimert, "Ben & Jerry's Names New Chief Euphoria Officer Freese to Assume Top Leadership Job at Vermont Ice Cream Company." Press release, Burlington, VT, November 2004. Published at www.benjerry.com/ our_company/press_center/press/WaltFreeseAnnouncement.html

10

SI AND CONFLICT
Thoughts About Getting Along

"We should go to the Arabs with sticks in hand and
beat them, and beat them, and beat them—until
they stop hating us."
—Tel Aviv cab driver

A TRUISM IN MEDICINE IS "Smiling doctors seldom get sued for malpractice."

Like most generalizations, this one contains a certain degree of validity. If we exclude the number of malpractice suits motivated mostly by greed, malice, and eccentricity at one extreme, and exclude those that result from egregious medical incompetence at the other extreme, the suits we see in the middle of the range—possibly over half of all suits, some experts believe—seem to involve relationships gone sour. It certainly seems that some significant fraction of them, a number subject to argument, of course, might never have gone forward if the medical providers had maintained closer personal relationships with their clients, or if they had moved quickly to acknowledge responsibility and actively atone in some very generous way.

People who lodge lawsuits against physicians and medical centers frequently cite an "attitude" on the part of the doctor or administrators. Perceived arrogance, lack of concern for human suffering, coldness, condescension, and an air of infallibility can set the conditions. "At first, I just wanted them to apologize," the plaintiff may say. "They would never even admit they made a mistake."

THE DOUBLE SPIRAL OF CONFLICT

Several thousand years of history have demonstrated pretty conclusively that conflict tends to create more conflict. Once it begins, it tends to escalate. Once it reaches a critical level of intensity, it tends to feed on itself. Some countries, political factions, clans, and neighborhoods have feuded for so long that no one seems to know how or why the conflict started. They only know that they have no choice but to respond to the atrocities of the other side, and usually go them one better.

I recall seeing an example of this in an old film starring the classic comedy duo of Stan Laurel and Oliver Hardy.

Laurel and Hardy had taken jobs selling Christmas trees, going door to door. The stopped their old jalopy in front of a house, walked up to the front door and knocked. The irascible owner opened the door, listened to their sales pitch for a few seconds, and bluntly told them to get lost.

Irritated at having the door slammed in their faces, they knocked again. Once more the owner appeared and turned them down even more rudely. An argument ensued and one of the angry salesmen decided to teach the impolite owner a lesson. With some fanfare, he desecrated the owner's house—I don't recall the actual atrocity; possibly he broke the door knocker—which caused the owner to fly into a complete rage.

The owner stormed out to the street and broke off the side mirror from their car, flinging it to the ground contemptuously. He defiantly brushed off his hands and glared directly at them as he went back into the house. The incident escalated, with each side inflicting ever more severe retaliation on the other. Laurel and Hardy broke his windows and he broke the windows of their car. When he had progressed to tearing off the fenders, they engaged in batting practice with his household belongings. Laurel flung a large vase out the window as Hardy smashed it with a baseball bat. Each act of aggression met with a new expression of outrage, and a new—thoroughly justified—counterattack.

By the time the episode closed, they had reduced his house to a shambles and he had reduced their car to little more than a chassis with wheels. They drove away feeling righteously indignant—and perversely triumphant—as he surveyed the damage to his house and congratulated himself on his resolute defense of his interests.

Unfortunately, many of the most costly conflicts in human experience have no such redemption in comedy. Onlookers may ridicule the protagonists for their mindless escalation of the situation, but too often innocent bystanders pay the price as well.

For those who observe and study continuing conflicts, the escalation of animosity tends to follow a very well-defined pattern, even though the parties who have become locked into it may not see it. But conversely, two parties who manage to maintain cordial and cooperative relationships—individuals, families, clans, companies, political factions, or countries—display the exact opposite of the escalating atrocities. Positive relationships can grow and strengthen over time, moving upward in a positive self-reinforcing spiral, just as continuing negative relationships move downward in an ever more destructive spiral. The upward spiral of cooperation looks like a mirror image of the downward spiral of conflict. Generally, in order to get from conflict to cooperation, the situation has to move back up the negative spiral to some kind of potentially neutral zone, and then find its way upward into positive territory, as illustrated in Figure 10.1.

Consider the progress of the conflict spiral, at the bottom half of the illustration. If *distrust* sets in for any of a number of reasons, or exists as a historical legacy to a relationship, then the situation has a bias toward conflict at the outset. A *provocation* by one party, or a series of provocations by both antagonists, provides each side with evidence of negative intent on the part of the other. After a few atrocities, the situation deteriorates into an *escalation* stage, at which point both parties have abandoned any aspirations for an amicable relationship. They typically see themselves as required to "fight back," or to retaliate for some unforgivable transgression by the other.

During this descent into irreversible conflict, the brain chemistry changes on both sides. Both antagonists have fully committed their energies to inflicting disadvantage on the others. Neither party can now seriously consider the possibility of allowing the other party to receive something of value. It becomes a win-lose proposition that, ironically, turns into a lose-lose proposition.

If the conflict relationship lasts long enough and does enough damage, it may eventually descend to the fourth level of complete *deadlock*. This happens notoriously with religious and ethnic animosities, and

Figure 10.1. The Double Spiral of Conflict

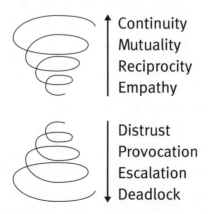

Continuity
Mutuality
Reciprocity
Empathy

Distrust
Provocation
Escalation
Deadlock

with long-running territorial disputes. In the case of the ancient conflict between Jews and Arabs in the Middle East, the conflict has become fully institutionalized; it shapes political structures, laws, educational doctrines, government policies, and commercial practices. In Northern Ireland, Protestants and Catholics murder one another in the name of the same deity.

It may seem idealistic to believe that a conflict situation that has degenerated to a fourth-stage level of deadlock has any possibility of a turnaround. Indeed, the sheer length of tenure of some of the world's most destructive conflicts seems to contradict the very proposition. However, many long-running relationships exist in which countries, ethnic groups, geographical regions, clans, and ideologies have managed to combine their interests for mutual benefit. The fact that some happy marriages do last a lifetime, that some countries get along well for hundreds of years or more, and some companies have done business together for many decades suggests that the positive, upward spiral of cooperation does work.

The upward progression of a relationship must begin with some adequate degree of trust—or *empathy,* in SI terminology. Circumstances may support a positive start-off to a relationship. Some of the players involved may have sufficiently high SI to engineer a state of affairs that invites others to communicate, share their interests and intentions, and seek common ground.

With sufficient empathy, the relationship can move to a level of *reciprocity,* in which the parties involved contribute positively toward one another's interests. Reluctantly at first, perhaps, but increasing as a result of seeing their own interests served, the parties may engage more voluntarily and proactively in finding ways to collaborate.

With luck, skill, and the passage of time, the relationship appears to have a long-term promise and payoff for all parties involved, and it shifts from a transactional proposition—"We'll give you A if you give us B"—to a proposition of *mutuality.* If it reaches that stage, the participants begin to think of it in terms of an enduring relationship. This involves the critical aspect of expectations: we have engaged with the other side for long enough that we see the likelihood of an ongoing, even institutionalized interaction.

And, in some fortunate circumstances, the parties arrive at a stage of *continuity*—a belief by all parties that the relationship serves their needs and interests so well that it takes on a life and an identify of its own. At this point we see the exact mirror image of the deadlock stage of conflict. Whereas in the deadlock stage of conflict, none of the parties feels any motivation to advance the interests of the other, in the continuity stage of cooperation, all parties understand the pragmatic value of helping the others meet their needs and satisfy their interests.

Perversely, the deadlock state actually has payoffs for those engaged in it. They get to feel like heroes defending their homeland, and they feel the squalid triumph that comes with inflicting hardship on their enemies. Unfortunately, they can't imagine a different state of affairs in which they don't have to disadvantage themselves in order to disadvantage others.

Case in point: while conducting a team-building session with a group of attorneys and their paralegals, one of my colleagues watched in amazement as an off-the-job issue had gained enough energy over time to become a big problem. At the start of the meeting, all of the attorneys sat on one side of the table and the paralegals sat across on the other. The consultant started by asking the chief paralegal her goals for the session. She replied, "We just want people to be happier, for work to get done better, and for everyone to get along better."

The consultant then asked the senior attorney his goals for the meeting. He pounded his fist on the table and shouted, "I want these women fired!"

Several of the paralegals burst into tears and things went downhill for quite a while until the consultant could determine the cause: when a former paralegal staff member who had passed away from cancer was in the hospital, she was not visited by any of the attorneys in the office. This was taken by the paralegals as a slight to her worth and it created a huge rift that included cold shoulders, work slowdowns, passive-aggressive behavior, and covert hostility.

In a typical legal office, the paralegals control much of the work flow. They keep the attorneys' calendars, schedule their meetings and court appearances, do research, and tabulate the billable hours and expenses. In many offices, they serve an invaluable back-office function, so the attorneys can concentrate on their cases or on acquiring new clients.

Because of their collective anger at the attorneys for their perception that they did not care about their paralegal colleague, their sabotage behavior became quite costly. Attorneys began to miss client meetings, court appearances, and filing deadlines. This had been going on for about three years.

In their defense, the attorneys were under the mistaken impression that the paralegal in the hospital didn't want any visitors and so they had honored what they thought were her wishes. When this miscommunication began to take on economic consequences (the work slowdown) and created real hostility, the senior partners decided to bring in the consultant to manage this mushroom cloud of conflict.

One group wanted "justice" (the attorneys) and the other wanted "peace" (the paralegals). The consultant realized they would make no progress with team building until this major issue was out on the table, discussed, and settled. Four hours passed, with more tears, cross-accusations, and thankfully, no more table pounding. In the end, they were finally able to work as a group to get closure, move on, and then discuss the tools needed to collectively solve future conflicts.

Perhaps we human beings will figure out how to turn deadlock into continuity, but even the most optimistic among us would probably concede that prevention offers a much greater promise than cure.

In an oft-repeated conversation, a middle-aged man asks his doctor, "How can I keep from going bald?" The doctor, in a paradoxical reference to the hereditary nature of baldness, says, "Get yourself a different grandfather."

The equivalent advice for reducing or eliminating deadlock says: "Don't let it start."

The Hatfields and McCoys Declare Peace _____

The legendary family feud between West Virginia's Hatfield family and Kentucky's McCoy family came to an end for certain in June 2000, when the two families held their first annual reunion in Pikeville, Kentucky. The feud had faded to an end almost 100 years earlier, and in the new millennium the age of commerce finally had its way with history. All that remains of the murderous feud is a modern tourist venture—a sort of "H&M enterprise." Several official websites, an official fan club, the annual festival, reenactments of historical events, videos and books, gift merchandise, and a genealogical database all testify to the time-less fascination of a thirty-year period of conflict that claimed the lives of twelve members of the families, pitted the state governments of West Virginia and Kentucky against each other, and created a legal bat-tle that went to the U.S. Supreme Court.

Perhaps the two families serve as historical icons of conflict, and the history of their feud might illuminate some of the ongoing con-flicts in today's world. The Hatfields lived in West Virginia, on the East side of the Tug Fork of the Big Sandy River; the McCoys lived on the West side in Kentucky. Both dominated by physically large, cruel, aggressive patriarchs, the families began fighting in about 1863. The first dispute involved accusations of hog stealing, and led to a shoot-out that killed a Hatfield.

Not long afterward, a drunken fight at an election celebration ended with the death of another Hatfield. The leader of the Hatfield clan, one "Devil Anse" Anderson Hatfield, had the three McCoys who killed his son rounded up and executed.

Things went from bad to worse, with Hatfields and McCoys raiding each other's farms and engaging in regular shoot-outs. Their battles escalated to include the surrounding communities, and the governments of the two bordering states got involved. The McCoys kidnapped a group of Hatfields and took them to Kentucky for trial. The government of West Virginia demanded their return, claiming Kentucky had no legal right to try kidnapped citizens of a neighboring state. The U.S. Supreme Court decided it had no legal basis to stop the trial; one of the Hatfields went to the gallows, and the other seven went to prison for life.

Eventually the feud had nearly decimated both families, economic development opened up the Appalachian region of America to more civilized governance, and the battles eventually stopped. After many years, the legendary feud passed into history as an archetypal example of escalating conflict. Eventually, the reference to "the Hatfields and the McCoys" survived only as a metaphor for a mindless state of war between two factions.

The Hatfields & McCoys T-shirts, coffee mugs, and other souvenirs advertised on the website, www.hatfieldmccoytradingcompany.com, offer testimony that some conflicts, at least, die of old age.

WHY ARGUE?

Many years ago I came to one of the most useful realizations of my young life, and the decision I made as a result of that realization became one of the most beneficial policies I've ever adopted. I simply decided to stop arguing with people. I didn't decide to stop trying to change their minds, or stop trying to get them to embrace my views or ideas. I just stopped arguing with them.

I finally concluded that I had really never won an argument with another person. Oh, I'd become very skillful at debating, at verbal swordplay, and at putting down the opinions and ideas of others with my quick thinking and sharp tongue. But I eventually had to face what I considered to be the primal truth of poet William Blake's verse:

> *"A man convinced against his will*
> *Is of the same opinion still."*

I realized that, with all of the skills of repartee I'd acquired during my university experience, I only ever succeeded in convincing people to my satisfaction, not theirs. I began to understand that defeating other people in verbal combat very seldom won me anything of real value, unless I considered my personal feelings of triumph as valuable to me. I concluded that every debate, every argument, every incident of win-lose swordplay has a cost as well as a payoff. While the payoff might involve gaining higher scores as a debater in the minds of the onlookers, the costs usually involved animosity, resentment, and desire for revenge.

I began to notice, over a series of arguments with my student friends, that one episode of verbal combat seemed to carry over to the next one. Two people who had clashed on the intellectual battlefield seemed more likely to clash again later. Arguing seemed to become a self-reinforcing habit pattern.

This realization caused me to back up, widen out my mental "zoom lens," and ask myself the key question: "What do I actually want from this situation?" Too often, I realized, I reacted to other people's opinions, especially those expressed strongly or aggressively, like a fish rising to a bait. I felt compelled to answer aggression with aggression; I could not let this obstreperousness go unanswered. I settled for less than I might have.

I began to realize that I could attract others to my points of view, induce them to listen more respectfully to my ideas, and maintain a positive empathy with them by passing up the opportunity to attack their ideas. By listening to them, affirming their entitlement to their views, and inviting them to express themselves more fully, I seemed to accomplish more and more of what I wanted with them. I also found that asking questions rather than making declarative statements often worked better in influencing them to change their minds.

Since then I've often reflected on the line from the ancient verse "The Way of Life," attributed to the Chinese philosopher Lao Tzu:

"The best captain does not plunge headlong
Nor is the best soldier a fellow hot to fight.
The greatest victor wins without the battle. . . ."

CRUCIAL CONVERSATIONS

Trying to avoid bad feelings causes more bad feelings than anything else. Most people find conflict with others, especially on a one-to-one basis, extremely unpleasant. And, except for a small population of highly combative people, most of us will go to considerable lengths to avoid it. We allow misunderstandings to continue without clearing them up, we permit others to take advantage of us or treat us inconsiderately without confronting them about it, and we hold ourselves back from asserting our moral and civil rights for fear that others will become angry with us.

For most of us, this knee-jerk avoidance reaction starts in childhood and never goes away. "Don't make Mom or Dad angry." "Don't make the teacher angry." "Don't make other people mad at you." If we carry it over into the countless social situations we encounter in our adult lives, and we interact with others who do the same, we fall into dishonest patterns of deception, false harmony, and covert warfare.

Conflict expert Dr. Steve Albrecht proposes that we "lower the bar on emotional censorship" and tell others what we think and feel more often. "People can benefit enormously in their lives," he says, "by making effective use of 'crucial conversations' basically clearing the air sooner rather than later. If I believe another person or group of people intends to act in ways that may jeopardize my interests in a situation, I have two main options. I can deal with their behavior covertly—cooking up my own interpretation of their behavior and imputing various disreputable motives to them, and ultimately trying to counter them in some roundabout way rather than confront them. Or, I can hold a 'crucial conversation' with them as soon as I discover any possible cause for concern.

"With option two—the overt course of action—I first let them know of my concerns and offer them the chance to either modify their actions or find some way to accommodate my interests. The earlier this crucial conversation takes place, the more options we'll probably have to work from. If I wait until I have a full-blown conflict going with them, we may have very few appealing options."[1]

Steve Albrecht offers a basic formula, or plan, for deciding whether and how to set up a crucial conversation:

1. Get Clear About the Situation. What do you know about the other party or parties involved? Do you understand their intentions? What evidence do you have that leads you to conclude that they have acted—or intend to act—against your interests? Do you need to have a conversation to clear things up?

2. Define Your Own Interests Clearly. What do you seek from your interactions or relationships with them? What do you seek to protect, preserve, or achieve?

3. Choose an Approach Strategy. Perhaps you can merely start a conversation with the other party, with little animosity involved. Sometimes you just have to express your interests and ask the other party to respect them. In a more delicate situation, you may wish to "telegraph" your concerns to the other party in some low-risk way. A private message, passed through a mutually trusted confidant, can get the other party thinking about the issue in advance of the conversation. You might politely broach the topic in an email, asking for a personal conversation. Choose a method that has the most chance of starting the conversation on a positive, cooperative tone.

4. Conduct the Conversation in a Positive Spirit. Make it a shared search for a mutually acceptable solution. Explain your interests to the

other party and tell how you see your interests as potentially jeopard-
ized. Make sure you fully understand their interests as well. Prepare
for possible hard feelings, defensiveness, or feelings of competitiveness
on the part of the other party.

5. Try for a Clear Outcome. If possible, invite the other party to
agree with you on a statement of principle, a specific point of agreement, or at least a policy that both of you can depend on going
forward. Maybe the meeting only serves to reduce feelings of apprehension or animosity. Or maybe it serves as a starting point for
improving the relationship as time goes on.

Notice that the process has less to do with achieving your goals and
more to do with opening the lines of communication and keeping
the conversation going. Couched in the language of SI, holding a crucial conversation means bringing all your S.P.A.C.E. skills to bear to
defuse a potential conflict and perhaps find ways to eventually meet the
interests of both parties.

Men of Cloth Disagree—Violently

Jerusalem, Israel (AP)—Greek Orthodox and Franciscan priests got into
a fist fight Monday at the Church of the Holy Sepulcher, Christianity's
holiest shrine, after arguing over whether a door in the basilica should
be closed during a procession.

Dozens of people, including several Israeli police officers, were
slightly hurt in the brawl at the shrine, built over the spot where tradition says Jesus was crucified and buried.

Four priests were detained, police spokesman Shmulik Ben-Ruby said.

Custody of the Church of the Holy Sepulcher is shared by several
denominations that jealously guard territory and responsibilities under
a fragile deal hammered out over the last centuries. Any perceived
encroachment on one group's turf can lead to vicious feuds, sometimes lasting hundreds of years.

Monday's fight broke out during a procession of hundreds of Greek Orthodox worshippers commemorating the 4th century pilgrimage by Helena, mother of Emperor Constantine, to Jerusalem. Tradition says that during the trip, Helena found the cross on which Jesus had been crucified.

Church officials, speaking on condition of anonymity, said that at one point, the procession passed a Roman Catholic chapel, and priests from both sides started arguing over whether the door to the chapel should be open or closed.

Club-wielding Israeli riot police broke up the fight, witnesses said. Afterward, the procession continued.

Greek Orthodox priests, dressed in black robes and donning elaborate headdresses, marched out of the church as bells rang loudly. Carrying gold staves and roses, they marched through the church courtyard and down a narrow stone alley as Greek Orthodox Christians clapped and cheered.

In 2003, Israeli police threatened to limit the number of worshippers allowed to attend an Easter ceremony if the denominations did not agree on who would lead the ceremony. Police brokered a last-minute deal, and the ceremony passed peacefully.

But a year earlier, the Greek patriarch and Armenian clergyman designated to enter the tomb exchanged blows after a dispute over who would be first to exit the chamber.[2]

ADDED VALUE NEGOTIATING

Some years ago I became interested in how conflict can affect the business world, and in particular how business people attempt to settle differences and come to agreement. I discovered certain prevailing doctrines—at least in the Western business world—that seemed to dominate and limit the process of negotiating.

Business educators—trainers, company training or personnel departments, publishers, seminar companies, conference organizers—have for several decades offered formal training courses dealing with negotiating. Reporters and members of the business press have typically saluted and praised people whom they've described as "tough negotiators." A tough negotiator presumably exacts something of high value for his or her "side," preferably while "giving up" very little in return. The language of negotiating, as used in business and the business press, leans heavily toward winning and losing; getting without giving; and gaining the upper hand.

The ideologies that seem to underlie these various approaches to negotiation span a spectrum from a sort of life-or-death combat, to a more cooperative view that accepts the idea that the other party may indeed receive value from the deal. The "pure win-lose" school speaks contemptuously of "making concessions," advises "exploiting your opponent's weaknesses," using various "negotiating ploys," and establishing a "power differential." The language implies that one party succeeds only at the expense of the other party.

The counter-view to the pure win-lose ideology goes by the admirable name of "win-win" negotiating. Some proponents do seem to advocate methods for helping both sides achieve their ends. Many others, however, seem to advocate a kind of "disguised win-lose" approach. Dressed in the language of cooperation, it often conveys the premise of "Yes, I want to see you win, so long as I win more than you." In some cases, the manipulative methods and ploys still signal the same mindset of winning and losing. At the extreme, the only difference is that its advocates do not promote aggressive, pure-power tactics; instead, they advise us to outwit the opponent.

A fairly comprehensive review of business articles, books, seminars, and conference programs shows a lingering bias toward an adversarial concept of negotiating. Further, very few proponents of either pure win-lose or genuine win-win negotiating have conceived of negotiating as a systematic process. Most schools of thought proceed from the same starting point: one side or the other presents a demand, an offer, or a proposal. This, presumably, marks the actual beginning of the negotiating process. Or one might advise us to "study your adversary" before making the opening offer or demand; perhaps that qualifies as the true first step in their thinking process.

Most of the currently accepted and popular negotiating methods characterize the process as a battle of wits. Consequently, it seems, the opening move depends entirely on the skillful negotiator's assessment of the situation. He or she has to meet the challenge of inventing a strategy for steering the other side toward a set of concessions they presumably would not otherwise make.

Some years ago, as I was reviewing the currently accepted ideologies and approaches to negotiating, it struck me that the lack of a methodical, stepwise process, accepted by all parties, imposed a severe handicap on the progress toward a solution. I began to experiment with a methodology that overturned several of the most basic premises of the traditional negotiating process, such as:

- The negotiation begins when one side presents an offer or a demand.
- The negotiation consists of a pushing contest (or a tug of war) around the first offer or demand; each side seeks to move the other away from the starting point.
- One must conceal one's needs, interests, and intentions from the other side; transparency weakens one's position while knowledge of the other side's needs creates an advantage.
- One must evaluate all potential deals from the point of view of relative advantage, that is, the extent to which the deal offers greater value for one's own side than for the other side.

However fundamental, and even sacred, these four assumptions may seem, they do not actually offer a very effective basis for achieving what we want.

The fundamental irony of power-based negotiating lies in the simple principle of *negative reciprocity*, often overlooked in the articles, books, and seminars that profess the "testosterone" model of negotiating. The principle of negative reciprocity tells us that, if both we and our negotiating counterparts approach the process with the intention of maximizing the value we receive and minimizing the value received by the other side, we will probably both fail at the first objective and both succeed at the second objective. Presuming that both sides have the same skills as "tough negotiators," both will succeed in depriving the other side of value.

This ironic truth makes the traditional power-based negotiation a *reductive* process rather than an *additive* process. And by overturning the four basic articles of faith just enumerated, we can actually come away from a negotiation with more than we might have originally hoped for.

Five Steps to "Yes"

After concluding that the conventional approaches would almost always yield suboptimal results, I began to experiment with a phased negotiating procedure that contradicted the entire paradigm as commonly accepted. After using it for several important negotiating experiences in my own business and personal life, I concluded that it showed merit and deserved further development.

Instead of starting with a demand, offer, or proposal, this unorthodox process began with a *dialog.* Violating both the first and second rules at a single stroke, the first step in the process involved disclosing one's interests to the other party and inviting the other party to share theirs.

I found that disclosing my interests to the other party did not seem to put me at any particular disadvantage; indeed, it tended to quickly bring the negotiating process to a focus. I also found that, more often than not, the person or people on the other side of the deal shared their own interests—at least to a degree one would not expect from using the conventional approach. After all, it seemed, how can I offer the other party something of value to them if I have no understanding of their interests?

This counterintuitive approach evolved to a very simple definition of a "deal," namely *an exchange of value that serves the respective interests of all parties involved.* To negotiate, then, means to search cooperatively for a workable deal. This precept immediately requires that we define the elements of value that can possibly go into the deal, and then find a way to combine them into a package that may appeal to both—or multiple—parties. And, before we can define the value elements involved, we have to first define the respective interests that those elements might possibly serve—ergo the first step of defining interests.

Another key part of this counterintuitive procedure involved violating the first rule in a second way. Not only does this added value negotiating method not *begin* with an offer or proposal, it calls for presenting the other party with *multiple* candidate "deal packages"—at least three of them—any one of which can meet one's own interests. However, the deal package stage comes *after* a careful identification of respective interests and a careful inventory of the elements of value that might serve those interests. Only then does it make sense to design several alternative combinations of value—each with a different relative emphasis—and then systematically evaluate them for mutual appeal.

The last element of the added value process requires evaluating the possible deals with respect to their total prospective value for *you*, regardless of the extent to which they create value for the other party.

I eventually formalized this unorthodox approach into a five-step negotiating procedure, based on building and maintaining empathy with the other party. The *added value negotiating* process follows five general steps, or phases:

1. Identify Interests. It helps for both parties to explain what they hope to get from the negotiation, not in terms of the provisions of any actual deal, but in terms of their own individual aspirations, needs, or goals. If the other party has little or no experience in this kind of exchange, you might find it appropriate to guide the process by stating your own interests first, and then interviewing them to help them articulate their interests. It often helps to express the two parties' interests in some kind of document, such as a letter or memo that can serve as the starting point and a reference for evaluating various possible deals.

2. Define the Elements of Value. Before either party proposes any kind of deal, both parties should enter into a "wideband" thinking process, to identify a range of possible elements of value that might go into a deal. This can include money, property, actions—what each party will agree to do, or refrain from doing—rights, and risks. The more creatively both parties consider the possibilities at this stage, the richer they can make the eventual deal.

3. Design Multiple (at Least Three) "Deal Packages." In a cooperative process, both parties confer to consider the various elements of value in light of their respective interests, and they use a "Chinese menu" approach to combine the elements of value into various alternative arrangements. By balancing the elements of value in terms of the respective interests, they come up with several different configurations, each with a different emphasis and a different set of tradeoffs. Each deal package should balance the relative interests of the two parties in its own particular way. If the other party has no experience with this kind of process, you can design three to five alternative deal packages, each balanced in a different way, and propose that the other party choose any of them. This approach tends to disarm the aggressive or suspicious party, because they understand that all of the optional deal packages meet your needs—just in different ways—and that your willingness to permit them to choose the best deal for their side signals your confidence in the balanced value.

4. Cooperatively Select the Best Deal. Selecting the best deal might just amount to checking to see if one or more of them gets a "yes" from both parties. If not, they can try various modifications, or simply go back to the drawing board and come up with several more designs. Once a deal emerges that suits both parties, it becomes the basis for the final settlement.

5. Refine and Perfect the Selected Deal. Often, one of the deal packages will appeal to both parties, and will need little or no refinement. Nevertheless, both parties can review the preferred solution and try to think of "extras" that they might contribute—elements of value that can enrich the value for one or both parties. This stage also includes pinning down the who, what, how, and when factors—the details that become part of the final agreement.

My favorite practical application of this added value negotiation method involved negotiating the contract to write a book about the method. I ignored the publisher's "standard contract" and invited them to consider various combinations of value that might meet their interests and mine. After completing the negotiating process, the editor of the firm acknowledged that they had gotten a better deal than they expected, even though they had granted a better deal than they usually agreed to.

These simple strategies—not arguing, holding crucial conversations, and conducting value-added negotiations—apply social intelligence concepts to age-old questions of human conflict. They are not the whole answer, or even a large part of the answer, to how human beings might get along better, but when coupled with a conscious effort to develop our S.P.A.C.E. skills they can surely move us a step or two forward.

Notes

1. Kerry Patterson, Joseph Grenny, Ron McMillan, and Al Switzer also use the term "crucial conversations" to refer to interpersonal exchanges at work or at home that we dread having but know we cannot avoid. Their book *Crucial Conversations: Tools for Talking When the Stakes Are High* (New York: McGraw-Hill, 2002) offers more techniques geared toward getting people to lower their defenses, creating mutual respect and understanding, increasing emotional safety, and encouraging freedom of expression based on their DialogueSmart training seminars.

2. News item posted on CNN website CNN.com, Monday, September 27, 2004.

EPILOGUE

SI and the Next Generation: Who's Teaching Our Kids?

> "We are discreet sheep; we wait to see how the
> drove is going, and then we go with the drove. We
> have two opinions: one private, which we are afraid
> to express; and another one—the one we use—
> which we force ourselves to wear to please Mrs.
> Grundy, until habit makes us comfortable in it, and
> the custom of defending it presently makes us love
> it, adore it, and forget how pitifully we come by it."
> —Mark Twain

CAN WE RAISE a generation of socially intelligent kids? What happens if we don't? Is it too late to do anything about the psychological kidnapping of our children by manipulative commercial messages and the cynical, narcissistic values projected by the popular entertainment media? Have we already lost the war to save our children from the worst of the modern American popular culture? And do problems with our media create problems with our culture?

This chapter is unapologetically "political" in its orientation—it's admittedly written with an attitude. It projects certain value judgments about the current state of the American culture at the time of this writing, and it advances certain opinions I have about "the way things ought to be." I imagine that this view will resonate with a large number of readers—possibly most—but I recognize that some may interpret it as anti-business and even "un-American." I ask the indulgence of those readers in other countries and cultures, and hope they will perceive it as something more than the customary narcissistic American self-preoccupation. Social pathologies that seem distinctively American have a way of migrating to other countries and cultures eventually.

We're living in strange times, and I believe we need to be looking around us to see what's going on, and to decide—individually and collectively—if that's what we want to have going on.

OUR CHILDREN ARE NOT OUR CHILDREN

At present, the concept of social intelligence is neither widely accepted nor authentically modeled in the current American popular culture. Ours is fast becoming an amnesic, now-oriented, temporary, throw-away society, based on the McDonaldization of ideas and behaviors; not just, "Do you want fries with that?" but an "I want mine—*now*" preoccupation and a chronic appetite for stimulation.

Faster is better; and if it breaks, just throw it away and buy another one. Whether it's people griping about slow Internet speeds, why they can't get their cell phones (with video cameras inside) to work, or their toss-away marriages (now known as "starter marriages"), the current social and cultural climate in America is not exactly the envy of the rest of the so-called modern world. The French philosopher and statesman Georges Clemenceau remarked many years ago: "America is the only nation in history that has gone from barbarism to decadence without the usual interval of civilization." On some days, I feel I'd have a difficult time debating the point with Clemenceau if he were alive today.

If we're to have any hope of launching a next generation of citizens into the world equipped with anything like a sense of social and cultural awareness; a sense of community; a sense of connection to the extended community of humans around the world; and a sense of altruism and service, we have a lot to overcome in the way they're currently being programmed for adulthood.

We modern human beings have become a species both blessed and cursed with an *exo-consciousness*: a shared environment of stimulating images, icons, ideas, ideologies, and impulses. Most of us are soaked, almost constantly, in the messages of the popular culture, which has now fully evolved to a commercial model of continuous amusement. The relentless march of commercial images and image technology is steadily converting one shared cultural experience after another to an entertainment format. Wars, famine, tragedy, terrorism, and human suffering are now the raw material for media products. Murder trials create overnight heroes, anti-heroes, and villains. "Reality" TV shows celebrate the most crass forms of human behavior. TV sitcoms have been forced to abandon all traces of subtlety as they desperately compete for viewers with ever more explicitly sexual shows. Cable and network news channels have become arenas for political combat instead of political thought, ultimately because personal conflict is inherently more entertaining than the contest of ideas. Even education must now be an entertaining experience.

Beat poet Allen Ginsberg commented two decades ago, "We're in science fiction now, man; whoever controls the images—the media—controls the culture." He was probably right. Shakespeare said, "All the world's a stage." This statement is now true—literally.

Many well-meaning and diligent parents like to delude themselves into believing that they "raise" their children—that they impart important values, attitudes, and standards of behavior by what they say and do. But, that parental influence competes constantly with other sources of guidance, and in some cases parental influence is the weakest of the influences. For most children, the set of influences consists of:

- Their parents (if they come from intact families)
- Their peers (other kids, typically their ages and older)
- Teachers, schools, and other authority figures outside the home

- Media figures—movie stars, TV characters, rock stars, and media delinquents
- Miscellaneous others—family members, neighbors, religious figures, and others

Increasingly we see that peer influence, as modulated by the influence of entertainment idols, popular music, TV shows, and movies, outweighs parental influence after the age range of about seven to ten years. Until that time, parents can have a significant influence on shaping a child's approach to life; after that, other influences tend to have a much stronger effect.

If we hope to provide children with positive influences and socially intelligent life strategies, we need to begin early, to diligently counteract and contradict the influence of the narcissistic messages that bombard them every day. One good starting point, particularly with children aged seven and above, is to teach them how television works. That means we have to understand for ourselves how it works. Let's begin with what many people still euphemistically call "the news."

THE (ONLY) TEN BASIC NEWS STORIES

Although many articles, books, and documentaries portray the news industry as cynical and committed to pandering to the lowest common intellectual denominator, few have noticed the curious irony that lies at the very core of the news paradigm. This irony may offer a better explanation of why the news is the way it is than any speculations about the ethics and motives of the news producers.

The curious irony is that, in this so-called Third-Wave age of information, as futurist Alvin Toffler named it, the commercial news process is actually imprisoned in a Second-Wave model, that is, an industrial model of news *production.*

Any subject expert who is regularly called on to appear in news interviews (such as I am, as a business consultant) soon discerns the unmistakable factory-like hum of the news operation. The process by which video editors interweave the live performances of news readers, the cutaways to remote units at the crime scene or the lawn of the White House, the obligatory "establishing shot" of the professor walking across campus to the laboratory, and the stock footage (the Rodney King beating, the Clinton-Lewinsky hug, or the lab technician testing the DNA samples) pays little homage to Toffler's Third Wave concept. Instead, it's straight out of the Industrial Age.

Probably the closest product analogy to the news is a fast-food operation, something like making hamburgers or baking pastries. Each little piece of news rolls down the line like a tidy, production-controlled PopTart® (with due respect to Kellogg's popular product): flavored, sweetened, glazed, and baked to perfection. Whatever the sacrifice in depth or insight, the fast-food news model is undeniably efficient and remarkably cost-effective.

What makes any industrial production process efficient and cost-effective is the use of *standard products*. In the news industry this translates into a few well-proven, reliable story structures. A basic inventory of about ten standard news stories makes the process of baking the news easy to manage.

One can switch on virtually any news show, from CNN's breaking news, to financial news, to the local stations, and see a mix of these ten figurative PopTarts rolling by in a varied sequence. This standard-product paradigm probably does more to explain the universal sameness of news programming, virtually around the world, than any supposed ideology or diabolical intent.

Perhaps those who criticize news producers as being cynical, exploitive, and shallow are right, but for the wrong reasons. They may be less the conscious purveyors of intellectual pabulum than they are helpless prisoners locked in their own PopTart factories. It's hard to give up such a comfortable way of doing business, and it's easy to rationalize: "People like our PopTarts."

What are the ten basic PopTarts—er, sorry, new stories? Just about anybody can tick them off, with a bit of thought. Here they are, for the record.

1. Shock and Horror.   As they say in the news biz, "If it bleeds, it leads." Murders, especially multiples, acts of unusual violence, brutality, or sadism, shark attacks, and the carnage left by explosions are sure-fire grabbers for the attention of a nation of gawkers.

2. Tragedy.   Preferably enhanced by the horror factor, as in a suicide bombing, the Tragedy category includes stories like natural disasters, airplane crashes, and hotel fires. The more lives that are wrecked, the better the material for the mike-in-the-face victim vignettes and the human interest stories about how the brave victims are "trying to put the pieces of their lives back together."

3. Hot Sex.   This is a plentiful product line, virtually addictive for news producers. It ranges from the intimate lives of celebrities to "socially responsible" stories about teen-agers having oral sex. It also includes derivative pornography, such as stories about the exotic dancers at the local club who are fighting to unionize. The story wouldn't be complete without the drop-in shots of pole dancers and interviews with busty entertainers.

4. Scandal.   Best teamed up with the Hot Sex story, for double effect, the misdeeds of government officials, politicians, and corporate bigwigs allow us all to cluck our tongues and enjoy seeing the sinners embarrassed and properly chastised.

5. The Fall of the Mighty.   Watching powerful people get knocked off their high horses has a special appeal, and could almost qualify as a national pastime. Combine a Fall of the Mighty story with good

Scandal, add a great Hot Sex story, and you have a grand slam. A head of state gets thrown out for having sex with the wrong person and trying to cover it up: "It don't get no better'n 'at."

6. Conflict. Just as people will always stop and gawk at a fist-fight, whether in the schoolyard or in Taiwan's Parliament chamber, conflict and the imminence of physical violence will always arrest attention. War is probably the most reliable news product of all; it always has been. In a polite society, violence is replaced by conflict between political parties, or among advocacy groups pursuing various social agendas. News producers will nearly always introduce an element of conflict into a story if they can figure out how. It's kind of a basic ingredient, like sugar or salt.

7.Worry. Journalists seem to suffer from a constitutional aversion to being perceived as naïve or overly optimistic. As a result, they seem compelled to find the dark side of just about any issue; the cynical motive, the reasons why it's too good to be true, and the looming possibility that something could go seriously wrong. Some economists have contended that more recessions are caused by journalists warning about recessions than by the business cycle. It is their sworn duty to help us worry about things like the possibility that the earth might collide with an asteroid within the next 1,000 years.

8. Voyeurism. The bizarre, the perverted, the weird, the sick and twisted, and the deviant, all make good entertainment for gawkers. The suicide jumper, the hostage standoff, the execution, and the demented old lady living with the 300 cats, all provide an element of curiosity or excitement that many people apparently need in their lives. In some cases, as with TV shows in the "bubba" genre, many people seem to enjoy peering at other people whose lives are clearly more screwed up than their own.

9. Dilemmas. News producers love stories about conflicts that can't be solved. The abortion issue, cloning, capital punishment, euthanasia, and the right to die, all arouse strong feelings and polarize opinion. The conflict ingredient comes naturally, and "balanced coverage" is easy to claim. The frequent use of two-sided moral Dilemma stories helps perpetuate the myth of "objective journalism."

10. Gee-Whiz Stories. And finally, we need a change-of-pace product, so we won't get the idea they're constantly pandering to our darker natures. This can take many forms, but usually has to be a novelty segment, a curiosity piece, or a heart-warmer. The local spelling bee, the dog that rescues the baby, astronauts in space, the Olympic athlete's mom crying tears of joy, and the President's hemorrhoids all help to round out the product offering and let us know that news people are actually regular folks like the rest of us.

So before we get too pious about the quality of journalism, let's remember that all products have to find receptor sites on the neurons of their intended customers, or they won't survive in the marketplace. Just as fast-food products find a strong and reliable response, fast news products arrest the attention of enough people long enough to sell them the fast food. Those of us who perceive the news as a mediocre type of information product aren't really the intended customers—for the news or the fast food.[1]

ANXIETY DRIVES ATTENTION

A major part of the design strategy in presenting "news" is finding a way to induce anxiety in the viewer. The operating principle of the news producer seems to be: "If I can make you uncertain and insecure—about your kids, your house, your job, your food, or your safety (killer bees, fire ants, the flu, SARS, AIDS, Mad Cow Disease, or West Nile Virus)—I can capture and hold your attention."

Case in point: after one particularly difficult period of monitoring terrorist "chatter," the U.S. Department of Homeland Security raised its color-coded "Threat Advisory Level" from "Elevated" (Yellow) to "High" (Orange). The American news media took a few snippets of information from the DHS and suggested that (overseas) terrorist groups might be planning to introduce some sort of biological weapon into the air in some as-yet-unknown U.S. cities. These dangerous airborne agents, the DHS spokespeople suggested, could be thwarted by using plastic sheeting and duct tape to cover the windows and air ducts for homes and business facilities.

As this story took on life, building supply stores actually saw a run on plastic sheeting and duct tape. Hardware stores that had plenty of these two items began running out. The story reached its peak when newspapers ran a photo of a homeowner in Bend, Oregon (population 57,000 give or take), on a ladder, taping plastic sheeting over the windows of his house.

Preparation is always a good thing, "forewarned is forearmed" is not a bad motto, and it's always useful to have plastic sheeting and tape around the house. But realistically, would a chemical attack on the United States start by targeting Bubba's house up there in Bend, Oregon?

Not everyone is equipped to realistically evaluate the kinds of anxiety-producing stories carried on TV news. Whenever my eleven-year-old granddaughter saw a frightening, violent TV news story involving a tragedy in some unfamiliar part of the world, she would often ask my son (her father), "How close is that to us?" What she was asking was not the geographic distance in miles, but the threat proximity—whether or not she should be *worried* because that event is dangerously close to her and her family.

Children who see a dead body on TV, shown as part of a news story in the Middle East, Miami, or Malta, may not have the maturity nor the presence of mind to see that death is being portrayed as an abstract concept—something that happened far away from their homes and/or has absolutely nothing to do with the quality or safety of their lives at that moment. Without the support of a significant adult to help the child understand the images he or she is seeing, the child cannot form an effective perspective for interpreting its meaning. Combined with the thousands of other disturbing scenes children see in watching TV an average of three to four hours per day, this flow of decontextualized imagery soaks into the child's brain and nervous system, and can form the foundation for a fearful view of life.

Ironically, the depersonalization of the information experience may eventually lead to the disappearance of the famous news persons themselves. Some digital technology experts are already speculating that, within five to ten years, animation techniques may become so advanced that the news reader you see on your TV screen will be an *avatar,* a synthetic character indistinguishable from a real human being. He or she won't have to be paid a multi-million-dollar salary, will never get sick, won't throw temper tantrums, and won't get caught in a career-destroying sex scandal. Some of the super-geeks even predict that, with "video on demand," you'll be able to choose your own avatar, and he or she will be different from the one streaming into your neighbor's TV, or even the one in your kids' rooms. You could have your favorite rock-star, Hollywood heart-throb, or even your mother delivering your news. Ah, progress!

BREAKING THE ADDICTION
TO TELEVISION

By commonly accepted definitions of addiction, the experience of watching television on a regular basis is addictive—not in the figurative, joking sense, but in a real, literal, clinical sense. The clinical definition of an addiction is an unhealthy attachment to something and the inability to function without it. If you have a television in your home and it's hooked up to receive commercial broadcasts or cable channels, it's almost a dead certainty that you disagree with the first sentence of this paragraph. It's also a near dead certainty that you're clinically addicted to watching television. Denial is part of addiction.

Brain wave studies prove conclusively that the experience of watching television for more than three to five minutes induces a brain state that is virtually indistinguishable from hypnosis: "alpha" brainwave activity, a semi-stupor, diminished capacity for information processing, diminished capacity for abstract or critical thought, and a high level of suggestibility. If you want to test this theory for yourself, try the following experiment: watch a typical popular TV show while standing up. Resist the urge to sit on the edge of the couch, put one foot up on the coffee table, or even lean against a wall. Stand flat-footed. While standing, your nervous system will remain active as your brain and muscles interact to maintain your balance. You'll soon discover two things: (1) a nagging desire to sit down (and slip back into the trance); and (2) the show itself will seem remarkably inane. *Television programming is specifically designed for the trance state.*

If you want to prove to yourself that you're addicted to TV—or evaluate your claim that you're not—here's a simple test: leave the television in your home turned off for one full week. I'll bet you can't do it. Right now, you're probably saying to yourself, "I could probably do it; I just don't particularly want to." Or, "There are some really good programs on; I don't want to give them up just to prove I'm not hooked." This is the ironic paradox: the only way to prove you can go for one week without watching television is to go for one week without watching television (does it sound like I'm taunting you?).

You see, I was addicted to television for many years, just as hundreds of millions of people now are. I suddenly broke my addiction in a single memorable event. I banished commercial television from my house several years ago; it's one of the most important and most rewarding decisions of my life. I was sitting in my living room one evening, channel surfing as I had done on many other evenings. I'd often noted that several hours would slip by as I flipped through the channels, seldom finding anything really interesting or worthwhile, but seemingly unable to just switch off the set and do something else.

On this particular evening I was emotionally raped: as I sat in my TV-induced stupor, the host of a variety show, one Maury Povich, cued a scene that portrayed an athlete getting injured, in the most shockingly graphic, horrifying way imaginable. Personally distressed and offended beyond belief, I snapped out of the TV trance. I became so angry at the injustice and insensitivity of presenting this man's unbearable suffering as a form of mass entertainment—Povich showed the same clip several times—that I switched off the TV set, unplugged it, and carried it out to my car. The next day I gave it to one of my staff members and never saw it again. I canceled my cable TV subscription and was thankful that only two local stations could even be received at my house.

I began to spend my evenings differently—reading, practicing the guitar, working on various projects I'd been putting off, and going out more often with friends. I began to notice that my general state of mind became brighter, more cheerful, and more open to new experience. I felt like I had cleansed my brain somehow, flushing out the accumulated pollution. Later, I brought some studio-grade video equipment from my office to my home and began to watch classic movies and comedies on videotape and later in DVD format.

If someone I meet discovers in conversation that I don't watch broadcast TV (I usually don't volunteer it), the first question is usually, "Well, how do you keep up with what's happening in the world?" My usual answer is "Are you assuming that TV programs represent what's happening in the world?" The second question is usually "But what about the major events? What if something really big happens?" My answer is usually, "Most of my friends know I don't have a TV. If something really big happens, somebody is sure to call me."

Of course, this is only one man's point of view. But since this is my book, I'll take this opportunity to tout the idea, in case a few readers might be motivated to kick the TV habit.

Oh, by the way: Thank you, Maury Povich. Much obliged.

THE BUYING OF OUR BABIES

In her book about the marketing of the consumer culture to children, *Born to Buy: The Commercialized Child and the New Consumer Culture,*[2] author Juliet B. Schor makes some blunt and bold claims: a typical ten-year-old has already memorized 400 brands and can identify 300 logos; the more a young child is submerged in the consumer culture (mostly through TV commercials, magazine ads, and product giveaways), the more likely he or she is to suffer from emotional or psychological problems. Her book features a survey of 300 kids, ages ten to thirteen, and it drew a correlation between kids who were firmly attached to consumerism, as showing more symptoms of depression, anxiety, and similar problems.

Her point is that the non-stop commercial advertising message aimed at our children says one thing: "You gotta buy this if you wanna be cool, stylish, or not be seen as totally lame and out of it."

The effect of brand advertising is that many children find their self-esteem tied to their ownership of prized brands, expensive clothing, and accessories (some ten-year-olds are equipped with cell phones that have more features than their parents' models). Since the commercialized popular culture never stops telling kids what to buy, what to wear, and how and where to spend their money, not having the "It" item of the moment in their homes or backpacks can cause an ego crisis for these impressionable and immature consumers.

Perhaps this explains how children in poorer neighborhoods can beg and whine until one of their underpaid parents shells out $130 for basketball shoes (which they soon outgrow). Perhaps this explains how Ronald McDonald and Mickey Mouse are more recognizable to kids in America than any current or former U.S. President. And perhaps this explains why most American kids who couldn't find Iraq on a world map for a cash prize can recite the lyrics, word-for-word, from the latest chart-topping songs.

Maybe a parent or caregiver who wants to help his or her child develop into a socially intelligent teenager needs to give the kid more doses of Vitamin N (as in "NO"). How about less economic retreat ("All right, already! I'll give you the money if you stop whining and leave me alone!") and more standing up for parental privilege, as in "No, I'm not buying that for you," or "No, you can't have my money to buy the expensive, poorly made clothes that you say every other child you know already owns," or "No, because I said so, and because I'm the adult and you're the child."

Ads Are Everywhere

Ubiquitous advertising is a trend that began a decade or two ago, and which is steadily gathering momentum. The only limiting factor is the ability of ad designers to find new ways to insert them into our consciousness.

Product placement is a strong and growing trend, in which commercial products are shown at strategic moments in movies and TV shows, presumably as natural elements of the cultural milieu for the story. The firm making the product pays part of the production costs of the show. It's a win-win deal all around, except for the viewers, who may have thought they'd already ponied up the cost of the production, either buying theater tickets or sitting still for the other commercials.

On the quintessentially tasteless show "The Apprentice," built around financial mogul Donald Trump, would-be apprentices had to design a new toy for Mattel and launch a new variant of Crest toothpaste. Both Mattel and Procter & Gamble saw sales increments immediately connected with the shows. The practice has become so common that watchdog groups have demanded that the U.S. Federal Trade Commission require producers to clearly identify the placements as commercial messages.

Another enterprising firm installs video screens in the elevators of high-rise buildings, charging advertisers by the second to impress their messages on defenseless passengers. The "elevator speech" on steroids, perhaps.

Not to be outdone for intrusiveness, one firm has invented the WizMark, to play audio commercials in men's restrooms. The hockey-puck-sized device sits in the bowl of a stand-up urinal and activates in the presence of a certain—er—fluid.

VIDEO GAMES: THE NEW SANDLOT

A Microsoft video game titled "Halo 2" sold $125 million worth on its first day of release in November 2004. That's about 2.38 million units, according to the people who follow these things. Brokerage analysts who study the billion-dollar video game industry estimated sales of $350 million in the three months following the release.

By comparison, the most successful first-day movie release in history (as of the date of this writing) was for *Spiderman 2,* which took in a paltry $116 million in ticket sales. (Keep in mind that the Gross Domestic Product and Gross National Product rates for many third-world countries won't break $100 million in a good year; American media firms can do it with one product and a lot of marketing clout.)

In their 2004 book, *Got Game: How the Gamer Generation Is Reshaping Business Forever,* authors John Beck and Mitchell Wade claim that some 90 million people make up the Echo Boomers or "Gamer Generation."[3] In their survey of 2,500 of these enthusiasts (who see video games as a primary form of entertainment and a focal point in their lives), Beck and Wade argue, among other conclusions, that video games actually make kids smarter. Further, all those ways to play outside in the old days—running, climbing trees, riding bikes, throwing a ball—are not necessary, once you have your good intellectually stimulating friends: the computer screen, the game disk, and the joy stick.

Speaking in November 2004 to *USA Today* Technology Editor Kevin Maney, Wade said (perhaps with a straight face), "Kids don't play sandlot ball the way we did or run through the woods. Everything they do is structured. This is a replacement for that unstructured time, and it's a lot more intellectually stimulating."

While we're marveling at all that intellectual stimulation our kids get, let's keep in mind that the best-selling violent video game series of all time (as of this writing), "Grand Theft Auto," features ways for gamers to initiate carjackings, shoot police officers, and murder prostitutes, scoring points for each "fun" act. (Not to be confused with sister product "Grand Theft Auto: Vice City," another game titled "GTA: San Andreas" was named the worst and most violent video game of 2004 by the family values watchdog group, the National Institute on Media and the Family.) Presumably, this is progress. And it beats playing ball or swimming?

Another popular game allowed kids to re-enact the assassination of President John F. Kennedy, playing the part of the shooter Lee Harvey Oswald, and competing for points by trying to kill the President in the shortest possible time. The game's promoters helpfully pointed out that it might get kids interested in history.

Video games aren't bad per se, and there is no prima facia evidence that they can turn every kid who plays one into a killer. However, they're not as harmless as they appear. The violent imagery in many of the martial arts, combat, war, flight, and sword-and-fantasy games is so strikingly realistic that the U.S. Armed Forces use some of the more sophisticated games to teach combat soldiers to fight in ultra-modern simulators.

It's not the video games alone; it's what the exposure to non-stop violence does, over and over, for the many hundreds (or even thousands) of hours some kids play and play and play these games. Some critics call it a form of violent "brainwashing"; others (who often make money off these products) refer to it as "entertainment."

One of the lone voices in the anti-violent video game war is David Grossman, a retired U.S. Army Lieutenant Colonel and Ranger, who teaches at the University of Arkansas and lectures internationally on the social impacts of violent video games. Grossman, an energetic professional speaker and a thoughtful, passionate former soldier, spends much of his time on the road, teaching police officers, school administrators, parents, juvenile justice administrators, and healthcare and mental health professionals about the rising tide of youth violence in the U.S. He blames much of this rise on violent video games.

Col. Grossman's website, www.killology.com, provides research and information on how societies teach soldiers, police officers, and even children, to kill. His take on violent video games is less than polite. He refers to them as "murder simulators" because he believes they very effectively desensitize children to violence and bloodshed.

Grossman conducted several experiments that indicated that video games make excellent firearms instructors. Starting with adults who had no firearms training whatsoever, he had them shoot a pistol at a gun range. As expected, they all shot poorly and all over the target, if they hit it at all. He then asked teenagers with no firearms experience, but hours of video game joystick and plastic pistol "trigger time" under their belts, to shoot a real gun at the same range. Their results were significantly better than the adults' and nearly as good as the people who practiced there regularly.

Grossman then had the adults practice at home with video games featuring shooting skills and then he retested them back at the range. You guessed it: they shot much better the second time, even with no real practice at the real range.

Grossman makes no claims that violent video games turn the average kid into a homicidal maniac. He acknowledges that the issue is much more complex than simply analyzing the exposure to one medium. But he does take significant issue with the creators and distributors of these games for their desensitizing abilities, believing that heavy exposure to these kinds of violent games (as opposed to golf, skiing, or mountain biking games, for example) makes it much easier for children to stop making the all-important dividing connection between real violence and pretend violence.

In his lectures, Grossman cites brain scans conducted by the Indiana University School of Medicine, which suggest that exposure to violent media may affect the brains of children with aggressive tendencies differently than the brains of non-aggressive children.

The most well-meaning, diligent parents often have no idea how to help children cope with the overwhelming diet of synthetic violence they get in their lives as media consumers. In fact, some of them even unwittingly aggravate the effects of violent media images.

Case in point: March 2001 was a particularly violent period for San Diego, California, schools. Within a seventeen-day span, two different high school students brought guns to two separate campuses and opened fire, killing two kids and wounding seventeen. Following these incidents, a colleague told me he and his wife had sat their kids down and "talked about what had happened at those schools."

Since his children ranged in age from five to eight, the effect was to confuse and terrify them. "Now the children are afraid to go to school," he lamented. These well-meaning parents had suddenly injected fear and doubt into their children's worlds. Was it necessary to speak about these incidents to kids who never knew they took place? Of course not. The choice to discuss this issue is age-appropriate. Are they mature enough to cope with this information? Is it relevant to their own situation? Or is this an example of parents lacking the social intelligence to say to each other, "Let's discuss this with them, gently and without scaring them, only if they bring it up."

TEACHERS, PARENTS, OR NEITHER?

Here's a great conversation-starter (or ender) at a party: why not liven up your next social gathering by suggesting to the parents in the room that *their parenting skills have very little long-term impact on the development of their children.* Say, "Your parenting style is one of the least significant factors in the way your kids turn out. It's really more about the influence of their peers than anything you do," and then see what happens. The responses will probably range from curiosity to outrage to exits.

As evidence of how much consternation this issue can create, consider that in her 1998 book, *The Nurture Assumption*,[4] author and researcher Judith Rich Harris said just that, in essence: "How parents raise their child has no long-term effects on the child's personality, intelligence, or mental health."

Harris, whose ideas on this topic are, not surprisingly, less than popular with many vocal parents, said this in a response to a scathing review of her book in the December 16, 2002, edition of *The New Yorker:*

> "Scientists have shown, for example, that parents have little or no ability (other than by passing on their genes) to make their children into churchgoers, though they can influence which church they will go to, if they do go to one. Parents can try to produce bilingual children by using a foreign language at home, but unless the children have a chance to use that language outside the home, they will usually fail. Children end up with the language and accent of their peers, not of their parents. Parents can influence some things but not others. The effects of parenting, and of the environment more generally, do not have to remain a mystery or a dogma—they can be investigated empirically. The results, however, may dismay those who have their own personal vision of how the human mind ought to work."[5]

Although what she seems to be describing (you have little to no influence) is far from a popular perspective, Harris is merely pointing out what we already know about subcultures (to which all children belong): they create their own rules, borders, and behaviors, and if you want to stay in that group, you adapt to those mores and values.

Harris' theory is similar to that discussed in Chapter 2: the behaviors of human beings (children included) exist in a context, influenced by whatever situation they find themselves in. Harris argues that, despite your best intentions for your kids (music lessons, soccer, Boy Scouts, Girl Scouts, limited Internet access, Sunday school, etc.) it's really more about how they interact with their peers than with you. By her logic, your best contribution to their healthy growth and development is to help them *pick appropriate friends.*

Her logic is hard to refute. At best, if you and your spouse or partner work full-time and your child goes to school, that is, you aren't with them all day because you can afford to stay home and home-school them, then they will be out of the range of your influence for the majority of the day. In many two-income families, it's not uncommon for one parent or partner to leave for his or her work even before the child is out of bed, sometimes not to return until the child is ready for bed again.

Whether you accept Harris' theory or not, all is still not lost. You can have some control over the growth and development of your kids; it simply means you must take an aggressive, active interest in their choice of friends.

This means knowing who they eat lunch with; who they talk to on the phone (or Instant Message via the Internet); and what they plan to do together on the weekends. If your child connects with another child enough so that a deeper friendship develops, it's appropriate to get to know the other child and the parents or caregivers as well. Before you ever let your child play at another child's house, you can meet the parents and take a quick tour of their home. This is not being nosy or prying; it's being reasonable. You want this social environment to pass your intuitive test: Is this a safe place to leave my child alone for any length of time?

BELONGING OR BE LONGING?

In her bestselling book, *Queen Bees and Wannabes: Helping Your Daughter Survive Cliques, Gossip, Boyfriends, and Other Realities of Adolescence,*[6] Rosalind Wiseman makes a compelling case for knowing how and why to help teenage girls cope with this trying time. While her text covers the junior and high school years in its depth, the focus really reflects the transition from junior high to high school. Much of her advice applies to boys as well.

She writes of kids who see themselves, or who are perceived by others, as being either "in the box" or "outside the box." As you may recall from your own high school experiences, or those of your children, being in the figurative social box is much preferred to being outside it. The box, of course, is where most teenagers strive to be, and for Wiseman, the rules to entry into this social cocoon are hard and fast.

For boys, being in the box means you have: good looks, nice hair, and an athletic build. You're smart without being "too smart," manipulative of teachers and other adults, macho, attracted to and attractive to girls, and blessed with a nice car and access to spending money.

For girls, in the box characteristics are similar to boys: you're physically attractive, with long hair, and an athletic shape that's neither too muscular nor too skinny. You're popular, with lots of friends, and access to goodies and perks (money for shopping at the mall, a driver's license, a boyfriend). You do well in school without really trying too hard and you can get things from your parents.

Every child in this social stratum knows (or quickly learns) what outside the box characteristics keep them on the other side of the looking glass.

For boys, it's any hint of nerdiness (computer game prowess, math, chess, or science skills), being physically awkward or not into sports, any "disability" ranging from bad hair, glasses, a chunky build, or a girlish laugh or voice. This last feature, compounded with the slightest hint of homosexuality (true or not), will make their junior and senior high school years difficult or even excruciating.

For girls, outside the box traits start with being fat, cursed with bad skin/hair/clothes, showing yourself as overly smart, or being "too good" at sports (which may suggest lesbian tendencies, as the ostracizing parallel for effeminate boys similarly reveals).

Ironically, the same behavior that serves as a barometer of popularity with boys, flirtatious or sexual behavior with a number of girls around campus, is terminal for girls. Overly sexual or provocative behavior for girls can keep them outside, largely because it is seen as territorially threatening to the relationships with boys the "inside" girls are trying so hard to create or nurture.

Recalling these times in your own life, the unspoken criteria for social "success" may seem achingly familiar, even after the passage of many decades. Most people, who dwelled outside the box, look back on those social collisions between the haves (status) and the have-nots (lacking) with relief that they never have to repeat this "in or out" experience of the schoolyard.

Perhaps the only thing tougher than being a student in this environment is being a parent or caregiver of such a child. You always want the best for your child and it hurts every parent or caregiver to see his or her child in emotional as well as physical pain. Your impulse is to ride to the rescue and save your kid from the same agonies you faced from your similarly oriented peers. This desire, to solve your child's problems by offering plenty of well-meaning advice, calling school principals, or haranguing the parents of "in the box" kids, is usually the wrong approach, says Rosalind Wiseman.

The solution to one group of kids making another group miserable is not as easy as complaining to other adults (who may have kept score in similar ways during their own school days). Wiseman argues that parents must allow their children to fight their own social battles, by supporting them, staying non-judgmental for as long as possible, and simply listening to them vent about how difficult their situation is at the moment it envelops them.

This is counter-intuitive behavior for most parents, especially those who see themselves as problem solvers, decision makers, or involved in their children's lives. But what may be good advice in a business setting (confront poor performance, give feedback, offer solutions, etc.) may not work as an intervention into the social microcosm of teens.

Two issues appear at work here: teenage overly emotional responses to social standings (bad, especially if your child sees himself or herself as "out of the box") and teenage intuition (good, if not yet fully developed). Kids often don't hear their parents when it comes to advice-giving sessions, because they're heavily preoccupied with the drama of the moment. Their feelings of anxiety, low self-esteem, and low maturity will tell them their parents don't "really understand" them, the issue, or its critical importance. They hear the words, but they can't apply them, especially if they don't seem relevant to getting into the box.

Parents typically get used to the role of Eternal Protector and Lecturer, building their repertoire largely during the safety patrol stages of the growing toddler, that is, "Don't touch that! It's hot! Get down from there! Don't put that in your mouth!" etc. It's hard to break these habits once the child is old enough to reason on his or her own. What sounds reasonable to the parent comes across like scolding to the child, and the child typically tunes it out.

According to Wiseman, the saying, "Help me by *not* helping me," is more appropriate, even when you're dealing with a loved one, your child. Here, the strategy is to be a good and patient listener, an empathic source of information (only when it's asked for), and finally, supportive of your child's thought processes, even if they diverge from your own. With this approach, the key is to allow the child's intuitive sense of the issue to come to the surface, with a bit of prompting by the parent.

For example, your son tells you a boy he admires (one who's in the box) has just been arrested for shoplifting. For many parents, the first attempt at a solution might be to lob a lecture-grenade: "I knew he was bad news! I don't want you hanging around with that thug anymore! He's going to get you into trouble along with him."

Wiseman's alternative strategy is to start with a non-judgmental approach and some careful questions:

Parent: "I know it must have been hard for you to tell me about that. Thanks for letting me know. You know, a long time ago we talked about how stealing from a store is wrong. So I know you already know that. What do you think about what he did?"

> **Son:** "Yeah, I know it's wrong to steal and so I can't believe he did that! I want to be his friend but I don't want him to get me in trouble."
>
> **Parent:** "I'm guessing that right about now he's wishing he hadn't done it. Have you thought about what you might say when you see him again?"
>
> **Son:** "Well, if he tells me what happened, like it was no big deal, then I'm gonna tell him it was stupid. If he tells me he did a dumb thing, then I'll probably stay friends with him."
>
> **Parent:** "Those are some pretty good ideas. It sounds like you've made a choice to see which way it goes before you decide."

The difference between this latter approach and the typical Parental Screaming Session is that the youngster in this example *arrives* at the solution, his truth (which is also close to yours) by his own intuitive process. Talking *to* kids rarely gets better results than listening to them or talking *with* them.

THE S.P.A.C.E. SOLUTION FOR SCHOOLS

So if we combine the thoughts and theories of Judith Rich Harris, Rosalind Wiseman, and others, and mix in the idea that the educational experience for many kids is their own shared environment, with mandatory attendance on a campus somewhere (save for the home-schooled kids), then are there some things we can improve in this small and specialized society? What should we expect of our schools?

In an effort to help schools foster social intelligence in kids, we might consider advocating the following efforts in our schools:

- *Provide more instruction in communication skills, especially at the middle school/junior high school level.* Mixing the highly volatile chemicals of hormones, puberty, the popular culture, and peer pressure can create a fairly stressful school setting. All of these toxins are present in large doses in the middle school environment. By high school, some real maturity becomes evident in a lot of kids. But those stuck in grades 6 through 9 tend to have the most problems coping with life, their parents, and each other, mostly because their maturity is insufficient. They may communicate poorly with each other, their teachers, and their parents. More structured programs that teach important communication skills might help. Because budgets and staff are always a problem, perhaps community volunteers, older student interns, and student-teachers could fill these instructional roles.

- *Provide and teach more anti-bullying programs.* School violence is a national problem in the U.S. and now, more disturbingly, on the rise internationally as well. The school violence that makes the news—on-campus shootings—is quite rare. The number of incidents of school violence (psychological as well as psychical) involving threats or bullying behavior is both large and largely unmeasured. The impact on fearful students is like a stone thrown into the pond—lots of ripple effects over time. Many school-based organizations provide programs, that is, the national PTA (www.PTA.org), www.drspock.com, etc., which include parental involvement as part of the anti-bullying curriculum.

- *Provide more empowerment programs to help build self-esteem for all students at all levels of schooling.* Everything from depression and suicide, to violence and dropout rates, to graduation rates and future college enrollments can be tied back to the self-esteem of the individual student. While lots of kids with varying degrees of low self-esteem manage to make it through school relatively unscathed, those who lack coping skills or support resources for this issue can find themselves at a huge disadvantage socially and scholastically. Like the communication programs listed above, empowerment programs are often best taught by younger instructors, who can connect to the respective ages or genders in the classroom.

- *Teach more programs related to safe dating (similar to Rosalind Wiseman's "Empower" program) to help teenagers understand the boundaries of their relationships.* Incidents of date rape, sexual harassment, and sexual battery (unwanted touching) in the school environment continue to rise at alarming rates in the U.S. Education and prevention programs in these areas often emphasize the need for healthy relationships, avoiding alcohol and drug use, establishing boundaries between the genders, and creating support systems, resources, and reporting methods to help current victims and prevent the creation of new victims.

- *Provide "safe Internet use" training for K-12.* Since the Internet is now an everyday part of many children's lives, it's time to teach them how and why they need to act safely in the Internet community. Creative and powerful Internet safety and education programs are offered by organizations like www.ISAFE.org and the National Center for Missing and Exploited Children (www.NCMEC.org).

A PRESCRIPTION FOR SOCIAL INTELLIGENCE AT EVERY AGE

Of any person, John Gardner (1912–2002) knew about service to his country and community. He was a Renaissance man in both the academic world and in government. As a Stanford professor, where he worked and taught until his death, he won the highest achievement award given by the university. In 1965, he was appointed the Secretary for Health, Education, and Welfare, and worked as an adviser on civil rights and social reforms to President Johnson. He founded Common Cause and helped develop public television through his creation of the Corporation for Public Broadcasting.

In his brief but insightful book *Self-Renewal: The Individual and the Innovative Society,* Gardner wrote of the need for people to take chances in their lives, to break old habits, to see things in new ways instead of always relying on what's certain and comfortable:

"As we mature we progressively narrow the scope and variety of our lives. Of all the interests we might pursue, we settle on a few. Of all the people with whom we might associate, we select a small number. We become caught in a web of fixed relationships. We develop set ways of doing things.

"As the years go by we view our familiar surroundings with less and less freshness of perception. We no longer look with a wakeful, perceiving eye at the faces of people we see every day, nor at any other features of our everyday world.

"It is not unusual to find that the major changes in life—a marriage, a move to a new city, a change of jobs, or a national emergency—break the patterns of our lives and reveal to us quite suddenly how much we had been imprisoned by the comfortable web we had woven around ourselves.

"One of the reasons why mature people are apt to learn less than young people is that they are willing to risk less. Learning is a risky business, and they do not like failure. In infancy, when the child is learning at a truly phenomenal rate—a rate he or she will never again achieve—he or she is also experiencing a shattering number of failures. Watch him or her. See the innumerable things he or she tries and fails. And see how little the failures discourage him or her.

"With each year that passes he or she will be less blithe about failure. By adolescence the willingness of young people to risk failure has diminished greatly. And all too often parents push them further along that road by instilling fear, by punishing failure, or by making success seem too precious.

"By middle age most of us carry around in our heads a tremendous catalogue of things we have no intention of trying again because we tried them once and failed—or tried them once and did less well than our self-esteem demanded.

"By middle life, most of us are accomplished fugitives from ourselves." [emphasis added][7]

The cliché "Our children are our future" has never been more true than today. With fear and self-doubt such a part of the American popular culture (terrorism, economic uncertainty, or simply fear of the future), will our children grow up to be accomplished fugitives, or will they grow to become effective, socially intelligent adults?

In the next twenty years, we're going to get the society we're creating now. What are you doing now, and what will you do in the near future, to make it a saner and more socially intelligent place to live for all of us?

Notes

1. "The (Only) Ten Basic News Stories" originally appeared on the author's website, KarlAlbrecht.com, 2001. Used with permission.
2. Schor, Juliet B. *Born to Buy: The Commercialized Child and the New Consumer Culture.* New York: Scribner, 2004.
3. Beck, John, and Wade, Mitchell. *Got Game: How the Gamer Generation Is Reshaping Business Forever.* Cambridge, MA: HBS Press, 2004.
4. Harris, Judith Rich. *The Nurture Assumption: Why Children Turn Out the Way They Do.* New York: Free Press, 1998.
5. Harris, Judith Rich. "Letters to the Editor." *The New Yorker,* December 16, 2002.
6. Wiseman, Rosalind. *Queen Bees and Wannabes: Helping Your Daughter Survive Cliques, Gossip, Boyfriends, and Other Realities of Adolescence.* New York: Random House, 2002.
7. Gardner, John. *Self-Renewal: The Individual and the Innovative Society.* New York: W.W. Norton, 1964, p. 64.

INDEX

H

Halo 2 (video game), 267
Hamper, B., 65
Hampton, E., 21
Hardy, O., 234–235
Harris, J. R., 272–273, 276
Hatfield, A. ("Devil Anse"), 240
Hatfields and McCoys, 240–241
Head games, 102–103
Helicopter language, 116–117, 128
Hierarchies, 193–197
The Hmong, 48–49
Hofstede, G., 193
Hoof-in-mouth disease: political, 113–114; using silence to deal with, 110–113; socially intelligence dealing with, 230–231
Hot sex news stories, 258
Howard, J., 51
"Hub Fans Bid Kid Adieu" (Updike), 101
Hugo, V., 1
Human Resources: General Dynamics, 184–185; toxic management dealt with by, 185–187
Humility, 100
Humor, 151

I

"I-messages," 5
Idea killing, 139, 141
Idea-selling statements, 141–142
Ideological civil war, 189
"In the box," 273–274
Inauthenticity: head games, power struggles, manipulation as, 102–103; left-handed compliments as, 94–97; narcissism as, 98–101; Puppy Dog syndrome as, 97–98. See also Authenticity
Individualism, 193
Influence, 226–227
Inhumanity, 26
Intelligence: disparity between social and abstract, 9–10; Gardner's model of multiple, 8–10; as human mental competence source, 6. See also IQ concept
Interaction skills: assessment of, 160–166fig; connecting with people, 179–180; priorities for improvement of, 179–181e; strength-weakness irony of, 177–179
Interaction skills assessment: step 1: examining toxic people you know, 160–161e, 162; step 2: examining nourishing people you know, 162, 163e; step 3: creating "Toxic Role Model," 162, 164e; step 4: creating "Nourishing Role Model," 164e–165; step 5: S.P.A.C.E. Radar Chart, 165–166fig
Interaction style: characterization of, 168–169; four patterns of, 170–172; individual preference for, 172; results focus, 169–170; social energy and, 169; social scenarios on, 172,

173e–175e; social scenarios scoring, 175e–176fig; strength-weakness irony of, 177–179
Interaction style patterns: diagram of, 170fig; Diplomat, 170fig, 171; Driver, 170fig–171; Energizer, 170fig, 171; Loner, 170fig, 171–172
Interactions: Adjective Pairs exercise, 167–168e; boss-subordinate relationships and, 213–214; children coping with peer, 272–276; four-minute empathy approach to, 154–156; game playing during, 102–103; gender politics during, 195–197; relationship maintenance through, 155–156; self-awareness during, 166–168e; zones of, 43–46. See also Conflict; Relationships
Interactions zones, 43–46
Internal competence, 11
Internet: Instant Message via the, 272; training for safe use of, 278
Interpersonal intelligence, 11
"Interpersonal skills," 4
Intimate space, 44
Intrapersonal intelligence, 11
Introversion interactive style, 169
IQ concept: debate over educational use of, 6–7; debate over measurement of, 7–8; described, 6; disparity between social/abstract intelligence, 9–10; g-factor theory of, 8. See also Intelligence

J

Jargon language, 132
Jensen, A., 7
Jethro, 197
Journalism news stories, 256–260

K

Keating, P., 50
Keep, Stop, Start, 181e
Keller, H., 159
Kennedy assassination, 20–21
Kennedy, J. F., 116, 268
Kerry, J., 113
Kerry, T. H., 113–114
Kidman, N., 81
King, M. L., 116
Korzybski, A., 53–54
Kozlowski, D., 217
Kubrick, S., 81, 100

L

Lamb, B., 100
Language: clean, 119, 145; dirty, 119–120, 121, 145; E-Prime, 130e, 130–132; EEO violations regarding native, 202–203; general

ABOUT THE AUTHOR

Dr. Karl Albrecht is a management consultant, executive advisor, futurist, researcher, speaker, and prolific author.

In his twenty-five-year career he has worked with many kinds of businesses, government, and nonprofit organizations in a wide range of industries world-wide. He has consulted with senior executives and lectured to conferences on all inhabited continents.

He is the author of more than twenty books on various aspects of individual and business performance, including *Brain Power: Learn to Improve Your Thinking Skills*; *The Northbound Train: Finding the Purpose, Setting the Direction, Shaping the Destiny of Your Organization*; *The Power of Minds at Work: Organizational Intelligence in Action*; and co-author of the best-selling *Service America!: Doing Business in the New Economy*, widely credited with launching the "customer revolution" in the U.S. and abroad, which has sold over a half-million copies in seven languages.

He devotes much of his effort to finding and developing promising new concepts for both organizational and individual effectiveness. His research and development activities have spanned a wide range of issues, from individual creativity all the way to corporate strategic vision. He is widely regarded as a key thought leader in the field of emerging strategic business issues.

He can be contacted at www.KarlAlbrecht.com.